LONELY COURAGE

LONELY COURAGE

The true story of the SOE heroines
who fought to free Nazi-occupied France

RICK STROUD

**SIMON &
SCHUSTER**

London · New York · Sydney · Toronto · New Delhi

A CBS COMPANY

First published in Great Britain by Simon & Schuster UK Ltd, 2017
A CBS COMPANY

1 3 5 7 9 10 8 6 4 2

Simon & Schuster UK Ltd
1st Floor
222 Gray's Inn Road
London WC1X 8HB

www.simonandschuster.co.uk
www.simonandschuster.com.au
www.simonandschuster.co.in

Simon & Schuster Australia, Sydney
Simon & Schuster India, New Delhi

A CIP catalogue record for this book
is available from the British Library

Hardback ISBN: 978-1-4711-5565-9
eBook ISBN: 978-1-4711-5567-3

Typeset in Sabon by M Rules
Printed and bound by CPI Group (UK) Ltd, Croydon, CR0 4YY

For Nell

CONTENTS

*Only the dark dark night shows to our eyes the
stars.*

(after WALT WHITMAN)

Suggestion for inscription on
SOE memorial at Natzweiler-Struthof
Concentration Camp for Women

*Three people can keep a secret if two of them
are dead.*

BENJAMIN FRANKLIN

*Women have a far greater capacity for cool and
lonely courage than men.*

SELWYN JEPSON,
SOE recruiting officer, to Winston Churchill

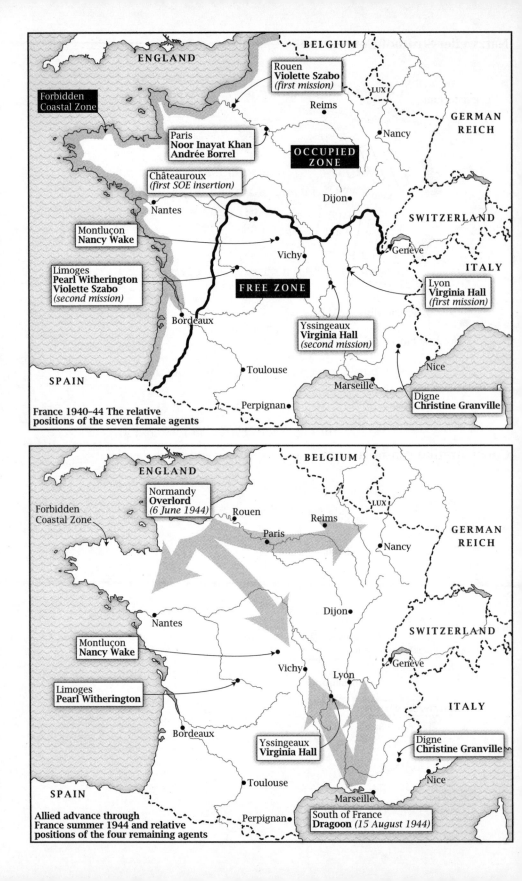

Map 1 (top):

ENGLAND

BELGIUM

Rouen
Violette Szabo
(first mission)

LUX

Reims

Nancy

GERMAN
REICH

Forbidden
Coastal Zone

Paris
Noor Inayat Khan
Andrée Borrel

OCCUPIED
ZONE

Châteauroux
(first SOE insertion)

Dijon

Nantes

SWITZERLAND

Montluçon
Nancy Wake

Vichy

Genève

ITALY

Limoges
Pearl Witherington
Violette Szabo
(second mission)

FREE ZONE

Bordeaux

Lyon
Virginia Hall
(first mission)

Yssingeaux
Virginia Hall
(second mission)

SPAIN

Toulouse

Nice

Marseille

Perpignan

Digne
Christine Granville

France 1940–44 The relative
positions of the seven female agents

Map 2 (bottom):

BELGIUM

ENGLAND

Normandy
Overlord
(6 June 1944)

Rouen

LUX

Reims

Paris

Nancy

GERMAN
REICH

Forbidden
Coastal Zone

Dijon

Nantes

SWITZERLAND

Montluçon
Nancy Wake

Vichy

Lyon

Genève

Limoges
Pearl Witherington

ITALY

Bordeaux

Yssingeaux
Virginia Hall

Digne
Christine Granville

Toulouse

Nice

SPAIN

Marseille

Perpignan

South of France
Dragoon *(15 August 1944)*

Allied advance through
France summer 1944 and relative
positions of the four remaining agents

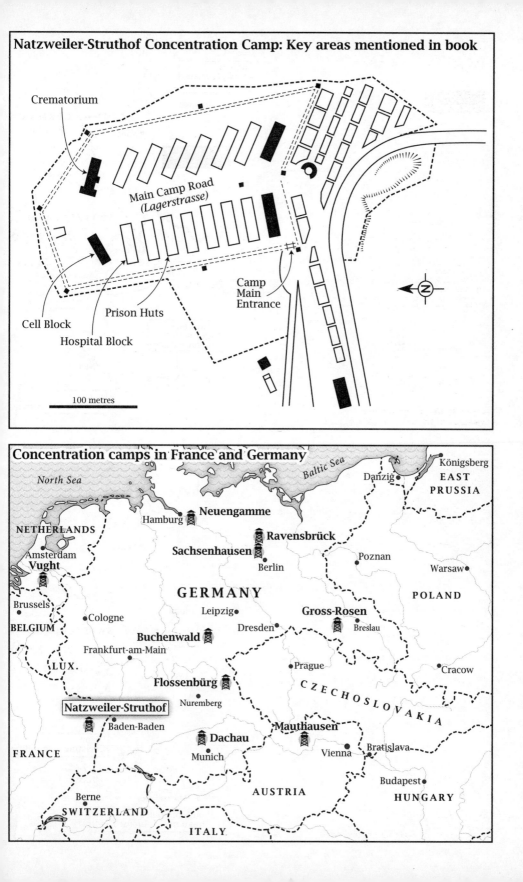

Natzweiler-Struthof Concentration Camp: Key areas mentioned in book

Crematorium

Main Camp Road
(*Lagerstrasse*)

Camp
Main
Entrance

Cell Block

Prison Huts

Hospital Block

100 metres

Concentration camps in France and Germany

North Sea

Baltic Sea

Königsberg

EAST
PRUSSIA

Danzig

NETHERLANDS

Hamburg

Neuengamme

Ravensbrück

Sachsenhausen

Berlin

Poznan

Warsaw

Amsterdam

Vught

GERMANY

Leipzig

Gross-Rosen

POLAND

Brussels

Cologne

Dresden

Breslau

BELGIUM

Buchenwald

Prague

Cracow

LUX.

Frankfurt-am-Main

Flossenbürg

CZECHOSLOVAKIA

Natzweiler-Struthof

Nuremberg

Baden-Baden

Mauthausen

FRANCE

Dachau

Vienna

Bratislava

Munich

Budapest

Berne

AUSTRIA

HUNGARY

SWITZERLAND

ITALY

INTRODUCTION

I have been fascinated with the women of SOE (Special Operations Executive) all my life. When I was nine the *Eagle* serialised *Carve Her Name with Pride*, the story of Violette Szabo. Each instalment became the high spot of my week. When I was about thirty I made a television drama series, *Diana*, about two SOE agents, a man and a woman. In the series we recreated Beaulieu (the SOE finishing school), described the life of an agent going into the field, blew up a train and rescued our heroine from a concentration camp. The series stayed in my mind long after it was shown. A few years ago, when I began to write history, I made a list of the subjects I wanted to tackle and that list included some of the female agents of SOE. Two years ago I decided the time had come to write their story. This book is about the women of F Section SOE, the ones who were sent undercover to work with the Resistance in France. There were thirty-nine, of whom twelve were executed and two died of illness. It would be impossible to write about all of them. I have therefore chosen to focus on seven and to use them as the lens through which we can look at the whole unit. The women came from all classes and walks of life, from a Polish aristocrat, to a shop assistant living in Stockwell, London. They all proved capable of great bravery and courage. Some of the young women came to lead hundreds of men and lived to see the liberation of France. Others were captured and endured endless torment before being executed. I hope I have done them proud.

A NOTE ON CODE NAMES

All the agents had code and field names, sometimes they had several. To give an idea of how confusing this can be, both Christine Granville and Pearl Witherington were at some time given the code name *Pauline*, the name *Solange* applies to a friend of Noor Inayat Khan's and was one of the field names given to agent Madeleine Damerment, while one of Noor's code names was *Madeleine*. At the time the proliferation of names was not only confusing, it could be dangerous. To avoid the same confusion in this book, once I have introduced an agent I use her real name.

PROLOGUE

On a March afternoon in 1942 a man wearing the uniform of a captain in the British Royal Navy sat in a bare hotel room interrogating a civilian. The two men were sitting on simple folding chairs separated by a plain wooden table. Blackout boards fixed across the windows blocked out the sun and a single naked light bulb glowed above their heads. The interview, which was conducted in fast, fluent French, was coming to an end. The naval officer switched to English: 'I'd like you to think about this. We'd both like to think about it. I don't want you to make up your mind too easily. It's a difficult decision to make, it's a life and death decision for both of us. I have to decide whether I can risk your life and you have to decide whether you are willing to risk it. Whatever you decide you must decide alone and not discuss it with anyone at all. Do you understand?' Then he stared at the civilian, his bright, dark-brown eyes unblinking, his face set, fixed and unreadable.

Later, when he was alone in the room, the captain, whose name was Selwyn Jepson, and who was not a captain at all but a veteran of the trenches and the successful author of detective fiction, sat deep in thought. He had interviewed many men in this room, looking for recruits for F (French) Section of the Special Operations Executive, the SOE. Some of his candidates were men who wore the old school tie and others who hated it; he had talked to varsity types, bankers, stockbrokers, lawyers and military men; Trotskyites, Stalinists, anarchists, burglars, bank robbers and pimps. Where they came from didn't matter, they had to share a hatred of the Nazis and be prepared to risk their lives to follow Churchill's command to 'Set Europe ablaze.'

One thing bothered him: he was not allowed to recruit women. When he told his superiors that he thought women were better suited for undercover work he met hostility and implacable opposition. Eventually he found himself in front of the prime minister who listened silently as he explained that women 'had a far greater capacity for cool and lonely courage than men' and he wanted to start recruiting them. Did the prime minister agree? he asked. Churchill thought, nodded his massive head, and said, 'Yes, good luck to you.'

Just over a year later, on the afternoon of 15 June 1943, two powerful cars sped through the sunlit fields of West Sussex. They were painted in brown and green camouflage and bore military identification plates. The leading car, an open-top Humber Super Snipe, was driven by a small, neat woman dressed in an impeccable civilian suit. On her fingers she wore expensive rings and in her right hand she held a lit cigarette. Her name was Vera Atkins, a 35-year-old Jewish refugee from Romania who had recently become the intelligence officer of F Section.

Next to her, in silence, sat an Indian princess, Noor Inayat Khan, twenty-nine, recruited by Jepson six months earlier. A radio operator, she had barely finished her training. The previous night she had stayed in London, at the flat of her closest friend. They sat up talking until dawn. In the morning, as she left, Khan had kissed her friend saying in her high, piping voice, 'It's the end of a phase, I shan't be seeing you again for a long time, so I will say goodbye.'

In the car behind were two more women recruited by Jepson. One was Cecily Lefort, a 43-year-old who spoke fluent French with an English accent. Beside her sat Diana Rowden, twenty-eight, with a pale face and auburn hair. Both women had been trained as couriers. In the front passenger seat sat a man, Charles Skepper, an expert in sabotage and the use of explosives.

They were nearly at the end of their journey. The road ran parallel to a chain-linked fence, which marked the edge of an airfield stretching away to their right as far as the horizon. Overhead, two Lysanders, stubby reconnaissance aircraft, flying one behind the other, dropped slowly to the runway.

The cars stopped at the airfield's heavily guarded entrance opposite a small brick-and-flint-built cottage covered in Virginia creeper. The group got out and stood in the sun taking in the buildings and the flat, empty airfield. Then Atkins led them in silence towards the cottage.

A young RAF officer wearing the insignia of a squadron leader greeted them. On the wall behind him was a large handwritten notice with the heading '161 Special Duties Squadron "A" Flight' beneath which were the words 'The Form:' followed by a long list of instructions. The officer began: 'Welcome to Tangmere. My name's Verity, I'm in charge, and we're happy to be at your service. You probably saw the chaps arriving.' As he spoke Noor read the notice, a string of things that the Lysander pilots had to do before flying into enemy territory. It included details about maps, flying times, drawing French money, checking flak positions over France and ended with the words 'Relax until take off time'. Someone had attached a typewritten note with the words 'EVERYTHING UNDER PERFECT CONTROL'. The front door banged open and two men sauntered in, dressed in flying gear, carrying bags and maps. 'Ah here they are now,' said Verity. 'We'll see you after supper when I've had a chance to brief them.'

Later the agents sat together at two trestle tables in a bare room with whitewashed walls and were served supper by a pair of khaki-clad mess stewards. As they ate, the French-language *Radio Londres* came on air, the voice of the Free French, broadcasting to people huddled round illegal radio sets all over France. The transmission started with the sombre opening notes of Beethoven's 5th Symphony, the Morse code for 'V for victory'. The announcer began: '*Ici Londres*', and went on to read out a string of 'personal messages', which in reality were coded signals to the Resistance. One message, 'Jasmine is playing her flute', was the signal that the four SOE agents were coming that night.

After supper Atkins took each agent into a room where she made a final check that they were not carrying anything that would give them away – bus or cinema tickets, English coins, letters, bills or labels on clothes. Khan noticed a silver bird brooch on Atkins's suit and remarked how pretty it was. Atkins took it off and handed it to her saying, 'Take it, it will bring you luck.'

Later, Atkins led the agents out of the house, the stewards following with their cases. The last rays of the setting sun lit the sky. Waiting for them outside was a big Ford estate car, the doors open and the driver standing quietly beside it. The stewards put the cases in the back of the car; Atkins dismissed them with a quiet thank you and they left without catching anyone's eye. Khan squashed into the car with the others. The armed sentries saluted as the car accelerated past the security barrier onto the airfield. Ahead of them were the Lysanders, their engines running, propellers spinning in an invisible blur, blue flames spurting from the exhausts, as the pilots tested the magnetos and checked the oil pressures. A huge full moon hovered on the eastern horizon.

Turbulence from the roaring engines pulled at the agents' clothes, making them hunch their shoulders. The air was heavy with the sweet, sickly smell of aviation fuel. Khan and Lefort were scheduled to fly together and before they walked to their allotted Lysander Atkins embraced them. Using the small iron ladder attached to the fuselage Khan and Lefort climbed into the small cockpit. As they had been trained, they stowed their bags under the plane's crude seats and plugged their leather flying helmets into the wireless and intercom system.

Through their headphones the two women heard the pilot saying, 'Good evening, welcome aboard Moonflight.' A calm voice from the control tower broke in, clearing them for take-off. The runway lights snapped on, the engine revved hard and the aircraft began to vibrate violently as it taxied forward. Through the wide windows of the tight cockpit the two women got a final glimpse of England: a few hangars silhouetted against the sky and the deep black tarmac of the runway disappearing into the gloom. Then both planes surged forward, climbing into the air.

*

Atkins stood by the car until she could no longer hear the sound of the aircraft engines. Earlier that evening she had seen one of the pilots reading a book called *Remarkable Women* and said, 'That book will have to be rewritten when these girls have done their stuff.'

Far below, the runway lights went out and the airfield vanished. Soon they were over the glinting waters of the Channel. 'Isn't it lovely in the moonlight?' the pilot said. They crossed the French coastline and for the next thirty minutes he pointed out landmarks and features to his passengers, forgetting that he had left his transmitter on and could have been heard by any German listening service or control tower tuned to his frequency.

They flew for nearly two hours, then their stomachs lurched as the plane began its quick descent. Below was the town of Angers and beyond it the field where they were to land. The pilot checked the map he had open on his knees and peered down, searching for tiny pinpricks of light from the torches of the waiting Resistance party. 'Ah got them,' he said as far below he spotted the light of a torch flashing Morse. Other torches flashed on, outlining the improvised grass runway. The ground rushed up and with a heavy thump the plane landed, the engine revved, suddenly loud as the pilot used it to brake. The Lysander bumped across the field for 600 metres, turned and taxied back to the reception party, turned again, into the wind then stopped, the propeller still spinning, ready for take-off.

Dark shapes of men came towards them. Lefort clambered out and Khan handed down their luggage. People crowded round the plane, five of them scheduled to return to England and anxious to get away. Two of them handed up suitcases which Khan heaved into the fuselage. Then she climbed out catching her green oilskin coat on the edges of the hatch. As her feet touched the ground two men brushed past her and clambered up the ladder; the others waved and shouted, wishing them a good trip, their voices drowned by the noise of the aircraft. A man dragged at Khan's arm, leading her away from the plane. The pilot pushed the throttle forward, the plane accelerated and was airborne, roaring low over Khan's head, making her duck.

The sound of the engine vanished into the night to be replaced by the noise of the second Lysander landing to drop off Skepper and Rowden and pick up the remaining outgoing agents. The time from landing to take-off had been just over three minutes.

Within half an hour all four newly arrived agents had split up and were on their separate ways, wobbling along on bicycles down moonlit roads.

'It was in Vienna that I formed my own opinion of the Nazis'

Over ten years earlier, in the Reich Chancellery in Berlin, at noon on 30 January 1933, the 85-year-old president of Germany, Paul von Hindenburg, had sworn in as chancellor Adolf Hitler, a man he detested and who detested him. The ceremony should have taken place at 11.00 a.m. but Hitler had spent the morning in quarrelsome meetings and had kept the president waiting. Now the old man could hardly bring himself to look as the new chancellor vowed to 'Protect the constitution and laws of the German people' and to 'Conduct my affairs of office with impartiality and with justice to everyone'.

In the streets outside people were pouring into the centre of the city to celebrate Hitler's appointment. After the ceremony he was taken in an open-topped car across Wilhelmplatz to the Hotel Kaiserhof, which had been his home for the last two years. The car travelled the short distance, slowed by crowds that roared approval at every wave and smile from the former labourer, now nearly forty-four, whose politics were based on the principle: 'Make the lie big, make it simple, keep saying it, and eventually they will believe it.' Inside the hotel he travelled in the lift to his suite on the first floor where he found waiters and chambermaids queuing to shake his hand. Hitler's campaign manager, Joseph Goebbels, had been hard at work choreographing the celebrations. Tens of thousands of troopers were arriving by lorry ready for the night parade through the Brandenburg Gate in the heart of the city. Goebbels had ordered the procession to be lit by thousands of flaming torches carried by the marching men. Hermann Göring was to narrate the evening's events, live by radio, across Germany. The flamboyant ex-fighter ace was now minister of the interior of Prussia and controlled the largest police force in the country. His first order as minister had been to tell his men: 'Shoot first and enquire afterwards, and if you make a mistake I will protect you.'

Most of the men in the parade were members of the Sturmabteilung, distinguished by their brown shirts and known as the SA. Their mottos included 'Terror must be broken by terror' and 'All opposition must be stamped to the ground'. The rest of the parade was drawn from the Schutzstaffel, the 'Protection Squadron' or SS, which had started life as Hitler's private bodyguard. The SS wore black shirts and swore to Hitler that they would bear him 'Absolute allegiance until death'. Every man in the parade wore an arm band emblazoned with a swastika and each detachment carried a distinctive unit banner. Goebbels wanted the evening's procession to be a fiery sea of red and black, scarlet and gold, surging to heavy thumping music from military bands.

The crowds streamed along the wide avenue of Unter den Linden and down Wilhelmstrasse towards Wilhelmplatz chanting 'Sieg Heil' to the rhythmic slow beat of drums and stamping feet.

Sebastian Haffner, a 25-year-old law student then training to be a civil servant, read the headline in the evening paper: 'Cabinet of National Unity Formed. Hitler Reichschancellor'. He said, 'For a moment I physically sensed the man's odour of blood and filth, the nauseating approach of a man eating animal and its foul sharp claws in my face.' The new Nazi vocabulary frightened him: *Einsatz* – Strike Force, *Fanatisch* – Fanatical, *Volksgenosse* – Racial Comrade, *Artfremd* – Racially Alien, and worst of all, *Untermensch* – Subhuman. Later he and his father agreed that the Germans who had voted for the Nazis were 'misguided ignoramuses ... victims of propaganda, a fluctuating mass that would fall apart at the first disappointment'.

Darkness fell, the torches blazed and the parade began. Göring took the microphone and described the scene to the nation. Later Hitler returned to the Reich Chancellery and appeared at a window with Göring at his side. The crowd went berserk, the cries of '*Sieg Heil*' thundered to a crescendo, the drums beat in deadly slow time, triggering wave after wave of cheering as the new chancellor raised his arm in salute. From another window President Hindenburg watched, incredulous.

Goebbels claimed that there were 1 million uniformed men in the parade, the British ambassador thought it was nearer 50,000. When the last thundering '*Sieg Heil*' echoed from the walls of the Reich Chancellery, Goebbels wrote in his diary: 'It is almost like a dream – a fairy tale. The new Reich has been born. Fourteen years of work have been crowned with victory. The German revolution has begun!'

Two months later, on 31 March 1933, the government announced an anti-Jewish boycott would take place the next day. That afternoon Sebastian Haffner went to the library situated in the Kammergericht, the law court in Berlin. On the way he passed crowds shouting '*Juda Verrecke*' ('Death to Judah') and behaving as if they were on holiday. Later, as he sat in the quiet of the library, the noise of tramping boots disturbed the silence. A young Nazi lawyer laughed and said, 'The SA, they're coming for the Jews.' A Jewish barrister stood up from his desk and quietly left. An official announced, 'The SA are in the building, the Jewish gentlemen would do well to leave.' A Brownshirt burst in shouting, 'Non Aryans must leave the premises immediately.' In the courts the judges quietly adjourned and filed out of the building past the SA men who were now lining the stairs. A senior Jewish barrister was beaten up for making a fuss. He was a veteran of the First World War and had been wounded five times, losing an eye. In the library a fat Brownshirt stood in front of Haffner and demanded to know if he was non-Aryan, staring intently at his nose. Haffner said 'No' and instantly knew that, by even answering the question, he had been shamed and defeated. On his way home he felt that the whole edifice of German law had ceased to exist and that his work no longer had any meaning. The next day he crossed Berlin to visit a Jewish friend. SA men stood with aggressive insolence in front of the open doors of Jewish businesses while their comrades painted anti-Semitic slogans on the windows.

On 7 April two laws were passed, one removing Jews from government office and the other forbidding the admission of Jews to the Bar. In a speech to the SA Hitler warned: 'I am resolved to suppress any attempt to disturb the existing order ... Anyone, no matter what his position, who rises against the regular authority of the state will be putting his head in a noose.'

That June, the American consul general in Berlin, George S. Messersmith, wrote to the State Department, declaring that Hitler and his new Teutonic order were a threat to world peace and that 'With a few exceptions the men who are running this government are of a mentality that you and I cannot understand. Some of them are psychopathic cases and would ordinarily be receiving treatment somewhere.'

None of these events made the slightest difference to the life of 20-year-old New Zealander Nancy Wake. Brought up by her mother in Sydney, Australia, she had run away from home at fifteen. In 1932 she inherited £200 from an aunt who wrote to her saying: 'I have been thinking of you always and hope this can help you.' A week later Wake sat in a first-class cabin aboard the *Aorangi 11*, the largest vessel of its kind, heading for New York where, in spite of Prohibition, she downed vast quantities of alcohol before heading for Europe. In London she taught herself to type and talked her way into a six-month trial working for the Randolph Hearst group of newspapers. Her job was to cover events all over Europe, based in Paris. Wake found a tiny apartment at the top of a building in the rue Sainte-Anne and moved in, determined to have a good time: 'I arrived there a sensitive young Australian romantic, determined not to be uncouth but I quickly felt at home, safe and very, very happy, I just loved it all. I loved the food, I loved their humour, I loved everything about it from the first.' She said: 'I was thrilled to be in Paris with all these gorgeous Frenchmen chasing after me. I was the dizziest person there ... For the first time in my life I was doing exactly what I wanted to do.'

Nancy was soon writing articles for Hearst newspapers across America, including the *San Francisco Examiner*, the *Houston Chronicle* and the *New York Journal*. She met French and American newspaper people and enjoyed their company. In the evenings she went to bars and cafes to meet fellow journalists. For Wake 'they were very funny and I used to learn a lot from them ... We were all friends. Most of the men were married with their wives in America or someplace, but we were mostly just friends. Mostly.' A favourite bar was Luigi's, where a regular topic of conversation was Germany.

Hitler's new laws became more and more repressive. The Jews were persecuted, trade unions and all political parties other than the Nazi Party were banned; clergymen who preached against Hitler were arrested as were members of the Reichstag who belonged to the Communist Party. Hitler pressurised Hindenburg into issuing a decree authorising the Nazi government to arrest and intern any person it deemed to be a threat to national security. A new word entered the vocabulary: Gestapo, an abbreviation for the Geheime Staatspolizei the State Secret Police.

By the end of 1934 Hindenburg was dead and Hitler was both president and chancellor of Germany, with the title of *Führer* – leader. The *Hitlergruß*, the Nazi salute accompanied with the words '*Heil Hitler*', became the compulsory greeting for everyone. Performances in the theatre ended with the singing of 'Deutschland Uber Alles' followed by the SA anthem 'The Horst Wessel Song'. Soldiers had to swear before God '... to obey without reservation, Adolf Hitler, Führer of the Reich, supreme chief of the Wehrmacht. I pledge myself as a courageous soldier always to observe this oath, even at the risk of my life.' The numbers of persecuted people leaving Germany kept rising and in 1937 reached nearly a quarter of a million. With Jews now excluded from the social, political and financial life of the country, Germany became a world that '... seems to be divided into two parts – those places where Jews could not live and those where they could not enter.'

On 26 April 1937 the Luftwaffe's Condor Legion appeared in the skies above Guernica in Spain. It was market day. The planes were armed with a mixture of blast, splinter and incendiary bombs. By dusk the town was in ruins and 300 civilians were dead. A month later the Spanish painter Picasso began work on a huge picture of the event. Simply entitled *Guernica* it was hung at the 1937 World Fair in Paris. The Nazi guidebook to the fair described the work as '... a hodgepodge of body parts that any four-year-old could have painted'.

By now, in London, the British authorities were concerned by what was happening in Germany and began to give the Hitler problem some thought. Three security organisations emerged. From the Foreign Office came one to investigate how propaganda could be used to influence German public opinion. It was called EH after Electra House, on the Embankment, where it was based.

The second body came from the Secret Intelligence Service, SIS, and was called 'Section D'. Its job was to 'Investigate every possibility of attacking potential enemies by means other than the operations of military forces.' The head of Section D complained that it was 'As if one had been told to move the pyramids with a pin.' The War Office also fielded an organisation it called General Staff (Research) or GS(R), just one officer and a typist. It was run by an engineer, Major J. C. F. Holland, who had spent time in Ireland during the Troubles. Holland decided that his area of research would be 'Guerrilla Warfare'.

Anti-Semitism was not confined to Germany. The mother of the young countess Krystyna Skarbek was a rich Jewess, heir to a banking fortune who had married an impoverished Polish aristocrat. There was a popular song about Krystyna's father: 'Listen Count and take heed not to step into debt. It may land you in a stew having as a wife the daughter of a Jew.' An acquaintance described Krystyna as 'A lovely young woman ... but in her presence Jewish topics were shunned ... just as one never speaks of the gallows in the house of a hanged man.' The same friend remembered a moment when, at a gathering, a woman in a traditional Jewish costume had called Krystyna's name and everyone present froze while Krystyna pretended not to hear the woman.

Krystyna's father counted royalty and a mythical dragon-slayer among his ancestors and lived on a huge estate bought by his wife. As a child Krystyna led a charmed life. She was pampered by servants and spent her days roaming the fields on a horse armed with a gun and a knife and followed everywhere by an adoring hound. At the age of twelve she had stolen and ridden her father's black stallion, a dangerous animal that had broken a man's leg. At school she was a quick learner, good at languages and sport. At her convent she had set fire to a monk's habit and been expelled. On her finger she wore the Skarbek signet ring, which included a sliver of iron, celebrating an ancestor who had refused to bow to a German emperor. Legend had it that he had flung his gold ring into the man's coffers declaiming: 'Let gold eat gold. We Poles love iron.'

In 1928 when Krystyna was twenty the bank collapsed, the estate was sold and her childhood idyll ended. Her father abandoned the family and died a drunk. Krystyna moved to Warsaw with her mother and very little money. In 1930, when she was twenty-two, she married a very rich man who described her as 'dotty, romantic and forever seeking change'. The couple soon divorced. Eight years later, in 1938, Krystyna was poised to marry for the second time. Her future husband, Count Jerzy Giżycki, was nearly twenty years her senior and a dashing adventurer who had worked as a cowboy, trapper, gold prospector and had been John D. Rockefeller's driver. He was well connected and had links with the Polish diplomatic service and British Intelligence, especially SIS. He described Krystyna as an 'excellent horse-woman, fair skier and the most intrepid human being I have ever met – man or woman'. She called him her 'Svengali'.

*

On 12 March 1938, Nazi troops marched into Austria. On 14 March the Anschluss, the formal union between Austria and Germany, was signed. Hitler burst into tears when he held the document. Then he made a triumphal procession into Vienna, the city where he had wandered penniless as a young man before the First World War. It was in Vienna that he had failed to become a professional artist or an architect and had been forced to live in shelters for the homeless as a down-and-out. Now his Mercedes swept through streets lined with cheering crowds and huge swastika flags billowed from the buildings. The car, flanked by outriders and SS security men, headed for the Hotel Imperial where the Führer had once laboured sweeping snow, forced to doff his cap to the rich and famous.

Hitler's arrival was the signal for a wave of anti-Jewish violence all over Austria. Thousands of Jews were jailed without reason. In Vienna Jewish men and women were seized as they walked the streets and humiliated, forced to scrub pavements and clean lavatories with sacred cloth ripped from their synagogues.

Refugees from the Nazi regime began to appear on the streets of Paris; some turned up at Luigi's and they all had stories. Nancy Wake heard a former socialist representative of the Reichstag describing how he had been forced out for not being a Nazi and how he had fled Germany in fear of his life. He told them what was happening in Vienna and begged journalists to write about it. Wake went by train to the Austrian capital where she found brown-shirted SA marching around the beautiful streets bullying and shrieking at anyone suspected of being 'non Aryan'. In the main square she watched a group of Brownshirts tying Jews to huge wheels, which they rolled along the cobbles while slashing at their victims with whips. Jewish stores were ransacked, the contents looted or thrown into the streets and the word JUDE was daubed on the plate-glass windows in huge red letters. Wake said:

> That trip was an important one for me … I was horrified and
> revolted by the public scenes … It was in Vienna that I formed

my own opinion of the Nazis. I resolved there and then that if I
ever had the chance, however big or small, stupid or dangerous,
I would try and make things more difficult for their rotten party.

Yet Nancy returned to Paris to find that she could not sell her stories. The world was not interested. To console herself she bought
a little dog, a wire-haired terrier, that she named 'Picon' after the
barman at Luigi's, and had him christened in the cafe by a visiting
American clergyman. She promised to bring the dog up as a law-
abiding citizen.

In 1938, another resident in Paris, Noor Inayat Khan, had just
graduated from the Sorbonne with a degree in child psychology. She
was born on 2 January 1914 in St Petersburg, Russia. Her mother
was American and her father was descended from the eighteenth-
century ruler of the kingdom of Mysore. Khan could play the harp
and piano and spoke several languages. She loved to write and to
play music with her brothers and sisters. Her mother, to whom she
was very close, wrote that Noor: 'Through all the stress and storms
of life, she moves in quiet delight . . . she has the gift that few possess,
the gift of love's sublimity.'

At the suggestion of a friend Khan began to translate some of the
Jataka Tales, 500 charming Indian allegories about the early life of
the Buddha. A theme that began to occur in her work was the tale
of a magical creature who brought joy and light into the world but
who in the end was called upon to make a great sacrifice.

On 7 November, a Polish Jew named Herschel Grynszpan walked
into the German Embassy in Paris. He carried a pistol and fired at
Ernst vom Rath, a diplomat, badly wounding him. The next day
the Nazi government banned all Jewish children from school and
closed down the publication of all Jewish newspapers and magazines. Rath died of his injuries on 9 November and there was a
public outcry. Joseph Goebbels announced that it was the Führer's
wish that 'demonstrations should not be prepared or organized
by the party, but insofar as they erupt spontaneously, they are not
to be hampered'. In his diary he wrote: 'Action against the Jews

will shortly be under way.' Early on the morning of 10 November, Reinhard Heydrich sent a telegram with orders that 'Business and private apartments of Jews may be destroyed but not looted. The demonstrations that take place shall not be hindered by the police. As many Jews, especially the rich ones, are to be arrested as can be accommodated in the existing prisons.'

That afternoon a boy, Alfons Heck, was on his way home from school in the small, quiet town of Wittlich, where the main businesses were farming and wine-making. Dark-green lorries roared past him into the town square. Armed SS and SA troopers leapt out, fanning across the square and into the streets. Their first target was a large shoe shop next to the town hall. They smashed the windows and flung the stock through the broken glass. The good Aryan citizens of Wittlich scrabbled in the dirt to steal the brand-new shoes that were falling like rain all around them. Alfons and his friends followed the rioters to Himmeroder Strasse and watched the SS and SA smashing down the doors of the synagogue. The delicate crystal glass of the large fanlight sailed through the air, splintering into a thousand pieces on the cobbles. A trooper climbed onto the roof waving the rolls of the sacred Torah shouting: 'Wipe your arse on it, Jews!' His voice was almost drowned out by the noise of the synagogue furniture crashing onto the road, hurled from the building's high windows.

Every Jewish business in Wittlich suffered the same fate. All the Jewish men were herded into lorries and driven off. Heck watched an SS trooper slam his fist into the face of the uncle of one of his classmates. The man collapsed, blood spurting from his nose. The soldiers picked him up and threw him 'like a bail of hay' into the back of a truck. The victim was a veteran of the First World War who had lost a leg fighting for Germany. As the victim's body landed in the lorry he let out a deep moan and Heck said that at that moment, he felt a surge of excitement and wanted to join in the destruction.

Similar scenes were played out all over Germany. The police did nothing while the fire services watched as Jewish buildings burned.

In Berlin a British journalist wrote that mob law ruled:

> ... throughout the afternoon and evening and hordes of hooligans indulged in an orgy of destruction. I have seen several anti-Jewish outbreaks in Germany during the last five years, but never anything as nauseating as this. Racial hatred and hysteria seemed to have taken hold of otherwise decent people. I saw fashionably dressed women clapping their hands and screaming with glee, while respectable middle-class mothers held up their babies to see the 'fun'.

The night of 9–10 November became known as Kristallnacht, or 'the night of the broken glass'.

In London, people in the War Office continued to work on the idea of guerrilla warfare. In June 1939 a paper was produced that concluded: 'If guerilla warfare is co-ordinated and also related to main operations, it should, in favourable circumstances, cause such a diversion of enemy strength as eventually to present decisive opportunities to the main force.' Roughly translated this meant 'Guerilla warfare might work and we should probably give it a go, or not, as the case may be.'

Lieutenant Colonel Colin Gubbins took a more robust view. He was a regular soldier who had served in India. Major J. C. F. Holland, head of General Staff (Research), took Gubbins to lunch and told him about his interest in undercover warfare. Then he asked him to write training pamphlets on the subject. One result was 'The Art of Guerrilla Warfare' which explained that 'Guerrilla actions will usually take place at point blank range as the result of an ambush or raid ... Undoubtedly, therefore, the most effective weapon for the guerrilla is the sub-machine gun.' Another pamphlet, 'How to Use High Explosives' proved to be very useful and popular.

In May 1939, Virginia Hall, an American who had worked in the US Consulate in Tallinn in Estonia, was in Paris and at the end of her tether. For twelve years she had tried to follow a career in the Foreign Service and at every turn she had been frustrated. One of her superiors had described her as a satisfactory clerk but a woman of unbounded ambition, with no self-awareness, who talked too much.

In 1931, on holiday in Turkey, Hall had gone shooting snipe with a group of friends. Towards the end of the afternoon she crossed a wire fence with her loaded shotgun under her arm and accidentally fired it. The blast hit her left foot at point-blank range. Gangrene set in and the lower part of her left leg was amputated. She was fitted with an artificial limb that she christened 'Cuthbert'.

An assistant secretary of state, who did not like women in the service, had discovered there was a ruling on disability and informed his superior that: 'The regulation governing physical examinations to the Foreign Service prescribe that amputation of any portion of a limb ... is a cause of rejection, and it would not be possible for Miss Hall to qualify for entry into the Service under these regulations.' She stuck it out as a clerk for another two years but in May she resigned and went to Paris. She was thirty-three years old.

In the City of Light she found that not all Parisians were as tolerant to the refugees from Germany as the journalists who drank with Nancy Wake at Luigi's. Hall wrote home to her mother in America telling her of slogans scrawled on the walls of Jewish businesses and of Jews being beaten up in broad daylight.

By August 1939 Noor Khan's career was blossoming. She wrote a gentle story called 'Ce qu'on entende quelquefois dans les bois' ('What You Sometimes Hear in the Woods'), which was given a spread in the *Sunday Figaro* illustrated with her own drawings. At the same time Radio Paris began to record her stories for their Children's Hour slot and *Jataka Tales* was published by George Harrap under their Folk and Fairy Tales for Girls and Boys list. The book was bound in handsome sky-blue cloth boards wrapped in a yellow dust jacket on which was an engraving of a deer and her fawn looking lovingly at each other. On the flyleaf the publishers claimed that the book told '... of animals and men who are moved to kindly acts by their appreciation of noble example'. The publication was a great success. Noor now also began a collaboration with a well-known journalist;

they planned to publish an illustrated newspaper for children with the title *Bel Age* (Beautiful Age)

Meanwhile Nancy Wake had fallen in love with a Frenchman, an entrepreneur called Henri Fiocca. She met him in the resort of Juan-les-Pins where Picasso took his mistresses and where celebrities like Coco Chanel and Somerset Maugham went to relax. Henri was an industrialist and a playboy. Wake said: 'I was madly attracted to him ... he was charming, he made me laugh and he was dead sexy.' He was fourteen years her senior and very rich. From the moment they met Nancy found every excuse to travel to stay with Henri in Marseille, a city she came to love. Henri for his part often went to Paris to see Nancy and meet her friends. 'I think it helped when Henri saw the way I lived my life with a large group of male journalists who were my close friends but not my lovers ... he saw the way we were all such great comrades together ... and he became friendly with a lot of them too.' Henri proposed to her in his favourite restaurant in Marseille, Verduns, and she accepted. The wedding day was set for the spring of the following year, 1940. Nancy said:

> There really was a sense that Europe was going straight to hell and that there was only a limited time to enjoy what you wanted to do. Everyone was packing as much pleasure into every day as we could, no-one knew what tomorrow would bring ... It might seem frivolous to do what we were doing ... but we thought that it was not only probable that this was our last summer before the war, it might just be our last summer full stop.

All through the year, Ribbentrop and Molotov, the foreign ministers of Germany and Russia respectively, had been negotiating a non-aggression treaty with each other. On 23 August 1939, in Moscow, the deal was done and the two men signed the agreement watched by a beaming Joseph Stalin. At the end of the treaty there was a secret protocol agreeing, among other things, that in the event of a 'political re-arrangement' of Poland that country would be divided between the two powers. The treaty was signed with much hand-shaking, back-slapping, vodka-drinking and photography. Very few people knew about the last clause.

In Berlin Hitler ordered the invasion of Poland, Fall Weiss (Case White). He told his generals that the object of the campaign was: 'physically to destroy the enemy. My "Death's Head" formations [have] orders to kill without pity or mercy all men, women, and children of Polish descent or language. Only in this way can we obtain the living space we need ...' He had also commanded his generals to: 'Close your hearts to pity! Act brutally! ... be harsh, be remorseless! ... Be steeled against all signs of compassion.'

In the early hours of Friday 1 September 1939, a German commando unit, disguised as Polish soldiers, attacked a German radio station sited very close to the border with Poland. They shot the guards, and then turned on some of their own unit, bludgeoning them to death and mutilating their faces beyond recognition. The commandos then destroyed the radio station and vanished, heading for their base deeper inside Germany. Similar attacks took place at other border wireless transmitting stations. The dead and mutilated 'comrades' were political prisoners dragged out of concentration camps to play a part in Operation *Himmler*. Their disfigured bodies looked as though they had been killed by the defending German soldiers. Hitler declared to the world: 'This night ... Polish regular soldiers fired on our own territory. Since 5:45 a.m. we have been returning the fire ... I will continue this struggle, no matter against whom, until the safety of the Reich and its rights are secured.' The invasion of Poland had begun.

On 3 September 1939, at 11.15 a.m. the British prime minister, Neville Chamberlain, broadcast to the nation announcing that the British government had given Germany until 11.00 that morning to withdraw its troops from Poland. In his calm, nasal, upper-middle-class voice he told the nation that as 'no such undertaking has been received ... this country is at war with Germany.' His closing message was 'It is the evil things that we are fighting against – brute force, bad faith, injustice, oppression and persecution . . .'

The same day in Stockwell, London, at number 18 Burnley Road, the Bushell family listened to the broadcast in silence. When it ended the children, four boys and a girl, all in their teens, broke into fast, fluent French spoken with a South London accent. Their father, Charlie, could not understand a word they were saying. Charlie had been an ambulance driver in France in the First World War where he had met and married their mother, Reine. The children had been brought up in France and England. The daughter, Violette, was pretty with black hair 'like a raven's wing'. She was eighteen years old and a lover of sport, especially gymnastics. She didn't get on with her father and had once run away from home to stay with her relatives in France. Her brother Roy described her as 'Pretty, smart and pig headed'.

Outside an air-raid siren began to wail and the family ran down the steep steps of the house into the street where all their neighbours were congregating. Overhead silver barrage balloons bobbed on steel hawsers, while higher still the silver silhouettes of aircraft twinkled in the blue sky. Nothing happened, it had been a false alarm, the aircraft were friendly. A strange silence filled the streets. Families drifted back inside. Charlie Bushell resolved to become an air-raid warden; his eldest son, Roy, announced that he was going to join the army. The other three boys were too young to enlist. Violette did not know what she was going to do.

In the days that followed German troops travelled to Poland in trains with '*Wir fahren nach Polen, um Juden zum dreschen*' ('We're going to Poland to thrash the Jews') chalked on the carriages. The Poles fought with great bravery as the German Army pounded and smashed its way to Warsaw. The recently harvested fields shook to the thud of heavy artillery; animals and humans fled from the crash of mortars and the stutter of automatic weapons; walls and buildings were smashed by twenty-ton Panzer tanks while all the time dive-bombers howled overhead. The Poles waited in vain for rescue by their English and French allies.

Behind the advancing army came special units with orders to eliminate the Polish middle classes in a plan named Operation *Tannenberg*. Soon, large groups of university professors, school-teachers, doctors, political activists, musicians, actors and retired officers were rounded up, led through the streets to public execution yards and shot. The Germans had compiled a list of 61,000 suspects to help identify their victims.

In three weeks Polish pilots destroyed more than 250 German planes but lost nearly two-thirds of their own machines. One pilot, Captain Roman Czerniawski, was ordered to round up as many reserve pilots as he could and fly the surviving aircraft of the Warsaw-based Pursuit Unit to Romania. On 17 September the Russians invaded, heading west to link up with their German allies. On 24 September nearly 1150 German aircraft bombed Warsaw. On the ground the Polish Army began to disintegrate, the German and Soviet armies linked up, Warsaw capitulated on 29 September, and seven days later the fight for Poland was over.

Krystyna Skarbek and her new husband were in South Africa when they heard the news of the invasion of their homeland. They went straight back to England on the *Capetown Castle*, a small mail-boat bound for Southampton, making agonisingly slow progress. Daily reports about the fighting were pinned to the ship's bulletin board and made depressing reading. On 29 September, the day that Warsaw fell, a notice on the board read 'Lost – a pair of lady's pink panties. Lost – Warsaw'. Krystyna had family in Warsaw.

They arrived in Southampton on 6 October 1939. Within days Krystyna managed to secure an interview with Sir Robert Vansittart, a senior figure at the Foreign Office, a first cousin of Lawrence of Arabia and a hard-line opponent of Hitler. No one knew how she had contacted him or why he had agreed to see her. Krystyna out-lined an idea she had to distribute propaganda inside Poland. Sir Robert was very interested and sent her on to his contacts in Section D. Next she was interviewed by a man calling himself 'Fryday'; in fact an intelligent and ruthless captain called George Taylor.

Krystyna launched straight into her plan. She wanted to smuggle anti-Nazi propaganda leaflets into Poland, crossing the border in secret and skiing over the Tatra Mountains to the winter resort at Zakopane, which she knew well. Earlier in her life she had helped boys smuggle cigarettes into the country by the same route, something she did just for the adventure. She knew the sporting men of Zakopane and was confident they would help her. She insisted that it was essential to start work at once to show solidarity with the Poles who now thought they had been abandoned to their fate. Then she told Taylor that the Germans were terrible bullies who needed to be intimidated with sabotage.

Taylor listened spellbound. When Krystyna left he wrote a report headed 'Notes on Madam G', the code name he had given her. 'Madame G visited me at 4 o'clock. She is a very smart looking girl, simply dressed and an aristocrat. She is a flaming Polish patriot. She made an excellent impression and I really believe we have a PRIZE.' He called her 'a great adventuress', 'an expert skier' and 'absolutely fearless herself'. He insisted to his colleagues that 'She says the matter is urgent' and she wanted to leave 'at once'. Taylor ended his report by saying 'She needs money for her work and I think she is going to earn it.'

Meanwhile, in Marseille Nancy Wake had brought her wedding arrangements forward. She and Henri were married on 30 November. The ceremony was followed by a lavish reception at the Hôtel du Louvre et Paix on La Canebière, the Champs-Elysées of Marseille. The hotel's stone facade carried four huge carved caryatids: a sphinx for America, an elephant for Asia, a dromedary for Africa and a fish for Europe. The statues stared down on the chauffeur-driven cars delivering the rich and important guests.

The head chef, Marius, had toiled for days over the menu. Deep-fried sole stuffed with the flesh of sea urchins was followed by lamb cutlets from Normandy roasted on improvised spits; then came fillets of beef and on and on. Each course was brought in on silver platters carried shoulder high and lit by secret lights hidden under the food. The guests cheered and stamped their feet with each new course. At the centre of everything was Nancy, beautiful in a wedding dress from Georges, the smartest couturier in Marseille. Her dress was made of black silk lined with pink and embroidered with rose-coloured orchids. Henri had invited three of Nancy's journalist friends from Paris, which she said 'was the nicest thing he ever did for me'. The dancing and drinking went on far into the night.

A fortnight before Christmas, in London, Krystyna received a telephone call telling her that the plan had been approved and she was being sent, as soon as possible, to Budapest. Once there her orders were to go straight to her hotel to meet a senior Section D officer who would brief her on local conditions. She was then to infiltrate herself into Poland, establish her contacts and set up a route to smuggle propaganda into the country. Her contacts in Hungary (code-named *15 Land*) and Czechoslovakia (code-named *14 Land*) were to be kept to the absolute minimum. She was told the fewer people she knew and could recognise the less she could give away if captured and tortured. Similarly the fewer people who knew who she was the less likely she was to be given away, either by chance or betrayal. It was emphasised that as a Jew and an aristocrat she was at special risk. She was given a new code name, *Madame Marchande*, and £250 to fund her mission.

The senior Section D operative in Budapest received a top-secret message about the operation. He was told Krystyna had been taken on for a six-month trial period and his orders were to 'Endeavour to form a definite impression whether the experiment should be continued or terminated.' On 21 December Krystyna left for Hungary.

THE PHONEY WAR

Hungary had relied on Germany for trade throughout the 1930s and had become pro-fascist. By the end of 1939 the Hungarian government was passing anti-Semitic laws and sliding towards a military alliance with Hitler. Krystyna arrived in Budapest in time for the New Year of 1940, which brought with it some of the worst weather for forty-five years. All over Europe snow, ice, heavy frosts and freezing rain made travel by road or rail difficult and sometimes impossible.

In Berlin, Hitler's generals, having conquered Poland, finalised the plans for Fall Gelb (Case Yellow), the invasion of the Low Countries. This was planned as the prelude to the invasion of France. Hitler wanted to start the campaign as soon as possible, irrespective of the weather or the army's state of preparation and ordered the invasion to begin on 17 January.

On 10 January 1940, the pilot of a German Messerschmitt Bf 108 Typhoon became lost in bad weather on his way to Cologne. With him was a passenger carrying a full set of plans for Case Yellow. When the plane crash-landed in a field in Holland, both men were arrested by the Dutch police and the plans fell into enemy hands. When he was given the news Hitler railed at the incompetence of it all and called off the invasion. The quiet that had descended on Europe after the fall of Poland continued. The British termed it the

Phoney War, the German press called it *Sitzkrieg*, and the French *drôle de guerre*. Europe waited, wondering what would happen next.

By the end of January Krystyna Skarbek was living in a small Budapest apartment arranged by Section D. Her cover story was that she was a foreign correspondent. One evening she was invited to a restaurant called the Café Floris. She walked into a crowded room and, by chance, saw a man she had met several years before. His name was Andrzej Kowerski, and when Krystyna came in he 'stopped and stared at her. She was slim, sunburnt, with brown hair and eyes. A kind of crackling vitality seemed to emanate from her.'

Kowerski was a tall, strongly built man with fair hair and powerful blue eyes. He held Poland's highest medal for bravery, the Virtuti Militari. Like Virginia Hall he had lost the lower part of one leg after a shooting accident. His orders were to stay in Budapest and organise the escape of interned Polish soldiers.

Krystyna invited him to have dinner with her the next night; he accepted but his work intervened and he stood her up. The next day he rang and arranged to meet her by the Chain Bridge, the suspension bridge linking Buda and Pest across the Danube. The night was freezing and his old Chevrolet unheated. As he approached the bridge he saw Krystyna, standing in the snow wearing a duffel coat with a hood pulled up against the cold. She walked towards the car 'In a dancing way, full of grace'.

They dined in a fashionable restaurant called Café Hangli, owned by one of the richest men in Hungary. They talked all evening, Kowerski drinking wine while Krystyna drank water. He told her that the Poles were bitter because England and France had not rushed to join the fighting as they had promised. German propaganda posters showing a badly wounded Polish soldier talking to Neville Chamberlain were all over Poland. The soldier points to a scene of utter devastation, exploding shells, burning buildings and dead civilians. The caption reads *England, This Is Your Doing*.

Krystyna told Kowerski about her idea to get anti-Nazi propaganda into Poland and how she planned to cross the Tatra

Mountains. Kowerski warned her that the pass to the Tatras was over 6000 feet above sea level, at night the temperature dropped to minus 20 or even 30 degrees. Many refugees had died trying to get out of Poland by this route and their bodies still lay frozen in the snow. She should at least wait until the spring he advised although even then the journey was going to be very difficult.

They spent that night in Krystyna's flat, which Kowerski found 'amazingly warm and cosy ... everything was magical and wonderful and funny'. When the maid appeared the next morning Kowerski slipped from the bed and hid in the wardrobe. When she had gone he ate 'every scrap of butter and crumb on the tray'. In the days that followed Krystyna badgered her new lover to find her a guide.

Eventually Kowerski found Jan Marusarz, a ski instructor from Zakopane and a former member of the Polish Olympic winter sports team. He was now working as a courier for the Polish military attaché, making regular journeys across the mountains into Poland. He too was horrified at Krystyna's plan. How did she think she would survive a journey that was dangerous, even for an experienced mountaineer like himself? She was a physically slight woman and he doubted she had the strength or the stamina for a mid-winter mountain journey. It took Krystyna an hour to persuade him otherwise. 'Very well,' he said, 'I'm a courier for the Polish Military Attaché and I have absolutely no right to take anyone with me, but I'll do it for you.'

Krystyna, Marusarz and an agent known only as 'Richard' set off about the middle of February taking trains across Hungary and Czechoslovakia and jumping from the last one in the dark, just before the Polish border. They spent the night in a safe house and the next day slipped into Poland and began their trek into the mountains.

Their wooden skis were heavy, the going was steep and thick snow slowed them down. They travelled in silence, their panting breath billowing in front of them, their exposed faces whipped by the freezing wind, sweat soaking their clothes. They often had to stop to recover their strength. By the end of the first day they were exhausted. As the light failed Marusarz brought them to a small shelter. He lit the Primus, melted snow in a small pan and made lemon tea. That night, fully clothed, they slept huddled together for warmth.

At dawn they strapped on their skis and continued up the endless mountain slopes, heads bowed against the wind. The temperature dropped, the wind blew harder and the sky ahead turned a dark threatening grey. In the late afternoon they entered Cicha Dolina, the Silent Valley, the ancient route into the Tatra Mountains. By the time they reached the next shelter the freezing wind was howling and visibility had dropped to almost nothing. In the hut they once again brewed tea, ate their rations and fell into a deep sleep. During the night Krystyna woke and thought she could hear voices shouting. She shook the men and made them open the door, but it was impossible to hear or see anything.

The next morning the storm had passed and the sun shone in a bright-blue sky. The jagged peaks of the high Tatras glittered in the distance. They moved on, black dots silhouetted against white, easy prey for border patrols equipped with field glasses and high-powered rifles. During the morning they came across the bodies of a young couple, frozen together in death. Krystyna covered them with the branches of a pine tree and drew a cross in the snow.

After six days they reached Zakopane and found the town full of German soldiers. Marusarz and 'Richard' travelled on to Warsaw leaving Krystyna to look up old friends and start the dangerous task of contacting the Polish Resistance.

A few days later a crowded steam train crawled into Warsaw main station carrying Krystyna and her anti-Nazi propaganda. The huge station complex was new, unfinished and devastated by the fighting. She stared at the tall central building, wrecked by Luftwaffe bombs and blackened by an accidental fire in the summer before the war. Where the architects' drawings had shown restaurants and cinemas, there were now only yawning caverns, open to the snow and cold. Acres of rubble surrounded the building, which was fenced off by splintered wooden hoardings. In the distance Krystyna saw the grey, blasted, smashed buildings of the city where she had grown up. Nothing moved in the wide, desolate streets, except for a few pedestrians huddled against the cold, and an occasional horse and cart.

Her first destination was 15 Rozbrat Street, where her mother lived. On her way there she saw Jews being beaten because they were walking in groups of more than three; she witnessed Jewish women and children running down the centre of the streets, forbidden to use the pavements. Gangs of Jews on punitive street-cleaning duty shovelled snow, shivering in ragged clothing.

She stayed with her mother for the next three days. She learnt that her brother Andrzej and several of her cousins had fought against the Germans and were now part of a resistance group. The city of Warsaw was under the control of a 39-year-old lawyer named Hans Frank who had ordered that all Jews must wear white armbands and blue Stars of David. Part of the city had been declared a Ghetto and 400,000 Jews were crammed into an area designed to house less than half that number. Krystyna tried to persuade her mother to leave the capital before she was forced into the Ghetto.

Krystyna met representatives of the most established Polish resistance group, the Union of Armed Struggle, the ZWZ. They were led by General Sosnkowski, an outstanding leader who, after the defeat of Poland, escaped in disguise to France to continue the fight against the Germans. The general's plan was to create a network of cells ready to rise up on the return of the Polish Army. His loyalties were to his government in exile and he did not trust Krystyna. He saw her as a pro-British danger, inexperienced and a liability.

She looked for other groups who might be more sympathetic to her. One day, while sitting in a cafe, a woman, an acquaintance from before the war, shouted out 'Krystyna, Krystyna, what are you doing here? We heard you had gone abroad with your husband.' Krystyna said no, she was not the wife of the diplomat Jerzy Giżycki, nor was she Krystyna Skarbek, the Jew. The woman was puzzled, she said the likeness was uncanny and went on her way.

She became friends with Countess Teresa Łubieńska, a 46-year-old aristocrat who had lost her only son in the September campaign.

The countess introduced Krystyna to Stefan Witkowski, an inventor and engineer. Witkowski was an eccentric maverick who had formed his own underground group, the Musketeers. He nicknamed Krystyna 'Mucha' – Fly. She gave him the propaganda material she had brought from Budapest. He explained how the Musketeers worked, hoping that she would use her influence to get funding from Whitehall.

Krystyna's first stay in Warsaw lasted three weeks. She found that the Poles wanted real news, not propaganda and came up with two schemes, one was for a mobile radio station and the other for a weekly clandestine paper. For the second she signalled London, asking for £100 a month to pay a journalist to run it. Another scheme to supply anti-tank weapons, guns, ammunition and money to a group wanting to start a revolt against the Russians (who now occupied eastern Poland) met with a firm refusal from London. Someone scribbled across her request 'No! – This on no account!'

Before going back to Budapest Krystyna wanted to make contact with resistance groups outside the city. She set off by train but was soon forced to use whatever transport she could find, getting lifts on horse-drawn carts and even walking. The deep snow that covered the fields could not hide the signs of the recent battles. The ruins of war lay everywhere, burnt-out vehicles, ruined farms, makeshift graves, and shattered trees. She saw endless convoys of vehicles grinding across the landscape transporting armies of shivering German soldiers. As she travelled she formed the impression that in spite of its new laws and restrictions the German administration was chaotic. She found German soldiers to be dissatisfied, fearful and often drunk. Back in Warsaw she was reunited with Stefan Witkowski who told her that the Gestapo had set up a headquarters in Zakopane and arranged for her to go back by a different route. Her guide this time was another war hero, Count Wladimir Ledóchowski. The journey took nearly a week, at one point they were fired on by border guards. They travelled by train and on foot and by the time they were back in Budapest Krystyna and Ledóchowski were lovers.

*

A month later on 10 May 1940, the American journalist William L. Shirer sat in a tiny Berlin radio studio feeling tired and sick to the pit of his stomach. He started to speak into the microphone talking to his listeners on the east coast of America: '... the blow in the West has fallen ... the Germans took the initiative today and at dawn their army, supported by a great air armada, moved against Holland, Belgium and Luxembourg ...'

The same day Neville Chamberlain resigned and his place was taken by Winston Churchill. The Phoney War was over.

1940: PARIS AND THE FALL OF FRANCE

On 13 May 1940, German tanks and infantry crossed the River Meuse and drove into France. Churchill flew to Paris and found the French government demoralised and beaten. The roads to the capital began to fill with retreating French soldiers and fleeing Belgian refugees. At first it was the well-off driving cars crammed with luggage, mattresses strapped to the roofs as a defence against the planes that were machine-gunning anything that moved on the roads. Rumours were everywhere: that parachutists had landed disguised as gendarmes; that poison sweets had been dropped at the Gare d'Austerlitz railway station and a child had eaten one and died; that Hitler was about to unleash a secret weapon against which there was no defence.

At the Gare du Nord and Gare de l'Est, trains appeared from the north carrying thousands of refugees. Clare Boothe, an American journalist, reported: 'They came off the trains with bewildered faces, white faces, bloody faces, faces beaten out of human shape by the Niagaras of tears that flowed down them ... The great stations echoed with the saga of their suffering and numbed your brain, sometimes almost your heart.'

By the beginning of May 1940, the British Army had assembled an Expeditionary Force of 394,000 men in France along the borders with Belgium and Germany. They were poised to resist a German advance and had been described in Parliament as being 'As well, if not better equipped than any similar army', which was not true. The advancing Germans rapidly overwhelmed the BEF, which was pushed back until an ordered withdrawal turned into a chaotic and full-scale retreat. By 21 May the British were trapped at Dunkirk with their backs to the sea. A plan, Operation *Dynamo*, was launched to rescue them.

Before Christmas 1939 Virginia Hall had joined the Services sanitaires de l'armée, a nursing service organised by the French Army. She was put through a four-week course in advanced first aid and self-defence after which she was ordered to drive ambulances adapted from Citroën lorries. Virginia had to use her prosthetic leg to depress the clutch pedal, which caused painful blistering. In March she was transferred to Metz, just behind the Maginot Line, the defensive fortification the French had built along the borders with Belgium, Luxembourg and Germany.

Throughout May and early June 1940, volunteer nurses were at work dealing with casualties all along the front line. Virginia Hall drove her ambulance, ferrying the dead and wounded back to field hospitals. Nancy Wake was doing the same driving an ambulance that she had made her husband buy her. She had worked as a nurse in Australia but was not prepared for the terrible wounds caused on the battlefield.

Another volunteer was a French woman, Mathilde Carré, who had told her husband of six years that she was leaving him because she was 'bored, bored, bored'. In the early months of 1940 she joined the Red Cross, looking for adventure on the battlefield. A small, sexy, energetic woman, she never seemed to tire and always wanted to be the best at whatever she was doing. One night she and a surgeon were sent up to the front in an ambulance to collect some wounded French soldiers. They were attacked from the air and forced to take cover in a ditch to avoid howling Stuka dive-bombers and the crashing detonation of explosions. When the raid ended

Carré told her companion: 'There's almost a sensual pleasure in real danger, don't you think? Your whole body seems to suddenly come alive.'

The fighting grew worse and the casualties mounted. Medical teams slept when and where they could, behind the steering wheels of the vehicles and on blood-soaked stretchers in the back. They were running out of medical supplies, food was rationed and water was scarce. The guns rumbled and the refugees pouring along the roads from the Belgian border made movement almost impossible.

At the end of May, seated in a pretty blue-and-white salon at the Ritz in Paris, Clare Boothe and three other American journalists sat talking about the war. They could hear the distant thudding of the heavy guns pounding away in the north-east. One of the four said he was tired of sending pieces with local colour about Paris under siege. 'What are we American journalists doing here?' he said. 'I'll tell you, writing thrilling little Baedekers for Armageddon ... [we ought] to ask our readers and editors back home a question ... If we let France fall, can we say that what we call Democracy is good enough anywhere?'

On 3 June 1940, the Germans bombed the Pont Mirabeau, a bridge across the Seine, badly damaging the nearby Citroën works and the surrounding streets. Crowds gathered and watched in silence as the fire brigade struggled with the flames. The Gare d'Austerlitz, Gare de Lyon and the Gare Montparnasse were jammed with people trying to buy rail tickets for the south.

At Dunkirk the last troops were taken off the beaches, leaving a rearguard of 4000 men. In all more than 338,000 men had been evacuated. They left behind thousands of vehicles, including tanks and armoured cars, all their heavy and medium weapons, millions of rounds of ammunition, and tens of thousands of gallons of petrol. Some of the equipment had been destroyed but a lot of it lay in the fields of France waiting for the Germans to salvage it.

The next day Churchill addressed the House of Commons: 'Even though large tracts of Europe and many old and famous States have fallen or may fall into the grip of the Gestapo and all the odious apparatus of Nazi rule, we shall not flag or fail ...' He went on to say that the fight would continue everywhere, that the British would never surrender, they would hang on until '... in God's good time the New World, with all its power and might, steps forth to the rescue and liberation of the Old.'

Two days later he asked his military planners for 'Proposals for transporting and landing tanks on the beach, observing that we have command of the sea, while the enemy have not.'

The flood of refugees continued to grow, fleeing from the fighting as the Germans advanced across northern France towards Paris. Pedestrians pushing prams loaded with children and possessions jostled with bicycles, horse-drawn carts, lorries and cars. By 10 June a haze of black smoke began to obscure the centre of Paris and a strange smell like burning pine filled the air. At the Musée national des arts, Agnès Humbert, a 45-year-old art historian, packed crates of rare books ready to be taken out of the city to safety. She was grateful that the work took her mind off the chaos and turmoil surrounding her. On the streets people stared into the sky, looking for airborne troops; bands of French soldiers roamed about in ruined uniforms shouting 'A bas la guerre', while the flood of people leaving the city continued to swell every day. Humbert finished her work and sat in the now silent museum, every now and then picking up the phone to listen to bulletins on the news service *Information Parlée*. She could not bring herself to utter the words 'Paris may fall' in case that 'by even saying the words she would make them come true ...'.

The next day the staff of the museum gathered in the courtyard, each carrying a suitcase. The smoke left greasy black marks on their faces. Lorries waited to evacuate them to the country. In a quiet controlled voice the museum director said that he would be grateful if Jewish colleagues would leave first.

Traffic jams stretched for miles along the roads out of Paris to the south and west. The once-distant sound of gunfire grew louder.

Huge queues built up at the petrol pumps. When cars broke down they were either abandoned, or the drivers paid farmers to hitch their vehicles to horses.

The fleeing citizens of Paris – the rich, the poor, the young, the old, the fit and the feeble – turned into a huge, slowly churning river of identical-looking refugees, terrified and sweating in the boiling sun. German aircraft roared overhead, machine-gunning and bombing at random, the shadows from their giant wings racing along beneath them. The planes disappeared into the sky leaving the dead and wounded lying among burning vehicles.

In London, Winston Churchill ordered Sir Maurice Hankey to summon the heads of Section D and Military Intelligence (Research) to discuss 'Certain questions arising out of a possible collapse of France'. The next day words travelled like lightning along the columns of trudging refugees – 'Paris has fallen.' On German radio the same phrase was repeated over and over for hours.

The Germans entered the capital on 14 June. An endless column of German vehicles wound into the nearly deserted city, led by tough, leather-coated men driving BMW motorcycles with machine guns mounted on sidecars, their goggled faces stiff as masks under steel helmets. German military policemen appeared as if by magic to guide the way, waving through the heavy lorries carrying the infantry, sitting upright with rifles between their knees, looking round at the fine buildings lining the boulevards and squares. Next came trucks towing giant 88mm guns that could blow a tank to pieces or shoot an aeroplane out of the sky. Then came the Panzer tanks, engines growling like animals, the commanders braced in the turrets, headphones clamped round their ears and pennants fluttering from whipping aerials while the heavy tracks gouged lumps of tarmac out of the roads. On and on they came, armoured cars, radio vehicles, engineers, signallers, mechanics and cooks, soldiers of every degree and rank rolled into the capital city of the country it had taken them little more than a month to defeat. Wireless chatter and the smell of hot oil, petrol and rubber filled the air. By the end of the afternoon enormous swastikas draped from the Eiffel Tower and over the Hôtel de Ville.

A little-known French general, Charles de Gaulle, had watched in silence, endlessly chain-smoking, as the chaos overwhelmed his country. He refused to accept the idea of the Vichy government and fled to England in a plane provided by the British, accompanied by his aide Lieutenant Geoffroy Chodron de Courcel. On 18 June, with Churchill's permission, he broadcast to France. To those few people who heard the transmission he asked: 'Is defeat final? No! ... France is not alone, France is not alone! ... She can align with England ... She can use, like England ... the immense industry of the United States ... Whatever happens the flame of French Resistance must not and will not be extinguished.'

On Monday 24 June, William L. Shirer found himself at the edge of a sun-dappled clearing in the forest at Compiègne where stood the railway wagon in which a beaten Germany had signed the Armistice at the end of the First World War. Hitler's standard fluttered from a flagpole close by. Hundreds of troops stood guard in rigid lines. The Führer's Mercedes arrived followed by other large black cars, swastika pennants flying, containing Göring and other senior Nazis. In the clearing Hitler walked over to a large granite block and read the words in French engraved on it: 'HERE ON THE 11TH NOVEMBER 1918 SUCCUMBED THE CRIMINAL PRIDE OF THE GERMAN EMPIRE VANQUISHED BY FREE PEOPLES WHICH IT TRIED TO ENSLAVE.'

Shirer could see the German leader's face 'afire with scorn, anger, hate, revenge and triumph'. Hitler was going to negotiate another armistice and he was going to do it inside the same carriage where the French and British had humiliated the Fatherland. The conditions he imposed on the French were harsh, a revenge for the terms imposed on Germany at the end of the First World War.

The treaty was signed the next day. The Germans were to occupy northern and western France, including the Channel and Atlantic ports, about two-thirds of the country. The rest would be a 'Free Zone' administered by a puppet French government from the town of Vichy. A few days later, on 2 August, the Vichy government found Charles de Gaulle guilty of treason and sentenced him to death.

Nancy Wake heard the news about the fall of Paris and cried for days. In Vienna she had seen the Germans humiliating the Jews and had vowed to do anything she could to oppose the Nazis. Now she had witnessed the German war machine at work on French civilians. The sight had put iron in her soul.

Sixteen-year-old Denise Domenach had been a part of the exodus from Paris, crammed into a car with six other members of her household including her parents and two brothers. She wrote in her diary: 'So that's it. The Armistice is signed. France has given in. When we heard this we were wiped out.'

'33 Hints for the Occupied'

The man who had signed the Armistice was the president of Vichy France, 84-year-old Marshal Philippe Pétain, hero of Verdun. The marshal soon introduced anti-Semitic laws, censorship and a new crime of 'felony of opinion'. The old motto of Republican France '*Liberté, egalité, fraternité*' was replaced by '*Travail, famille, patrie*'. Huge quantities of French farm produce were requisitioned and sent to Germany.

Virginia Hall continued to drive ambulances. She was transferred away from the front into the Free Zone where she joined a new unit driving the wounded from Valence to Paris in the Occupied Zone, a round trip of about 700 miles. She discovered that the boundary between the Occupied and the Free Zones of France was as absolute as any frontier. To cross it the citizen needed a *laissez-passer*, issued by the Germans. The possession of one was a privilege, not a right, and it could be withdrawn without warning. Petrol was now rationed and Virginia had to spend time queuing for petrol coupons, passes and the endless rubber stamps she needed to travel in and out of Vichy France. At the end of July she was demobilised and went back to Paris.

Agnès Humbert returned to Paris feeling like an invalid 'recovering from a long and serious illness'. On the train her papers had been examined by the first German soldiers she had seen. The men showed a grunting Teutonic politeness, and waved their lantern in her face. The experience terrified her.

She arrived at the Musée national des arts and found a notice announcing in gothic script that entrance was free to all German troops. Books and exhibits had been removed from the library and replaced with volumes about racial purity. On her way home she was shocked to see a French gendarme saluting German officers in an obsequious and servile manner. The next day she told a colleague that if she did not do something she would go mad. On the Metro someone thrust a leaflet into her pocket. It was headed: *33 Conseils à l'occupé* ('33 Hints for the Occupied'). The thirty-three tips started by describing the German soldiers now arriving in the city on leave from garrisons all over occupied Europe: 'Tour buses unload waves of them in front of Notre-Dame and the Panthéon; each one of them has a little camera screwed to his eye. Don't be fooled, they are not tourists.' Another hint went on: 'On the outside pretend you don't care; on the inside stoke your anger. It will serve you well.' Finally: 'You won't find copies of these tips at your local book shop . . . Make copies for your friends, who will make copies too. This will be a good occupation for the occupied.' Humbert went home and typed out copies, realising that she was not alone, that there was a 'glimmer of light in the darkness'.

In Whitehall senior members of the security services continued to discuss guerrilla warfare, even wondering what they could learn from Sinn Féin and the IRA. They concluded that underground armies must use any method available to them, including propaganda, industrial and military sabotage, terrorist acts and rioting. The people who ran such organisations must be fanatical in their pursuit of the cause, capable of total secrecy, politically reliable and ruled by a controller with almost dictatorial powers.

Three days later the prime minister signed a 'Most Secret' document authorising the creation of a new organisation 'to coordinate all action by way of subversion and sabotage against the enemy overseas'. The organisation was to be known as the Special Operations Executive, the SOE. It was envisaged that the SOE would send small teams into all the occupied countries of Europe to make contact with local guerrilla movements and organise them into groups known as 'circuits', which could be armed and supplied, and brought under British control. The circuits were to be directed towards gathering intelligence and harassing the occupying powers. Eventually they would be used in support of an Allied invasion. The SOE teams were usually made up of three people, a leader, a wireless operator and a courier. The code name of the leader often became the name of the circuit.

The SOE was an ad hoc, amateur force and was not trusted by conventional military men or the established security organisations. Fierce arguments about the SOE soon broke out among representatives of the Foreign Office, the ministries of Information and Economic Warfare, MI5, MI6, the Army, the Royal Navy and the Royal Air Force.

Not everybody living in occupied Paris was French. Pearl Witherington, twenty-six, had been born and raised in France but both her parents were British citizens and she had a British passport. Pearl's father was dead and she lived with her mother and three younger sisters. The family subsisted on what Pearl earned working as a personal assistant at the British Embassy. Her fiancé, Henri Cornioley, was a French prisoner of war. After the invasion Pearl had tried but failed to get her family out of France. She now had no money and no idea what to do. A rule was soon introduced that British nationals in Paris must sign in at the police station every day. It became illegal to move anywhere without properly registered and stamped identity cards. A curfew was introduced between 11.00 p.m. to 6.00 a.m. Food was rationed and could not be purchased without coupons. Loudspeaker vans toured the streets issuing proclamations and reminding people that acts of aggression against the occupying forces were punishable by death. Pearl knew that it was only a matter of time before she and her family were arrested and sent to a concentration camp.

For Virginia Hall, things were easier. As an American citizen she could come and go as she pleased. After her demobilisation she felt she had seen enough of how the Germans were behaving and decided to move to England. She left Paris on a train bound for Spain and then Lisbon where she could get a boat to Southampton. On the train she met an Englishman, George Bellows, who introduced himself as a businessman. Virginia told him about herself and her time in France. He thought the fact that she could speak four languages, had spent a lot of time in Europe and knew France might interest his contacts in London. Before they parted he gave her a list of telephone numbers and suggested that Virginia ring them.

The summer turned into autumn and the faint feelings of hope that Agnès Humbert had felt when she first read '33 Hints for the Occupied' continued to grow. She was now part of a small group of academics, lawyers and museum staff dedicated to opposing the invaders. That September the group produced their first tract, 'Vichy at War'. Copies were printed on the museum's Roneo machine. Humbert used the museum's large-font typewriter to print *Vive le général de Gaulle* on sticky labels, which were plastered all over the city. A colleague typed more labels printed with *Nous sommes pour le général de Gaulle*, which he carried round on his bicycle, fixing them onto the side doors and tailgates of German lorries, a crime that carried the death penalty.

Without warning and with no explanation Agnes was dismissed from her job. She went on working for the group and helped produce the first edition of an underground news sheet, *Résistance*. The opening paragraph read: 'Resister! It is the cry from your heart to all, in the distress that the disaster that has overwhelmed our country. It is the cry of all of you who won't give up, and of all of you who want to do your duty.' Hundreds of copies were secretly distributed throughout the Occupied Zone.

Before the Armistice Mathilde Carré had been ordered to Bordeaux, and was told to 'Get there any way you can.' She arrived, tired, filthy and hungry to find there was no organisation for her to report to – her war was over.

One lunchtime she sat in a crowded restaurant, now wearing an elegant black suit when a waiter asked if she would mind sharing her table. Carré looked up and saw a handsome dark-haired man in ill-fitting clothes. Nodding, she waved her slim fingers for him to sit. They began to talk. The stranger was charming and introduced himself as Armand Bori. He claimed to be a Frenchman though he spoke with a strange accent, which he explained was because he had been born and brought up in Poland. As the afternoon wore on Bori suggested that she might agree to give him lessons in pronunciation and Carré agreed. In the following weeks they became close. Bori revealed that he was a major in the Polish Air Force, a fully trained intelligence officer with orders to set up a network of agents in the Occupied Zone. He was already in regular communication with London through a secret radio located in Marseille. His real name, he told her, was Roman Czerniawski. Then he asked her if she was interested in helping him, warning her that the work was dangerous, arrest meant the death penalty. Carré agreed and became his lover. He nicknamed her La Chatte – The Cat.

On Bastille Day, 14 July 1940, General de Gaulle held a parade at the Cenotaph in Whitehall. It was a lonely moment for the French general, the British government had recognised him as leader of all the Free French but he had failed to get the support of the French diplomatic community exiled in London. His attempts to rally support among French servicemen impounded in temporary camps in England had proved disappointing; many opted to go back to France rather than join him. On 3 July 1940 the British Navy had sunk the French fleet at Mers el-Kébir to prevent it falling into German hands. Killed in the operation were 1300 French sailors, leaving many Frenchmen bitter towards the British.

The large crowd of Londoners that came to watch the proceedings at the Cenotaph fell silent as de Gaulle approached the memorial. In his hands he carried a wreath; behind him stood a group of French officers flanked by a guard of honour drawn from French troops loyal to de Gaulle. He laid the wreath gently on the steps of the monument, stepped back and saluted. The officers with him did the same while the soldiers presented arms, many of them in tears. De Gaulle shouted '*Vive la France ... Vive l'Angleterre*'; a massive cheer went up, and the crowd roared in unison '*Vive la France, Vive l'Angleterre*'.

Among the men on parade was a Foreign Legionnaire, Sergeant Major Etienne Szabo. In the crowd lining the pavement stood Violette Bushell with instructions from her mother to find a homesick French soldier and bring him to their house in South London. That night Szabo sat with the Bushells in Stockwell eating supper and talking in French. Before he went back to his barracks in Farnborough he asked Violette if they could perhaps meet again.

The next month they were married at Aldershot Registry Office. Violette was nineteen and Etienne thirty. A week later Etienne Szabo was on board a ship, part of a convoy carrying General de Gaulle to Dakar to persuade the Vichy French in West Africa to change sides. When the general failed in that mission he wrote to his wife saying, 'The ceiling is going to fall in on my head.'

In Marseille, Nancy Wake stood in a crowd watching the leader of the Vichy government, Marshal Pétain, review a parade of 15,000 veterans, men of the Légion française des combattants, an organisation set up by the Vichy government to honour French veteran soldiers. One witness reported that: '... without a smile he surveys the electrified crowd, which he salutes with a wave of his stick. His head white as snow and pale blue eyes. His calm has a powerful effect.' When the crowd surged round him, an old woman kissed the hem of his coat in a religious fervour.

Nancy was not impressed. She found Pétain a fraud, and said they were all sick of 'Daddy and his preachings of morality and virtue.' France was an occupied country and Nancy did not like the experience: 'it was something you carried with you from the moment you woke until you went to bed. And you didn't know who to trust, even members of your own family.'

Denise Domenach complained to her diary:

> Now we have to have cards for everything: bread, meat, sugar, oil, butter, flour, soap, coffee, coal. If German gentlemen are passing one is obliged to stand aside. The other day Bernard and I failed to get out of the way and were squashed by a car full of the Boches. We know now what it is like to live in an occupied country ... It seems that in London there is a French general who thinks of us.

Later she wrote, 'We continue to encounter the Boches in the streets. Everyone has a different reaction. I know some who spit on the ground. Others make a face. Me, I whisper just loud enough for them to hear "Tchistrack" it seems that is the word for "Merde" in Boche.'

In Marseille Nancy Wake met a French Army officer, code-named *Xavier*, who was involved in the Resistance. When he found out that she travelled a lot in the south of France he asked if she would take a letter to the coastal town of Cannes. She agreed and soon became a regular courier delivering papers, and sometimes equipment, including a wireless transmitting set. With the help of her husband Henri's money she quickly became skilled at obtaining false identity papers and coupons for food, petrol and clothing.

The Hôtel du Louvre et Paix in Marseille where she held her wedding reception was now a favourite haunt of German officers. Wake and her friends spent their evenings in the small back bar, drinking and keeping an eye on the invaders lounging in the sumptuous foyer, nicknaming them *Fridolins* – a version of the name Frederick. Here Wake met a British officer, a POW on parole from his prison camp and through him met Captain Ian Garrow of the Highland Light Infantry, also on parole. Garrow was a tall, dark-haired man of twenty-two. He broke his parole, went into hiding in Marseille and began to organise an escape route into Spain for trapped Allied personnel. Before long, Nancy, again with the help of Henri's money, was working for him as a courier.

Mathilde Carré and her lover Roman Czerniawski moved to Paris looking for recruits for their Resistance network which now had the code name *Interallié*. Their apartment at number 14 rue du Colonel Moll became their headquarters. On a wall in the living room Czerniawski pinned a large-scale map of France and drew lines on it in charcoal, dividing the Occupied Zone into thirteen sectors. Michel Brault, a well-known lawyer, was persuaded to allow them to claim to be on his part-time staff dealing with legal matters outside Paris. This would help them explain why they were in contact with so many people. An old childhood friend of Carré's, René Aubertin, introduced them to the president of the Association of Chemical Engineers, Marc Marchal, who ran a small underground network recruited from his close friends. He agreed to bring them under the wing of Czerniawski and was given the code name *Uncle Marco*. Carré moved round Paris, almost always dressed in a brown fur coat and red beret. She identified contact after contact, using her charm to persuade each one to join *Interallié*. Before long the network included Charles Lejeune, a senior policeman, who provided access to blank identity cards and police documentation. When Lejeune's wife, Mireille, introduced Carré to her neighbours the Hugentoblers, the couple agreed that their house could be used as a secret letter drop.

By the end of 1940 *Interallié* had a network of nearly 200 agents working all over France. Reports went to London on a daily basis and every week Mathilde Carré typed out a sixteen-page report on thin rice paper to be smuggled to Lisbon and from there to London by plane. The fog of secrecy that had descended on France was clearing. Intelligence teams in London were beginning to piece together a picture of what the German war machine was doing.

On 1 September 1940, Virginia Hall reached London from Lisbon. She found a city braced for invasion. Barrage balloons bobbed over the city. The entrances to official buildings were protected by sandbags and the windows of shops and houses were taped to prevent injuries from splintering glass. Official signs sprouted on government buildings. Wooden boards with the word 'Shelter' and an arrow pointing to the nearest place of safety were on every main street. Main roads out of the capital were closed so that priority could be given to the busloads of children being evacuated to the country. At night cities were blacked out and lamp posts painted with white rings to make them more noticeable in the dark. A law had been passed requiring everybody to carry a gas mask and every other person seemed to be in uniform.

Virginia rented a room at 4 Queen Street in Westminster, made contact with the American Embassy and briefed the ambassador about life in occupied France. She told him she wanted to go back to America to be reunited with her family, especially her mother. For this she had to get permission and visas. In the meantime the embassy offered her a job as a secretary.

On 17 September the full-scale bombing of civilian targets began, the Blitz. For night after night British cities were battered by thousands of tons of high explosives. London's docks disappeared in sheets of flame fuelled by the sugar, paint and alcohol stored there in huge quantities.

At the beginning of December German security forces, in collaboration with French police, began to round up the last few British citizens marooned in Paris. The police officers at the station where Pearl Witherington had to go every day to register warned her to get out, saying that she and her family were in danger of arrest. The Witherington family went into hiding, protected by neighbours. A few days later Pearl got them on a train travelling into the Free Zone. The family had no passes and no way of knowing how they were going to cross the Demarcation Line. On the way Pearl met a man who was taking horses across the line and asked him to help. With his assistance they left the train, hid in ditches to dodge German border patrols, caught another train and got safely across. Pearl's new-found friend paid for the extra tickets and even bought them coffee. Eventually they reached Marseille where they hoped to find a way to get to Spain.

In Budapest, Krystyna Skarbek's flat had become a store for weapons and explosives. She found that her local Section D contact, a journalist called Hubert Harrison, was unreliable; he was often late paying her salary and she wondered if he read the reports that she and her contacts risked their lives to gather. The Polish underground, loyal to the government in exile, were still wary of Krystyna and her association with British Intelligence. One officer said, 'We do not want the British to poke inside our underpants.'

Krystyna had many admirers. One rejected suitor threatened to castrate himself with a revolver, but failed, hitting himself in the foot. Later he tried to commit suicide by throwing himself in the Danube, only realising that this was not going to work when he crashed onto frozen ice.

During the battle for Poland in 1939, a new Polish high-velocity anti-tank rifle had proved very effective against even well-armoured German tanks. Its presence on the battlefield had been a secret and the weapon was kept in boxes marked 'Do Not Open, Surveillance Equipment'. After the surrender the blueprints for the gun were destroyed. Krystyna discovered that one of the weapons had been smuggled into Hungary and was hidden under the bed of the agent who had rescued it. She took the rifle just before pro-German police raided the agent's flat. Then she sawed off the barrel and the stock and got it out of Hungary in the diplomatic bag.

Krystyna made another trip into Poland with Wladimir Ledóchowski. They carried rucksacks packed with American, Polish, Czech and Hungarian currency, false identity documents, microfilm, maps, a compass and photographs of Winston Churchill standing with the Polish general Władysław Sikorski. On the first leg of the journey they crossed the border into Czechoslovakia on foot at sunset. They were spotted and fired on, just managing to escape into the woods, bullets smacking into the trees around them. They marched through the following day until exhaustion forced them to try to find a train to take them into Poland. At the first railway station they disturbed the stationmaster's dog, which barked, giving them away. They were arrested by a lone guard who held them until a patrol arrived to take them to the police station to wait for the Gestapo. While they waited Ledóchowski said they were brother and sister trying to get home to Poland from a Hungarian internment camp. Krystyna took up the story distracting the guard while Ledóchowski destroyed some of the incriminating material he had in his rucksack. The patrol arrived and marched them off, stumbling through the dark, wet night. At an iron bridge over a river Krystyna began to limp and make a fuss about her feet. Ledóchowski used the diversion to throw the packet of photographs into the water. The guards saw what he was doing and began yelling, shouting that the pair would be shot. They were put up against a wall and interrogated for hours. The contents of the rucksacks were spread on the ground. One of the men held up a necklace belonging to Krystyna. She snatched at it, screaming and scratching the man's face, ordering him to return her 'diamonds'. In the confusion they bolted, the guards firing wildly into the darkness after them. It took two days to get back to the Hungarian border. On the way they were fired on again and Krystyna fell down a slope, injuring her leg.

Krystyna then went to Poland and returned with microfilm carrying information about ammunition factories, aircraft manufacture, and submarine warfare, including details of a new torpedo. The intelligence had been gathered by agents who had infiltrated forced labour groups working in Germany. She also bought a large Anglo-Russian dictionary in which was hidden cypher information to be used to establish an undercover radio link between London and Warsaw. She got back to Budapest at the end of November, tired and ill. She had been in the field for nearly a year. The networks she had helped set up gathered intelligence about troop and freight movements all over Poland and provided information about Romanian oil fields. She organised escape routes, sabotaged communications and helped blow up petrol barges on the Danube. Gestapo agents trying to keep track of her in Budapest were baffled by her wild cover stories. In Poland posters appeared carrying her picture and offering £1000 for her arrest. Sir Owen O'Malley, the British ambassador in Budapest, said that Krystyna was the bravest women he had ever met, adding that she could 'do anything with dynamite except eat it'.

1941: F SECTION
V THE ABWEHR

One contact Virginia Hall had been given by George Bellows, the man on the train, was Nicolas Bodington. She contacted him early in the new year and he invited her to dinner. She arrived at his house to find a man of about her age with a small moustache and large round glasses. She did not know about his pre-war relationship with a Gestapo officer named Karl Bömelburg or that he had spent several months failing to join MI6 before being taken on by F Section, the branch of the newly formed SOE that dealt with France. F Section's officers were impressed that Bodington spoke French and had been educated in the country.

Over supper Hall discovered that Bodington and his American wife loved food, drink and the arts. As they ate Virginia told him she wanted to go back to France for a few weeks on a relief mission. She reminded him that as an American citizen she would be able to move about with comparative freedom.

The next day Bodington sent a memo to 'F', the abbreviation for his boss, telling him about Virginia Hall, saying that: 'This lady ... might well be used for a mission.' He wanted to fund her trip to France in return for whatever information she might be able to send back. He ended saying that he was going to 'put her through the cards' which meant he would run a security check on her.

He asked Virginia to come for a formal interview. He found that she was from an affluent background, was well travelled, fluent in French, German and Italian, and could get by in Russian. In spite of her disability she claimed to be able to ride horses, sail, climb mountains, shoot and ride a bicycle. She admitted that she could not run and had no knowledge of wireless communications. Her service as an ambulance driver in France gave her the right to claim that she had already been on active service. Bodington was impressed and wrote saying that he recommended her for use as a 'Class A liaison in France – unoccupied territory with journalistic cover.'

At 4 a.m. on 23 January 1941, the pro-Nazi Hungarian military police burst into the flat where Krystyna and Kowerski were sleeping. After spending an hour turning the flat upside down they found nothing but still took the pair in for questioning. As they were led away Kowerski was astonished to see Krystyna smiling as though they were going to a cocktail party.

In her cell, Krystyna was shown a set of false papers in the name of Zofia Andrzejewska, one of her cover identities. Staring at the photograph of herself she admitted a similarity, 'but it seems to me that the girl in the picture is much prettier'. She and Andrzej were brutally interrogated for nineteen hours. Finally, knowing that the Germans were terrified of tuberculosis, she bit hard on her tongue causing it to bleed. She convulsed and appeared to be coughing up blood, one of the symptoms of the disease. A prison doctor was called who demanded that Krystyna's chest be X-rayed. Years earlier she had worked for a Fiat dealership and the fumes from the garage had damaged her lungs. The damage showed up on the X-ray as shadows and the doctor confirmed it was tuberculosis, recommending that she be released. He warned that Kowerski might also be contagious.

The two were let out on condition that they did not leave Budapest, or even their flat, without permission. They could only travel round the city by tram and had to report by phone to the police every three hours. Another condition of release was that they were to go straight to the Café Hangli, which the police suspected they were using as a rendezvous. The couple left, followed by two plain-clothes policemen. Their resistance friends had been warned about the arrest and at the cafe no one approached them. Eventually they went home and discovered that the phone was tapped and the flat under observation. They decided it was time to leave Hungary.

The police knew that Kowerski had a car, the Chevrolet in which he had first wooed Krystyna. They did not know that he had a second car, an Opel, hidden in an old greenhouse. One night a friend acted as a decoy, driving the Chevrolet out of the city. The police followed, thinking the couple were escaping. With the coast clear Kowerski and Krystyna took the Opel and drove to the British legation to ask the ambassador, Sir Owen O'Malley, for help.

O'Malley gave them British passports and new names, Christine Granville and Andrew Kennedy. For good measure Christine knocked seven years off her age, her new passport showing her as twenty-six. A member of O'Malley's staff was ordered to drive Krystyna across the border.

In the embassy garage the boot of the car was opened, Krystyna climbed into the tiny space, contorting her body, 'like a penknife' then the boot was gently closed. Kowerski set off first in the Opel, followed by the embassy car with pennants fluttering from the wings. The cars reached Lenti, the border crossing with Slovenia, and Kowerski ostentatiously pulled over to let the diplomatic vehicle go first. Trapped in the darkness Krystyna heard the guards asking to look in the boot. There was a short argument followed by laughter and the car accelerated on. Once out of sight of the border the car pulled up and, like a butterfly, Christine Granville unwound herself from the steel cocoon and climbed blinking into the light.

In occupied Paris Agnès Humbert climbed the stairs to the clinic where her mother was recovering from an operation. Waiting for her at the top were two men who declared themselves to be 'German Police' and asked her to go with them back to her house which they were going to search. They broke furniture, rummaged through her clothes, found a few half-finished copies of *Résistance* and arrested her. What the Germans missed, hidden under the floorboards, was a list of 400 people who were associated with *Résistance*, complete with addresses and telephone numbers. There were also copies of every edition of the paper. They took her to Gestapo headquarters where they interrogated her, making her stand while they circled her, screaming in German.

After three hours they let her glimpse a fellow Resistance worker. He had been beaten and could not stand or walk properly. The interrogators sniggered and said, 'He's changed a bit since he's been with us don't you think?' Humbert thought that the look of sadness in the prisoner's eyes would haunt her for ever. For another four hours the interrogators bawled at her. By eight o'clock that evening Humbert was in Paris in solitary confinement in the military Cherche-Midi Prison. There were bloodstains on the walls.

In Britain de Gaulle's Free French authorities became aware of the existence of SOE F Section. When they realised that they had been kept in the dark about the secret organisation operating inside their own country they became angry. As a result, and to placate them, SOE set up a parallel organisation called RF Section with headquarters in a house rented from Bertram Mills Circus in Dorset Square. Although ultimately it reported to Colin Gubbins, RF Section was directed by de Gaulle and the Free French. Most of the recruits were native French patriots. From the start relationships between F Section and RF Section were not simple or easy.

On the moonlit night of 5 April 1941, a bomber droned low over the estate of Philippe de Vomécourt, near Châteauroux in central France. Inside the fuselage Georges Bégué, a radio operator and the first SOE agent to be sent in, waited with his legs dangling over a hole in the aircraft's floor. Watching him was a dispatcher, the operative responsible for his well-being on the flight, for making sure his parachute lines were attached properly and that he jumped on time. A green light flashed on, the dispatcher gave the thumbs up and Bégué dropped into the darkness, followed by his radio set. Five days later three more agents fell from the sky, one of whom was Philippe's brother Pierre, a handsome and capable 35-year-old. Radio contact with London was quickly made and a month later two canisters floated down, thudding onto the lawns of the de Vomécourt estate. The tommy guns, knives, plastic explosives and anti-shipping devices they contained were hidden in the shrubbery round the chateau.

After nearly a year F Section was in business and ready for action. In London there was a flurry of papers debating exactly what that action should be. A document arrived on Churchill's desk, which made the exaggerated claim that F Section SOE was now ready to 'set in motion large-scale and long-term schemes for revolution in Europe'.

In 1925, in his political manifesto *Mein Kampf*, Hitler wrote that the communist Soviet Union was an ideological enemy of Germany. Nevertheless Germany and Russia had invaded Poland together as allies. Hitler was a capricious ally and on the afternoon of 22 June 1941 he turned on Russia and initiated Operation *Barbarossa*. Four million German soldiers, transported by 600,000 vehicles and 700,000 horses, crossed the Russian border on a 2000-mile-wide front. Hitler had ordered that the plan was to be carried out with unprecedented, unmerciful and unrelenting harshness. He told his countrymen:

National Socialists!

The German People have never had hostile feelings towards the people of Russia ... However the Jewish-Bolshevist rulers in Moscow have attempted to set not only Germany but all of Europe aflame ... The results of their efforts were chaos, misery and starvation ... Today an attack [on Russia] unprecedented in the history of the world in its extent and size has begun ... The purpose of this front is the safety of Europe and therefore the salvation of everyone.

May God help us in this battle.

Nicolas Bodington wanted to get Virginia Hall into action as quickly as possible and set about organising her cover as an American journalist. He persuaded George Backer, the editor and president of the *New York Post*, to accept her as an accredited member of his staff and to publish any articles that Hall might send from France. Now Bodington had to give her the skills she was to need in the field. He sent her away for a few weeks to be given a fast version of the SOE training course.

The expert teaching the latest intake of SOE trainee agents about explosives was puzzled. He thought he saw a woman among his class of men. Nonplussed, he continued with the lesson, describing a new plastic explosive that could be moulded like putty and concealed in the complex shapes of engines and machine housings. Correctly used it could destroy vital parts that might take weeks to replace and bring factories and communications systems to a halt. As he talked about the vulnerable parts of railway signal boxes and a fuse called a 'time pencil' that could be set to explode anything up to twenty-four hours ahead he tried to get a good look at the new student's face. In the darkness of the gloomy lecture hut he could not be certain if it was a man or a woman. His mystery pupil was Virginia Hall.

As well as explosives she learned to use the Fairbairn–Sykes Commando knife, a slim and lethal weapon that the instructor told them to use 'delicately' with an upward stabbing motion. At first Virginia and her class practised sneaking up behind straw-filled dummies, grabbing them round the neck and slitting their throats. Then they were given a wooden knife and told to do the same thing to a human. Hall smeared her blade with red lipstick and crept silently behind her victim, grabbing him, and slashing his throat. The victim turned round to reveal a smear of bright-red lipstick across his Adam's apple.

She was taught about radio communications, weapons and security measures. Her false leg prevented her from attending parachute training. One night she was pulled from her room by two men who appeared to be officers in the Abwehr, the German counter-espionage service, accompanied by a French gendarme. She was taken to a room where she was screamed at, bullied and threatened but never faltered from her cover story that she was a fully accredited American journalist.

On 23 August she left England by aeroplane for Lisbon from where she took a train through Spain into the Free Zone of France. In her memory were the only contacts SOE had been able to come up with, a list of five people. Her train pulled into Vichy on 4 September. Virginia's first act after renting an apartment was to present herself and her papers to the American Consul and the French police.

To substantiate her cover story she began to write articles about life in the defeated country. They appeared in the *New York Post*. She stayed in Vichy until she had established her cover then felt it was safe to move to Lyon. Soon after she arrived she met a young British pilot, Flight Lieutenant William Simpson, who had escaped from a blazing aeroplane in May of the previous year. He had lost all his fingers, his face was badly burned and he was waiting for repatriation to England. The two met almost every day and eventually Hall revealed that she was a British agent, telling him how difficult she was finding it to build up her network of contacts. Simpson warned Hall that Lyon was full of imposters, false friends and Nazi sympathisers who would not hesitate to double-cross her. Then he began to introduce her to people he trusted.

One was Mme Germaine Guérin, the madame of a brothel who entertained anyone who could pay, especially German officers, French police officers, industrialists and members of the Vichy government. She used some of her takings to rent apartments where she hid people on the run, Jews, Poles and escaping Allied prisoners of war.

Mme Guérin had a friend, an engineer who regularly travelled to Paris, crossing in and out of the Occupied Zone. Another of her friends was a gynaecologist, Dr Jean Rousset, a stooping grey-haired man with a dark moustache, who looked after the girls in the brothel. The prostitutes picked up a lot of gossip from their homesick German clients and passed it all on to the doctor, providing information about what the units around Lyon were doing and where they were going. Pillow talk was also a good indicator of German morale. Rousset was a source of false medical certificates, especially useful for people who had been selected for obligatory work in Germany and wanted to show they were too ill to travel. Hall and Rousset came up with an idea to use a psychiatric clinic to hide escaping British pilots and agents among the inmates.

Another recruit brought in by Simpson was Robert Leprevost, an organiser for an escape route for aviators who had been shot down. Leprevost was also a source of false papers and identity cards. Soon Simpson, whose injuries were very bad, was put aboard an ambulance train, heading for Spain and repatriation. Virginia was sad to lose a useful ally.

By the end of the summer, on the Eastern Front, German troops were within forty miles of Moscow, where they had captured nearly a million prisoners and thousands of guns and tanks. Diplomats and civil servants in the city prepared to evacuate. Then came the autumn rains and with it mud – Rasputitza. The advance bogged down, supplies ran low and tanks had to be used to drag bogged vehicles out of the mire.

When winter arrived it found the troops equipped for summer, without heavy boots, thick woollen socks, or winter clothing of any sort. Fuel froze, oil thickened, machine guns jammed solid with ice and men went down with frostbite. The Russians fought back with a fury that none of the invaders had ever experienced. One German staff officer wrote in his diary: 'The moment must be faced when the strength of our troops is at an end.'

While the Soviet Union and the Third Reich slugged it out, SOE's F Section acquired a new chief, Maurice Buckmaster, a 39-year-old, French-speaking, hard-working man. Like many old Etonians he was popular with some and disliked by others. He had survived Dunkirk and before the war had worked in France. His new boss, Colin Gubbins, told him that F Section was 'highly embryonic'.

In the first two months of his command Buckmaster sent fourteen agents, a record number, into France. By November 1941 they were all behind bars.

Buckmaster appointed a civilian woman, Vera Atkins, as his personal assistant. Atkins looked and behaved as though she was a member of the British upper-middle classes. Her accent was clipped, her vowels drawn out, her clothes immaculate, her jewellery expensive and her hair coiffed. Every day a taxi collected her from the Chelsea flat where she lived with her mother and delivered her to the SOE office at 64 Baker Street. Atkins was a small, chainsmoking woman, known for her formidable memory and her ability to intimidate her colleagues. One of her staff confessed that Atkins 'was the SOE'. Her duties included attending the daily meetings of section heads which Buckmaster chaired. Buckmaster found that her memory and her brilliant organisational abilities made her 'indispensable'. Unusually for someone working in such a top-secret world, Atkins was not British but a well-born Romanian refugee. Her name was Vera-May Rosenberg and in 1940 she and her mother had escaped from Europe with the help of the Resistance and an Abwehr officer she had bribed.

The Polish-run *Interallié*, continued to flood London with intelligence from all over France. Its agents gathered information about ammunition dumps, airfields, and factories working for the German war effort. Men operating undercover within the French railway system monitored trains, noting where they were going and the precise details of their loads. Propaganda experts provided accurate summaries of what was appearing in the German-controlled French press and assessments of the morale of French civilians and German troops.

To handle the growing traffic a powerful radio transmitter was built from spares and installed on the top floor of an apartment near the Trocadéro in Paris. The first signal received from London read 'To Interallié Congratulations'. Soon *Interallié* had four radio sets transmitting and receiving.

The organisation outgrew the apartment in the rue du Colonel

Moll and moved into the upper part of a red-brick house found by Carré, 8 rue Villa Léandre in Montmartre. Carré told the owner that Roman Czerniawski was her cousin and that he had dealings in the black market and kept odd hours. Czerniawski invited a former lover, Renée Borni, to join him and train as a radio operator. She was a young, unsophisticated, pretty, dark-eyed girl. Carré hated her on sight and moved out of No. 8 into an apartment round the corner in the rue Cortot, a steep hill where Maurice Utrillo had once lived and worked.

By Christmas 1941 Roman Czerniawski felt able to throw a small party, to celebrate the end of the first year of *Interallié*'s activities. The guests gathered in the red-brick house in the rue Villa Léandre and listened to a broadcast from London – 'We wish happy birthday to our reunited family in Paris'. They sent a reply – 'Always and everything against the Boche' and drank a toast. The atmosphere in the room was difficult. People felt the tension between Carré and Czerniawski's lover Renée Borni. Earlier in the evening the two women had squabbled over a new fur coat that the leader had given his girlfriend.

The same evening, at Abwehr headquarters, Hugo Bleicher was interrogating a captured *Interallié* agent and persuading him to change sides. Bleicher was a small but effective cog in the German security service. Fluent in Spanish and French he had answered an advertisement calling for volunteers to join the censorship service vetting military and civilian mail. He found himself instead a private in the Geheime Feldpolizei, the plain-clothed secret military police. Bleicher passed his days arresting and interrogating fugitive French prisoners of war and people who had been denounced by their neighbours. Private Bleicher was good at his job and very soon was transferred to Military Intelligence, the Abwehr, where he was promoted to *Feldwebel*, a senior NCO.

The Abwehr had a rival: the Sicherheitsdienst or SD, a sister organisation to the SS-controlled Gestapo. The Gestapo were the secret police while the SD dealt with intelligence; both used intimidation and torture as part of their interrogation technique.

Czerniawski spent the day after the party in his room with Renée Borni. While he worked on the organisation of the circuit Renée typed out messages for transmission to London by two wireless operators housed in the attic. Night fell and the couple went to a small restaurant in Montmartre for supper. In the corner was a three-piece band and when Roman and Renée had finished their supper the violinist came over and asked 'What does Madame wish us to play?' Borni replied, 'Could you play "Sombre Dimanche"?' The room filled with the melancholy sad tune about a man lamenting his lover, knowing he will never see her again. Czerniawski had heard it the year before in Bucharest, just after the collapse of Poland and had been told that a friend had committed suicide listening to it.

In the pouring rain the pair walked back to the apartment, sheltering under an umbrella. Inside Czerniawski shook the umbrella to get the rain off. Renée grabbed and closed it, saying it was bad luck to open an umbrella inside a room. Czerniawski told her that he was not superstitious. At just after three in the morning they went to bed, tired and tense, falling into a deep sleep.

The winter sun had not yet begun to rise over the streets of Paris when the front door of 8 rue Villa Léandre was smashed in by soldiers bawling in German. Hugo Bleicher, wearing a trenchcoat and a beret, burst into Czerniawski's room and fired a pistol into the air, shouting 'Hands up', yelling at the soldiers to search the house. Feet thumped on the stairs leading to the attic containing the two radio operators, their transmitter and code books. Renée sat up in bed, sobbing. Czerniawski, wearing silk pyjamas, stood in the middle of the room, his hands on his head, saying, 'I am a Polish officer and I wish to be treated as a prisoner of war.'

Bleicher stared at him, his sharp eyes obscured by light from the bulb in the ceiling reflecting in the thick lenses of his glasses. He smiled, lowered the gun and said, 'Get dressed.' The house filled with the sound of smashing furniture as cupboards were torn open, drawers flung onto the floor and papers scattered everywhere. Czerniawski had no idea what had happened to the two radio men in the attic. To divert the hunters he said, 'The papers you are looking for are in that wardrobe.'

A soldier pulled Renée out of bed and made her stand against a wall, naked except for a sheet, her eyes wide with fear. Bleicher pressed close to her, speaking quietly in French. Czerniawski said, 'She has nothing to do with us. She is just my girlfriend.' Bleicher ignored him and went on talking.

A soldier burst into the room and shouted, pointing towards the attic. Bleicher grabbed the now fully dressed Czerniawski by the wrists and handcuffed him. Outside hobnail boots clattered along the cobbles, fists thumped on doors and lorry engines revved. A soldier hit Czerniawski in the back with his rifle. The tall Pole looked at his mistress and murmured 'Goodbye' before being forced out of the room, down the stairs and into the road where several cars were waiting, engines running, doors wide open. Czerniawski was thrown into the back of one, two soldiers bounced in on either side of him and it accelerated onto the Avenue Junot, swerving to avoid the soldiers running and shouting to each other. The heavy vehicle skidded through the steep streets of Montmartre, heading for Abwehr headquarters.

Back at 8 rue Villa Léandre, Bleicher continued to murmur softly to Renée Borni who began to nod and speak while a soldier stuffed handfuls of *Interallié* papers into a suitcase. It was six o'clock in the morning, the sun had just begun to rise. Somehow the radio operators had escaped.

Mathilde Carré had spent the night in another part of the city and came home after the curfew had finished. Climbing the steps that led to the rue Cortot where she had her room, she could see the commotion of soldiers and a vehicle at the turning to the rue Villa Léandre. In front of her a group of men in long raincoats and trilby hats lurked by a cafe called the Lapin Agile. Carré hurried past, ignored the men and headed for the Place du Tertre, trying to work out what to do. She stopped by a print shop to check if she was being followed. A voice at her shoulder said, 'What are you doing here so early in the morning?' It was one of the men in the long raincoats.

She said she was looking for a present for a friend with whom she was having lunch. The man smiled and said, 'Why don't you have lunch with me instead?' Suddenly she was grabbed from behind by two more men who lifted her off the ground. 'We've been waiting for you. Come with us.' Then they bundled her into a police van. The doors slammed and as it sped off Carré heard her landlady shouting, 'Don't hurt her, she has done nothing wrong!' Seconds later it stopped, the rear doors were pulled open and Carré found herself staring at Renée Borni and Hugo Bleicher. Bleicher looked at Borni who nodded, saying, 'Yes that's her, the Cat.'

That night Carré lay in the dark on a wooden bed in a cell in La Santé Prison wearing all her clothes. It was freezing cold – the tiny room was filthy and stank of urine. She wanted to die.

At dawn she was woken by a guard screaming at her to stand to attention when she was spoken to and to clean her cell. Then she was taken back to Abwehr headquarters where she found herself in a pleasant, light room at the top of the building. A steward came in and served her real coffee, milk, butter, sugar and rolls. Bleicher appeared. He offered her a cigarette and told her she was too intelligent and interesting a person to rot in prison. He asked for her help in destroying the *Interallié* network. He told her they had captured many documents in the raid on 8 rue Villa Léandre and had a long list of suspects. He had to make arrests and needed her help. The war was over, he said, England had lost. As she finished eating the breakfast he said: 'Work with me loyally and you shall be free: but if you try any tricks with me it will mean your immediate execution.'

The first to be arrested that day was an agent who had arranged to meet Carré at the Café Pam Pam on the Champs-Elysées. He was introduced to Bleicher and accepted a lift from him, thinking he was a friend. As they sped through the streets Bleicher pulled out his gun and said: 'Monsieur you are now in a car of the German police and I beg you not to make a painful scene.' Bleicher was relentless in the pursuit, pausing only to have a lavish lunch with Carré at the Café Graff. By the end of the day all the early recruits to *Interallié*, Lejeune the senior police chief, René Aubertin, Carré's childhood friend, and *Uncle Marco*, were in separate cells in Fresnes Prison.

The last to be arrested that day were the Hugentoblers whose house was used as a letter drop. Bleicher pushed into their apartment waving his gun. At the sight Madame Hugentobler became hysterical, crying out that she had a fourteen-year-old daughter and a baby that was not even a year old. Bleicher stared at her and said, 'France will look after your baby.' She was dragged out of the building screaming and sobbing. By midnight the Hugentoblers were in cells in separate prisons.

Bleicher's work was over for the day. He bought Carré a sumptuous dinner and then, to her surprise, drove her to the outskirts of Paris, to the Villa Harry Baur in the exclusive Maisons-Laffitte complex where he and some senior men of the Abwehr were billeted. The car pulled up outside the large, luxurious house and when Carré asked Bleicher what was going to happen next, he said, 'We are going to bed.' That night she became his lover. 'I found myself in the presence of the most disgusting sentimental beast – and I began to think with regret of my cell,' she said. The same night, in the women's prison at La Santé, Madame Hugentobler hanged herself.

Carré soon became a favourite of the officers billeted in the Villa Harry Baur. They called her 'Kleines Kätzchen'. Each evening she wore a pair of black silk pyjamas as an evening dress. After dinner she flirted with the officers while her new lover played the piano.

Bleicher took over Czerniawski's headquarters in the rue Villa Léandre and filled it with English-speaking counter-intelligence men. Carré led Bleicher to agent after agent. Among the victims were *Interallié*'s first wireless operator and courier, Stanislas Lach, and Wladimir Lipsky, who had been second in command. Lipsky was arrested with his daughter and his teeth smashed during his interrogation. Father and daughter ended up in Mauthausen concentration camp, known to the Germans as 'The Bone Grinder'.

Few of the arrested realised they had been betrayed by Carré. Whenever she was present at an arrest Bleicher treated her as though she too was under suspicion, shoving her about and shouting at her before appearing to take her into custody.

The organisational plans, the reports, the maps and lists of contacts captured from Roman Czerniawski, were examined, catalogued, cross-referenced and filed. With each new arrest came more intelligence, which was processed in the same way. Before long Bleicher had discovered, and taken over, *Interallié*'s four radio transmitters. At a secret meeting called by his commanding officer, Oskar Reile, Bleicher outlined an idea to use the transmitters to fool London into thinking that *Interallié* was still functioning. Reile agreed to give the plan a try.

Masquerading as 'Colonel Henri', Bleicher commandeered the Little Priory, a mock-Tudor villa in the lower part of St-Germain. It stood in its own small grounds, had two floors, an attic, central heating and even a small bar in one of the downstairs rooms. Bleicher took over one of the bedrooms for himself and Carré while the others crammed into what was left. He rechristened the house 'the Cattery'.

One of the arrested was a radio operator who Bleicher persuaded to change sides and send a signal to London that appeared to come from Carré. In it 'she' admitted that there had been a disastrous series of arrests but that she was still at liberty and working to rebuild the shattered network. The transmission over, Bleicher waited to see whether London had taken the bait. The reply was short – *Message Received*. Bleicher's link with London was up and running.

In the days that followed a stream of disinformation flowed from the Cattery. Real intelligence was woven in with half-truths and outright falsehood. Bleicher wanted to persuade Buckmaster that it was safe to resume sending agents.

RADIO GAMES

Pierre de Vomécourt had worked hard to build up his circuit, code-named *Autogiro*. The circuit had nearly 10,000 men whom he commanded first from Paris and then from Le Mans 130 miles to the west. De Vomécourt's security was sloppy, names and addresses were handed out with abandon, wireless transmissions were sent from the same safe house and were too long. The Germans were very good at finding secret radios. Vans equipped with special direction-finding equipment toured the streets looking for clandestine signals. Once found two vans were used to pinpoint where the transmission was coming from. The longer a set was on air the greater the chance of detection. *Autogiro* eventually fell foul of a Vichy police counter-intelligence team, key agents were arrested and the detector vans pinpointed de Vomécourt's radio operator and his transmitter. In the struggle that followed the radio operator was shot and wounded. He was hauled off for interrogation and his equipment confiscated. Without a radio de Vomécourt's circuit was deaf and blind with no way of passing information to London or receiving instructions. He became more and more desperate as the weeks of silence slipped by. Eventually he met Michel Brault, the lawyer who had helped Mathilde Carré and Czerniawski get started and who had no idea she was now working for Bleicher. Brault told him about *Interallié* and offered to introduce him to Mathilde Carré. On Boxing Day

1941, de Vomécourt and Brault walked along the Champs-Elysées to the Café Georges V. Waiting inside was Carré. Sitting quietly across the room, concentrating on his newspaper, was 'Colonel Henri' as Sergeant Hugo Bleicher now termed himself.

De Vomécourt and Brault came in and sat down. The charming, dark-haired Resistance leader shook Carré's hand. As usual, she was wearing her brown fur coat and red beret. She listened sympathetically as he outlined his predicament, telling her about the arrests and the loss of the radio operator and his radio. When he had finished she said she might be able to help but needed time to talk to her friends. De Vomécourt suggested they meet again in a few days in a small office he rented nearby.

When the two men left, Carré told Bleicher that de Vomécourt was someone she could work with, 'a man of the world ... material to improve and direct properly'. Bleicher was uneasy, he did not like the idea of her meeting the handsome Frenchman on her own. Reluctantly he agreed to the plan, warning her not to try any tricks, reminding her what would happen to her if she double-crossed him.

Once in de Vomécourt's office, Carré told him the same story she had fed to London about the near destruction of *Interallié*. She did not tell him about Bleicher or her arrest, claiming instead that, thanks to her, the circuit was still transmitting to London and she was prepared to let him use the link.

Later Bleicher and Carré argued. She wanted to leave the Cattery and rent an apartment where de Vomécourt could contact her at any time of the day or night. Eventually Bleicher gave in; she could move out but he was going with her. Carré found a place near Gestapo headquarters on the avenue Foch and the pair moved in posing as M. et Mme Jean Castel. Bleicher pretended to be an anti-Nazi Belgian businessman eager to help the Resistance. Pretending to be Belgian helped to explain his odd, thick accent. Once the arrangements were in place they allowed de Vomécourt to send his first message to London. He wrote it in code and gave it to Carré to take to her radio operator.

The signal was passed to F Section, and Buckmaster read it with relief. Someone queried the signal – de Vomécourt had been off air for a long time, how could they be certain it was really him? Then it was pointed out that de Vomécourt had included a code word known only to himself and London, therefore the message must be genuine.

De Vomécourt asked for two things: a large sum of money along with a replacement radio plus an operator so that he could communicate directly with London. The reply came, was decoded and taken to de Vomécourt: the money was not a problem, but there were no radio operators available. With many apologies Buckmaster instructed him to go on communicating through Mathilde Carré. By this means, every message sent or received on behalf of de Vomécourt was copied, translated into German and placed in the rapidly expanding Abwehr SOE F Section files. Using the information Bleicher began to make arrests, one of whom was a friend of the lawyer Michel Brault who began to suspect there was something wrong.

He shared his worries with de Vomécourt and the two men agreed that they were uneasy about the man that Carré was spending so much time with, Jean Castel the 'Belgian businessman'. Fearing that Brault himself was soon going to be arrested they decided he must disappear. Then de Vomécourt confronted Carré with his suspicions. She broke down and told him exactly what had been going on. Through her tears she claimed to be a helpless woman trapped in the clutches of 'Jean Castel' who was really an Abwehr agent called Hugo Bleicher who had the power of life and death over her. She claimed Bleicher had made her life a misery. She said that she wanted to redeem herself and 'get my revenge on the Germans'.

In the next few minutes de Vomécourt came up with a plan he hoped would wrong-foot Bleicher. He told the sobbing Carré to go back to Bleicher and tell him that, a few days before, just after the New Year, there had been a meeting in Paris of senior Resistance leaders from all over France, convened to negotiate new methods of liaison between France and SOE in London. Carré was to say that he, de Vomécourt, had been at the meeting and been ordered to go to England and bring Buckmaster up to date with the new arrangements. Then he was to come back to Paris, bringing with him a high-ranking member of British Intelligence, possibly a general, with the authority to finalise the negotiations.

Bleicher was delighted with the information Carré brought him, not realising that she was now working against him. He pictured his men following de Vomécourt and the British general to a meeting of the most important underground leaders in France. His mind whirled with the possibility that he was soon going to be in a position to wipe out the entire leadership of the Resistance and humiliate the British Secret Service. He set about getting permission to implement his grand scheme and took it to his superiors. The Gestapo quickly got wind of what was happening and wanted to step in, arrest de Vomécourt, then shoot him and all his accomplices. The Abwehr in Berlin sent a senior officer to find out what was going on. He gave the plan his approval, the Gestapo backed off and Bleicher was given the go-ahead.

A few days later Mathilde Carré had another surprise for Bleicher: de Vomécourt wanted to take her with him to London and leave her there in a liaison role. Bleicher seized what he saw as a heaven-sent opportunity to insert his own agent in the heart of the enemy. In his excitement he told Carré that she was going to become famous throughout the Reich as the Mata Hari who had penetrated SOE. What neither Bleicher nor Carré realised was that de Vomécourt's plan was to get Carré out of the place where she had done so much damage. Once in London, she could be interrogated and forced to reveal everything she knew about what was really happening in Paris.

Pretending to be Carré, Bleicher sent a signal to London asking for a Royal Navy motor launch to pick up the agents from the Breton coast. In London Buckmaster dutifully organised a launch to make the pick-up on the night of 12/13 February. A tough young SOE officer, Ben Cowburn, who knew the area well, was ordered to act as a guide. Bleicher saw to it that troops guarding the coast were given orders to ignore the presence of spies on the beach and German naval vessels were instructed not to engage the British motor launch. Bleicher was delighted, thinking he had set the stage for phase one of his great coup: the despatch of de Vomécourt to England combined with the insertion of Carré, his agent, into SOE headquarters.

On the afternoon of 11 February an undercover German surveillance team mingled with the crowd on a platform at the Gare Montparnasse waiting for the train to Brest. Standing separately on the same platform were Mathilde Carré, Pierre de Vomécourt and Ben Cowburn, ignoring each other and pretending they did not know they were being watched. The train pulled in and Carré climbed aboard. In her suitcase she had packed a black dress, some blouses and the black silk pyjamas that her German admirers found so entrancing. As usual she wore her brown fur coat and red beret. De Vomécourt and Cowburn got into separate carriages. Whistles blew, the engine heaved and the train began to move. At the last minute two of Bleicher's surveillance team jumped aboard.

By nightfall the agents were huddled together on the beach. De Vomécourt thought he could see two figures crawling about in the nearby rocks watching them. Cowburn began to flash the recognition signal out to sea and after about half an hour a man appeared from out of the dark wearing wellington boots; he whispered that his name was Redding and that he was a new agent. He told them that a Royal Navy motor launch was moored in the bay and the dinghy that had dropped him was too small to take more than one passenger and had gone back to pick up a second agent. As they waited the wind got up and the flat sea suddenly became choppy. A small rowing boat appeared, a rating struggling with the oars in the heavy sea. The passenger, the second agent, was clinging to the sides to avoid being thrown into the sea. Finally a second dinghy appeared rowed by a rating and carrying a naval officer. Shouting to be heard above the noise of the surf, he said he was an Australian lieutenant sent ashore to make certain that everything went smoothly. De Vomécourt told the new agents that the beach was being watched and they were likely to be arrested so they decided to abort the mission and return to the safety of the motor launch. Waist-deep in water, with waves now crashing over them, the group struggled to heave themselves into the small dinghies, which capsized, hurling the new arrivals' radio and Carré's suitcase into the foam. Unnoticed the oars drifted off into the darkness. The ratings managed to push the overturned dinghy through the surf, using it as a float to help them swim back to the motor launch. A few minutes later the party on the beach heard the roar of the motor launch's powerful engines heading back to England. The noise faded and they were left with just the wild wind and the crashing sea. Drenched and freezing, they decided to abandon the effort that night and split up, planning to return to try again the following night.

The two agents and the naval officer set off together, vanishing into the night. De Vomécourt, Cowburn and Carré walked until they found a hotel. It was locked, forcing them to spend the rest of the night sitting in the rain. At dawn Carré went to telephone Bleicher who told her that his men had arrested the two new agents and the naval officer. Bleicher used the deception radio to contact London and arranged another attempt at the pick-up. This time the sea was dead calm, but no launch appeared. Once more the scheme was abandoned.

There was nothing left for Cowburn to do so he set off back to the Free Zone heading for Lyon where he had been told there was an American woman who might have a radio and be able to help him. Carré and de Vomécourt headed for Paris.

A few nights later they were back on the beach, hidden among the rocks, signalling to the boat that they hoped was standing off ready to pick them up. The night passed and no boat showed. A hidden Abwehr officer saw that the launch had appeared, but off the wrong beach, where it could not see the flashing torch.

Bleicher, desperate for his plan to work, ordered the German intelligence team operating the false radio to transmit again to persuade London to have another try. The message that was passed to Buckmaster asked for a fourth attempt, saying that the two arrested agents were safe and about to become operational. It added that the naval officer who had been left on the beach was going to be smuggled into Spain as soon as possible. Buckmaster believed the fiction and requested another motor launch to go over on the night of 26/27 February. He took the unusual step of allowing his second-in-command Nicolas Bodington to go with it.

This time Bleicher joined his observers hiding on the beach. The launch appeared, signals were exchanged and a large rowing boat appeared. Armed men leapt out, guns at the ready to drive off any German opposition. Bodington waded ashore wearing a white duffel coat, carrying a cosh in one hand and a revolver in the other, waving everybody to get on board the rowing boat. When de Vomécourt and Carré finally stepped onto the deck of the big motor launch a rating said, 'Oh Christ, it's a bloody woman.' The launch turned for England. Bleicher stood on the shore watching it power away, carrying all his hopes for glory.

In Dartmouth harbour they found Buckmaster waiting for them. Over a full naval breakfast he was briefed about what had been going on in Paris and told that the radio he thought was one of his own was actually being operated by the Germans. Carré teased Bodington, impressing Buckmaster and causing one of the people who met her to say, 'That Cat woman has got some guts.' Now fully aware of the deception, Buckmaster sent a message to *Autogiro* saying that de Vomécourt and Carré had reached London and that de Vomécourt was soon to return with a general in the security services.

Vera Atkins was given responsibility for interrogating Mathilde Carré. To win her confidence Atkins set her up in a comfortable flat overlooking Hyde Park and for the next six weeks wined and dined her in expensive restaurants and went round the West End buying her new clothes. In Harvey Nichols Carré bought Atkins a thank-you present, a black choker. She was encouraged to talk, especially in the flat, which was heavily bugged. By the time Atkins had finished with her Carré had revealed everything she knew about the German intelligence operation, the arrests, Bleicher and the wireless game.

At his headquarters Bleicher waited anxiously for news that de Vomécourt and the general were on their way to Paris. Signals arrived assuring him that he was not to worry, everything was going according to plan but the pair had been delayed.

On 1 April, de Vomécourt returned to France, in secret. He had no radio and had to communicate by sending a courier to Virginia Hall who forwarded the messages on from her own wireless transmitter. Towards the end of April the courier was on his way across the Demarcation Line between the Occupied Zone and the Free Zone when he was arrested in a routine document check. He was carrying messages written in long hand by de Vomécourt. When the papers arrived on Bleicher's desk he recognised de Vomécourt's handwriting and realised that he was being double-crossed. While interrogating another agent Bleicher discovered where de Vomécourt was living and arrested him. More agents were arrested and de Vomécourt's circuit was finally destroyed. Mathilde Carré's days of usefulness to SOE were over. The well-dressed, sexy, short-sighted woman in the red beret exchanged the comfort of the London flat for a narrow cell in Holloway Prison. There was no prospect of a review of her case until the war ended. As a traitor to both the Allies and the Nazis, she could expect little mercy, whichever side won.

Back in France, Cowburn arrived in Lyon and found the 'American lady' who turned out to be Virginia Hall. She sent him on to Marseille and told him who to contact when he got there. On his way to England he travelled along the Pat Line, the underground escape route into Spain, and although he did not meet her, one of the people who helped him was Nancy Wake. The Pat Line had its own problems; its founder, Ian Garrow, had been arrested and was awaiting trial.

The year 1941 was drawing to a close and had seen a series of setbacks for Buckmaster and the men and women of F Section. Sloppy attention to security had led to the arrest of the majority of agents sent in. Baker Street had failed to understand that the heart of any circuit was its radio operator and the transmitting equipment. SOE activity had produced negligible results and had not won over the French people who still resented the British for failing to help them. The head of the Political Warfare Executive, Robert Bruce Lockhart, summed up the position in an appreciation written for the British foreign secretary: 'It is the plain truth which will be denied by no honest person ... that most of the energy which should have been directed against the enemy has been dissipated in inter departmental strife and jealousies.'

At 7.48 a.m. on 7 December 1941, 353 Japanese fighters, bombers and torpedo planes appeared in the skies over the American fleet moored at Pearl Harbor. When the sun set the place was in ruins; all seven main battleships had been sunk or damaged, along with three cruisers, three destroyers and an anti-aircraft training ship. Also, 188 American aircraft were blazing wrecks and 3500 personnel were dead or injured. The next day Japan declared war on the United States. Two days later Germany did the same.

In Washington, General Dwight D. Eisenhower, a new member of the War Plans Division of the War Department, insisted that the war against the Japanese was more important than anything happening in Europe, which he described as a 'side show'. He argued against any plans to invade Europe or even to assemble American troops in Britain.

'IF YOU COULD EVER SEND ME A PIECE OF SOAP I SHOULD BE BOTH VERY HAPPY AND MUCH CLEANER'

In occupied Europe, at the beginning of 1942, spirits were low. The ordinary citizen lived in fear of the Germans and inhabited a world where everything was rationed and in short supply, especially happiness. In Lyon the eighteen-year-old Denise Domenach continued to keep her diary and wrote that if the war went on for much longer she would die without ever having achieved anything and without ever having loved anyone.

Also in Lyon the usually indefatigable Virginia Hall lay in bed ill with a cold, a typewriter on her knees. She was writing to Nicolas Bodington, complaining about the weather, which was 'mingled snow rain and slush out of doors ... the dark days are fairly abysmal and a short English word describes one's mood. The word, you know, is written *h** purest anglo saxon.' She described the lack of food and the impossibility of buying new shoes ending 'I get so "fed up" queer isn't it? ... I'll get over it.' She signed off with 'Cheers' and her nickname 'Dindy'.

In Paris the trial of Agnès Humbert and her seventeen fellow collaborators on the underground paper *Résistance* started. The

German judge began by expressing his respect for those on trial
and the service they had performed for France. He went on to say
that it was his 'harsh duty' to conduct himself towards them as a
German. Humbert was accused of the offence of 'writing and distributing the anti-German newspaper *Résistance* and of the crime
of espionage'.

The trial dragged on for nearly six weeks. At its close Humbert
was found guilty and sentenced to five years slave labour. Ten of her
comrades were condemned to death. On her return to her cell the
female warder, with tears in her eyes, whispered 'They've got no
heart these people, no heart.'

Across the city, Picasso had not been allowed to exhibit his work
since the invasion. His paintings reflected the sombre mood of the
country. He became an object of curiosity, often visited by German
officers curious to meet the man who their Führer described as a
'degenerate artist'. When one colonel looked at a reproduction of
the Guernica picture and asked him who did it, Picasso answered,
'You did.'

At the end of January 1942, Germany celebrated, the ninth anni-
versary of life under the Führer. A crowd of 14,000 people gathered
in the Sportpalast in Berlin to hear Hitler promise that the result
of the war would be 'the complete annihilation of the Jews'. The
hour was near he said, when 'The most evil universal enemy of all
time will be finished for at least a thousand years.' The crowd went
mad, cheering and shouting '*Sieg Heil*' until long after Hitler had
disappeared. While the Germans were celebrating Singapore fell to
the Japanese, which Churchill described as 'The worst disaster and
largest capitulation in British history.'

In spite of the disaster in the Far East, Eisenhower changed his
mind and declared: 'We've got to go to Europe and fight ... and
we've got to quit wasting our resources all over the world – and still
worse – wasting time ... If we're to keep Russia in, save the Middle
East, India and Burma we've got to begin slugging with air at western Europe; to be followed with a land attack as soon as possible.'

He began to formulate a plan, code-named *Roundup*, to land 1.5 million men on the French coast between Le Havre and Boulogne on 1 April the following year.

From Moscow Stalin demanded that the invasion take place at once, arguing that with most of the German Army fighting in the east Allied troops would find little resistance. In Berlin that spring Hitler gave the order for an immense fortification, an 'Atlantic Wall', to be constructed, stretching from the coast of Norway, down and along the Channel as far as the border between France and Spain in the Bay of Biscay.

On 7 March, Roosevelt sent a memorandum pointing out that by June 1942 the United States would only be able to transport 130,000 men to Britain. The invasion called for a force of at least 400,000. Even with the huge increase in ship production that was underway this could not be achieved before the beginning of 1944. It was Roosevelt's view that the earliest realistic date for a cross-Channel invasion was June 1944. In an attempt to rally the military planners on both sides of the Atlantic, Churchill declared that, nevertheless, the United States and Britain were marching forward in a 'Noble brotherhood of arms' and 'Our agreed programme is a crescendo of activity on the continent'.

In Baker Street, Buckmaster and his junior assistant, Vera Atkins, had become inseparable. He began to call her Vera, and was often with her in the Operations Room and took late suppers with her in the canteen. While Buckmaster travelled in every day on the bus and was always early, Atkins had an arrangement whereby she was picked up by the same black cab every morning. She was often the last to arrive, though always in time for the daily ten o'clock meeting. When it was suggested that all staff should sign in each morning Atkins refused, saying that mornings were not her time of day. Buckmaster wrote in a report that she was 'Somewhat disinclined to accept instructions without argument. Requires handling.'

*

In the south of France the Germans had become interested in a mysterious woman they nicknamed 'The White Mouse' and Nancy Wake knew that this was her. She was asked to take important and highly incriminating papers to Paris. Nancy's cover for the trip was that she had been born in Grasse, a place where perfume was manufactured and that her trip to Paris was for a cosmetics company. She knew that this story would not last an Abwehr or Gestapo interrogation. She carried Grasse bus tickets in her pocket and had booked a room in Paris, even though she was not planning to use it. Finally she wrote a long and touching letter to Henri saying she could no longer bear to live with him and was leaving Marseille. This was a cover to explain her absence if she got trapped in Paris and could not get back. On the train, as she crossed into the Occupied Zone, Resistance workers secretly watched her to make sure she got through the ticket and identity-paper inspections.

The trip went off without a hitch. Nancy arrived at the address of the safe apartment she had been given where she was welcomed in to find a maze of huge rooms which the fuel shortages had made impossible to heat. In the middle of the drawing room she was puzzled to see a small wooden hut had been erected containing sleeping bags, two armchairs, candles, a lantern and a small kerosene stove. The owners explained that this was where they spent the freezing nights. The huts were on sale all over Paris. They made Nancy very welcome, cold but safe in one of the huge bedrooms.

Nancy delivered the documents hidden in parcels, then she and her hostess wandered round the expensive area carrying string bags and looking like housewives. This was her first trip to the capital since the fall of France. What she saw depressed her. German uniforms, flags and propaganda leaflets; well-dressed women openly consorted with immaculately turned-out Nazi officers while the ordinary people had a 'look of resignation and quiet despair'. For Nancy the worn-down appearance of everyday Parisians was far more depressing than the sight of the collaborators. She got back to Marseille and was told she had done the Resistance a great service.

The arrest of de Vomécourt and the collapse of his *Autogiro* circuit left F Section with no agents in the Occupied Zone. There was some activity in the Free Zone including three agents building a circuit called *Urchin*. At the centre of *Urchin,* but not its leader, was Virginia Hall, no longer 'fed up'; the gloom that had hovered over her at the beginning of the year had lifted.

Ben Cowburn, the SOE agent who had been on the beach with de Vomécourt and Mathilde Carré, said that:

> If you sit in [Virginia Hall's] kitchen for long enough you will see most people pass through with one sort of trouble or another which [she] promptly deals with ... Everybody brought their troubles to her and our HQ in London sent their troubles in the form of agents who were told to contact her to find [wireless] operators. She was so willing to help that when a needy visitor came she would give her ration cards away, wash clothing and make contacts for him.

Another agent said that in the same kitchen you could meet 'every British [circuit] organiser in France'.

Earlier in the year, two men, one a badly needed radio operator, had been parachuted into France near Tours. They were dropped into a vineyard nearly nineteen miles wide of the planned landing place. The pair set off to find help and got hopelessly lost. They travelled hundreds of miles, first round Occupied France then crossing into the Free Zone and ending up in Perpignan. Here they at last made contact with a man who sent them on to Marseille and a rendezvous with Hall. She found them in good spirits even though they had been on the road for a month with no access to food coupons or travel permits.

Another radio operator rescued by Hall was Denis Rake, a brave man and a flamboyant homosexual. Rake had landed by felucca on 14 May. Lax security on the part of a colleague had alerted the police to Rake's presence in the country. He went on the run and was arrested crossing into the Occupied Zone. Somehow he persuaded the police to let him jump off the train. He linked up with another agent and went to Lyon where Hall arranged for a new wireless to be delivered to him.

Virginia Hall's workload grew and she told London: 'We could use about six clever chaps in various centres this side. It's a snowball, but we need a number of perfectly and utterly reliable persons – persons from "home".' She added that she would do the job herself but 'The only trouble is that I am doing too much as it is and find it hard to swing around the circuits fast enough.' In another signal she added: 'If you could ever send me a piece of soap I should be both very happy and much cleaner.'

In Paris, at the Abwehr HQ in the Hôtel Lutetia, a stocky, 36-year-old priest called Robert Alesch sat in front of Major Karl Schaeffer. Alesch was an ambitious man with contacts in the French Resistance. In public he pretended to be anti-Nazi, but in fact he had become a German citizen and an informer. He had already been paid 10,000 francs for his work.

Schaeffer told the priest that they knew about Hall and were listening to her wireless transmissions. He was now to become an official Abwehr agent with the code name *Axel*, officially registered as agent GV 7162 number f385.42 gZ. His mission was to make contact with Hall and to find out everything about her. The pointy-nosed priest nodded, agreeing to his new rank and task.

While Virginia Hall and her comrades struggled to make headway against the Germans, the chiefs of staff in Whitehall had their minds on bigger things. In spite of Roosevelt's reservations they were thinking about a 'large scale descent on Western Europe in the spring of 1943'. They told SOE to train and arm Resistance forces to be ready for the invasion. When the fighting started it would be SOE's job to harass the Germans and hinder the reinforcements moving to the beach-heads. Roads, railways and airfields were to be sabotaged, communications cut and the enemy demoralised by spreading black propaganda and disinformation. This was a tall order. The reality was that in the field F Section was still finding its way. The Resistance was untrained and badly equipped and SOE did not have the resources to help them.

Then, an artist, André Girard, appeared with what seemed to be the answer to all the problems. Out of the blue he contacted London, claiming to have 300,000 men trained and ready to rise up when the longed-for invasion started. He called his circuit *Carte* and said that what he needed was support, especially money and equipment.

A new SOE agent, Peter Churchill, who was not related to the prime minister, was sent from London to discover what was really going on inside *Carte*. He found Girard to be an immensely likeable man claiming to have high-level contacts in the Vichy French Army. One of Girard's dreams was to use those contacts to establish a secret pro-Allied army inside the Vichy force. Peter Churchill was impressed by Girard's organisation. The details of *Carte* recruits were filed on forms, including an agent's name, address, telephone number, date of birth, experience, technical capabilities and anything else that might be useful to know, sixty-one headings in all. They were not written in code but in 'clear' French and kept in Girard's study. Sometimes they were carried around by agents who might need them for reference. They formed an immensely useful resource for the *Carte* circuit or to anyone else who got their hands on them, like the Germans.

On his return to England, Peter Churchill wrote a glowing report on what he had found. Buckmaster began to explore ways for the new circuit to be funded and used. As Girard's *Carte* began to dominate the thinking of F Section, the Cabinet Office formally ratified the decision by the prime minister to allow women to be sent into the field. The hunt began for suitable candidates.

Not far away from the Cabinet Office, in Wandsworth, South London, stood an enormous, bleak Victorian building known as the Royal Victoria Patriotic Building. It had been requisitioned by MI5 as a place to interrogate foreign nationals arriving in England and was called the London Reception Centre. One of the detainees was a 23-year-old French woman called Andrée Borrel who had just arrived from Portugal.

Borrel had trained as a nurse with the Association des dames de France (ADF) and in the battle for France had treated wounded soldiers. After the armistice the ADF came under the control of Marshal Pétain, which Borrel would not accept and so joined the Resistance. In 1941 she had worked for Ian Garrow helping to organise the Pat Line, running a safe house outside Perpignan with her lover Maurice Dufour. Towards the end of the year the pair were betrayed and had to use the line themselves to get to Portugal from where Dufour flew to England, leaving Borrel to follow on. For a while she worked for the Free French Propaganda Office at the British Embassy, then on 24 April she was put on a flight to London. The MI5 officer who interviewed her in Wandsworth concluded that: 'She is an excellent type of country girl, who has intelligence and seems a keen patriot. From a security point of view, I can find nothing against Mlle Borrel and recommend her for release to the FFF [Free French Forces].' The FFF were very distrustful of any French person who collaborated with the British. They asked Borrel to reveal details of her work with Ian Garrow's Pat Line, including names, addresses, places and details of how she operated. She refused.

Her lover, Maurice Dufour, had been taken by force to the basement of the Free French HQ in Duke Street, London, which, like an embassy was effectively French soil and not under the jurisdiction of the British. He was interviewed by two French captains, Girard and Wybot. They told him they had arrested Andrée Borrel and they would 'Make her talk using every means, even if we have to rape her one after the other.' They ordered him to strip and began to hit him in the small of the back with a leather-covered steel rod. He had been wounded in France and they concentrated on the half-healed scar, which caused great pain. This went on for more than a month after which Dufour said, 'Because of the beating, which was repeated almost every night, I was unable to lie down, neither could I stand, and spent many days and nights crouching and whimpering.'

When F Section heard about Borrel they asked her to come for an interview with Selwyn Jepson, who discovered that her parents were working class and that after leaving school at fourteen she had spent eighteen months training as a dressmaker. Then she worked as a shop assistant in a bakery and finally as an assistant in a fashionable dress shop. What she really liked was bicycling, spending her weekends going for long rides into the country. If she was not bicycling she was hiking and climbing, wearing trousers and heavy sweaters and carrying a backpack. She liked boys' games and wanted to be one. She was a strong woman with a lot of stamina. Jepson reported that:

> The Free French movement ... have made it a condition that she would give them all the intelligence concerning the organisation for which she was working in France. This she refuses to do and apparently they refuse to employ her unless she does. I think she would make an excellent addition to our own Corps Feminine and it should not be difficult to get her ... she said she was perfectly willing to let us have the information she refuses to give to the Free French.

Borrel was enrolled in SOE on 15 May 1942.

In France Ian Garrow was still waiting to be tried. The 34-year-old officer had spent six months in jail, three of them in solitary confinement. He wrote to Nancy Wake telling her that he was starving and asked her for help. At first Wake's husband, Henri, thought it was too dangerous for her to get involved, especially as the Germans were on the lookout for her. When she told him that she would not stand by and do nothing, he gave in and promised to help. A friend drove Nancy to Fort Saint-Nicholas, outside Marseille, where Garrow was being held and waited in case anything happened to her. Nancy's request to see him was turned down. She was told that she could bring him food parcels, which she began to do, three times a week. She kept up her demands to see him and on days when she did not visit the prison she wrote to him. In May Garrow was tried and sentenced to ten years in Meauzac concentration camp. When Nancy was finally allowed to see her former boss she was shocked at his condition, wondering what he had been like before she began bringing the food parcels. Then a man visited her who had been in the cell next to Garrow and told her he knew of a guard at Meauzac who, for the right bribe, might help him escape. The day came for Garrow's transfer to the camp. Nancy and Henri went to the Gare de Marseille-Saint-Charles to wave him off. Garrow arrived in a truck with a group of other prisoners, all manacled together at the wrist and with heavy leg chains. Garrow looked old and emaciated, hobbling across the platform to the prison train. Nancy found the sight as upsetting as anything she had seen in her days driving ambulances full of wounded men.

In St Mary's Hospital in Paddington, London, on 8 June, Violette Szabo gave birth to a daughter she named Tania. She had not seen her husband, Etienne, for seven months. Several weeks later she received a letter from him saying that he would come home to see his daughter as soon as he could get leave. The next she heard was that he had died of wounds inflicted while fighting the Afrika Korps at Bir Hakeim in the Western Desert. He was thirty-two years old.

Andrée Borrel's training was intense, and suited her interests. It started with a tough preliminary course in the south of England based on Commando training and designed to weed out unsuitable candidates. Everything was so secret that some candidates became confused. One asked, 'What are we being trained for exactly, I applied for a job as a bilingual typist.' Buckmaster's line was that there was 'no use trying to do things by the book – there is no book!'

Having passed the initial test, Borrel and her group were sent to Scotland to Arisaig, a remote estate in a restricted naval area far from prying eyes. In the weeks that followed she was taught to handle boats, read a map, and initiated into the mysteries of the Fairbairn–Sykes knife. The students learned about firearms, plastic explosives and unarmed combat. One trainee said, 'By the time we finished . . . I would willingly enough have tackled any man whatever his strength, size or ability . . . [The instructor] taught us to face a fight without the slightest tremor of apprehension . . . [We could] hurt, maul, injure or even kill with the greatest of ease.'

After Scotland the trainees were divided into two groups: some became radio operators of which there was always a shortage, the others were sent to Beaulieu in the New Forest, the SOE's finishing school. At Beaulieu, Borrel was taught how to be inconspicuous. The rule was that anyone with a secret to hide should not only hide it but hide the fact that they had it to hide. The trainees developed skills in concealment, changing addresses, and being able to spot when they were being followed. They were taught about the types of German and French military and police uniforms.

The Beaulieu course ended with a four-day exercise. Agents had to travel to a designated part of the United Kingdom, make contact with other agents, using prearranged passwords, and then go through the motions of placing plastic explosives on a target such as a factory or telephone exchange. The police were alerted to the presence of the agents and could arrest and interrogate them. Like their male counterparts the SOE women were going to be in action twenty-four hours a day and had to be self-reliant, highly motivated, aggressive and able to seize any chance that the enemy left open for them. Fear and loneliness were their constant companions.

While training, Borrel met a mentor, Adèle le Chêne. Le Chêne gave her some tips in the ways of the world and summed her up as 'cool calm and brave ... a good comrade for men, but nothing more, you understand?' Her supervising instructor thought that 'She has little organising ability' ... but was 'Thoroughly tough and self reliant with no nerves. Has plenty of common sense and is well able to look after herself in any circumstances ... absolutely reliable ... she should eventually develop into a first class agent.'

At the end of her training Borrel was commissioned as an ensign in the First Aid Nursing Yeomanry, the FANYs, a quasi-military organisation and the only women who were allowed to bear arms. It was hoped that, because they were FANYs, the female agents, if captured, would be treated as soldiers and not spies. Before being sent into the field Borrel reported to the parachute training centre at Ringway near Manchester where she did the required five jumps and

earned her parachute wings. She was ready to be sent into action; all
she could do was wait for her orders.

On 4 August, Robert Alesch arrived in Lyon looking for Virginia
Hall. He was accompanied by a radio operator called Petit John.
Alesch made contact with her second in command, Dr Jean Rousset,
and told him that he had been sent by Jacques Legrand, leader of
the *Gloria* circuit and explained that there were problems in Paris.
He handed Rousset a roll of film, and said that Petit John was on
the run from the Germans and needed help. Then he left, saying he
had no time to wait and meet Mme Hall but must get straight back
to the capital. When Virginia was told about Petit John she said that
he must go to Marseille and from there head to Spain. The radio
operator vanished and was never heard of again.

A week later Alesch arrived at Abwehr headquarters. With him
he had a package that the circuit leader Legrand had asked him to
take to Virginia. He handed it to Oskar Reile, the head of Abwehr
III, the department responsible for counter-intelligence. It contained
detailed plans of the defences at the port of Dieppe. Reile knew that
this was very sensitive information and ordered the destruction of
the *Gloria* circuit. In the next few days more than sixty agents were
arrested, including Legrand. The network was finished – *brûlé*.

Six days later Virginia Hall heard someone banging on her door.
She opened it to find Dr Rousset, who wanted her to come at once
and meet the new courier waiting in his surgery. At Rousset's house
Virginia met Alesch, someone she had never seen before. He told
her that there had been more problems in Paris, an agent had been
arrested with an incriminating list in his pocket. He asked her for
money towards the cost of operations in the city and for instructions on what to do. Virginia was suspicious of him; she could not
explain why, it was just a feeling she had. She told him to go back
to the capital to try to restore order to the compromised circuit. He
was to come back in ten days when she would have the money and
more instructions.

When Alesch had gone Virginia contacted Baker Street, asking them to instruct their agents in Paris to check up on the priest. Baker Street replied that Alesch was genuine and that she should give him the help he needed. When he returned she gave him 100,000 francs and unexposed microfilms.

Later Virginia heard about the arrests and wondered why Alesch had not mentioned them on his last visit. When he reappeared she asked him point-blank what was going on. Alesch became embarrassed and told her there had been problems; he knew about them but had not wanted to overwhelm her with bad news. He explained that things in Paris were confused. He had lost contact with the *Gloria* network and, worse, with the agent to whom he had handed the money. Next he asked Virginia what would happen if she herself were arrested or disappeared. He suggested that she give him the names of her contacts as a back-up in case of an emergency. By now Alesch was quite agitated, almost begging her for help. Virginia told him to go back to Paris, find out what had happened to the people he had lost contact with and to try to reorganise things. When he had done this he must come back and tell her what was going on. Later she signalled Baker Street asking if they knew anything more about Alesch. London told her not to waste her time.

Alesch turned up a month later with intelligence he said came from *Gloria* for urgent transmission to London and added that he needed more money. Virginia gave him another 100,000 francs and when he had gone repeated to F Section that she was worried about Alesch and thought he might be a double agent. She admitted she had no hard evidence. The reply was that the intelligence coming from Alesch was first class, that he was totally trustworthy and that he could not possibly be a double agent. Virginia stopped arguing.

For the next few weeks Alesch returned to Lyon on a regular basis. Each time he brought intelligence concocted by his masters in the Hôtel Lutetia. Some of it was true and some of it was false, yet all of it appeared to be genuine and London declared themselves very satisfied with the quality.

*

At 5 a.m. on 19 August, 6000 Allied troops, mostly Canadian, were preparing to disembark onto Dieppe's steep shingle beaches. The plan, Operation *Jubilee*, formulated by Rear Admiral Louis Mountbatten, was to seize the port and hold it for twelve hours. In that time the invaders were to destroy important buildings, equipment and defences. They were also to look for and gather military intelligence.

Thanks in part to Alesch the Germans knew the raid was coming and were waiting in force. Allied intelligence about the beaches was based not on the work of the Resistance but on picture postcards and inadequate aerial reconnaissance. One intelligence report stated that 'reports indicate that Dieppe is not heavily defended and that the beaches in the vicinity are suitable for landing infantry, and armoured fighting vehicles ...'

As they came onto the beaches the invasion force was cut down by heavy fire from artillery and machine guns. Their armoured vehicles were halted, stuck in the shingle and destroyed. Six hours later the order to withdraw was given and by teatime the Germans were dealing with the aftermath. Around 60 per cent of the force were lost, dead, wounded or prisoners of war. The Royal Air Force lost 106 aircraft and the Royal Navy a destroyer and 33 landing craft. The failed raid was a lesson in the difficulties of landing men on open, defended beaches.

In North Africa, on 30 August, Erwin Rommel gave the order for his troops to start an advance intended to sweep the Allies out of North Africa and give control of the Suez Canal to Germany. He told his colleagues: 'The decision to attack today is the most serious I have taken in my life ...' Rommel was heading for the British headquarters in Cairo.

Denis Rake, the wireless operator Virginia Hall had rescued earlier in the year, had again been arrested trying to get to Lyon after a failed affair in Paris with a Wehrmacht officer called Max. Hall heard about the arrest and asked her police contacts for help. She had asked for many favours in the past and this time they said that it was 'probably impossible' to do anything. Then she heard that Rake was to be sent to Castres, known as 'The worst prison in France'. Later the police told her they had Rake's wireless and stock of forged identity papers and were going to help him escape. Hall was confused and had no idea who to believe.

Over the course of the year her apartment in Lyon had filled up with radio parts, forged identity papers, weapons and large sums of money. Agents came and went and strangers appeared wanting help to get out of France. She decided that it was too dangerous to go on living there and moved into a flat on the rue Garibaldi owned by the brothel-keeper Germaine Guérin.

A man called Bradley Davies turned up in Lyon, looking for Virginia. He claimed he was a British agent, code-named *Blanchet* and that he needed 75,000 francs to get across the mountains into Spain. Virginia checked up on him with Baker Street who told her he was a double agent and on no account to let him near her and ordered her to kill him if necessary. When she asked for poison capsules to be sent they told her not to worry, arrangements had already been made to deal with him. A few days later Davies was captured by the Resistance in Marseille and shot.

Later she radioed London saying 'My time is about up' and asked them to get her out in October. Her plan was to travel in the open to Portugal, relying on her cover as a correspondent for the *New York Post*.

About the same time 300 Abwehr agents, dressed in civilian clothes and carrying identity cards provided by the French police, crossed the border into the Free Zone. They travelled in vehicles carrying local number plates. Many of the men were specialists in wireless communications. They headed for Lyon, Marseille, Montpellier, Tarbes, and Pau. Wireless detector vans followed. The operation was code-named *Donar* after the German god of thunder and was the result of a collaboration between the Germans and French. German agents had always been able to enter and move around the Free Zone but now they were doing so with the protection of the French police who provided communication facilities and garaging for the vehicles.

Thanks to Operation *Donar* radio operator after radio operator was arrested. Among them was 24-year-old Brian Stonehouse, who before the war had been a successful graphic artist specialising in fashion for magazines like *Vogue*. Hall wanted to send a team of agents disguised as SS officers and gendarmes to rescue him and three others who had been arrested. Getting the uniforms for the disguises proved too difficult and the plan was abandoned. A few days later she asked London to put off her departure until November, so that she could leave everything in good order.

On 7 September in the port of Greenock, two Special Branch officers escorted a former French stunt pilot, Henri Déricourt, down the gangplank of a tramp steamer that had brought him from Gibraltar. He had been in Aleppo when it was overrun by the Allies in July 1941, and because he was a pilot had been offered a job by the British airline Imperial Airways. Before joining the Pat Line escape route he had managed to return to France and spent some time in Paris getting married and sorting out the affairs of his wife.

The next day he was interrogated by MI5 at the London Reception Centre. They knew he had contacts with American intelligence, and that he had been working for Air France flying German VIPs into North Africa and round the south of France. Déricourt admitted that he was in touch with, a high-ranking officer in Nazi intelligence in Paris. After four days of interrogation he was issued with an Alien Registration Card and registered as RPS9435/E.1a(USA). The last part of the registration referred to the fact that it was American intelligence who had asked for him to be brought to England. On the fifth day, even though the investigating officer was not satisfied with his story, Déricourt was put up at a secret London address.

What Déricourt had not revealed was that he had been working for a racketeer on the black market supplying apartments and luxuries to the Germans in Paris. One of the racketeer's most important contacts was SS *Sturmbannführer* Karl Bömelburg, head of the Gestapo in France. Déricourt had been introduced to Bömelburg before the war by Nicolas Bodington.

Maurice Buckmaster heard about Déricourt and asked to see the interrogation notes. MI5 said that while Déricourt had 'produced no suspicious evidence ... He would have been a likely subject of German attention ... we do not feel [he] can be cleared from a security point of view.' Selwyn Jepson was told to interview him.

In his dingy interview room in the Victoria Hotel in Northumberland Avenue, Jepson learned that Henri Déricourt was an experienced pilot with a good knowledge of the geography of France and was familiar with a French aircraft similar to the Lysander. Even though he found him arrogant and untrustworthy, Jepson thought Déricourt was just what the SOE was looking for. Up to then RAF pilots and planners had grown to distrust SOE's ability to organise landing strips and reception committees. To Jepson, Déricourt's flying experience made him the ideal man to rebuild that trust. When Vera Atkins saw him she said, 'My heart sank because I felt he wasn't a man I could trust. Why I had that impression I don't know ... Possibly it was his slightly mocking attitude, perhaps he didn't seem to look one straight in the face ... I didn't like him [and I] wouldn't trust him.' Nicolas Bodington assured Buckmaster that: 'Déricourt is first class material.'

Andrée Borrel's wait for orders came to an end. One of her fellow agents was a 32-year-old lawyer called Francis Suttill, a charming, dark-haired man with clear grey eyes, a classic profile and a strong personality. His mother was French and he had been educated in France. Buckmaster thought Suttill had a mind that 'cut like a knife into the problems we put before him', and planned to send him into France with Borrel as his courier. Suttill was given the code name *Prosper*.

Andrée Borrel was parachuted into France on 24 September. She was accompanied by Lise de Baissac, whose brother Claude was already an SOE agent. De Baissac's orders were to establish her own small network. Her commandant had described her as 'quite imperturbable and would remain cool in any situation ... she was very much ahead of her fellow students'. The two women flew to France in a Whitley bomber. Circling over the drop zone the pilot saw the indication lights had been set too near the trees that hedged the field and the lights themselves were wrong. He aborted the mission.

The next night the mission was repeated. Before take-off Borrel and de Baissac drew straws to see who should jump first. Borrel won. The atmosphere in the plane on the second attempt was tense. This time the pilot saw that the lights were white instead of red. A torch flashed the correct recognition signal and he decided to go ahead with the jump. The dispatcher opened the hatch, Borrel sat with her legs dangling into space, the green light flashed and she jumped into the slipstream of the plane. Her chute opened with a thump and she floated down, followed by de Baissac. Both women landed as trained, rolled on their sides, collapsed their parachutes and punched the quick-release buttons on their chests. Men ran up out of the darkness to help bury the parachutes and jumpsuits. In the bright moonlight they were led off the tiny field and taken across country to a primitive shed where they spent the night. In the morning a horse and cart took them to a safe house. Andrée and Lise were the first women to be parachuted into France.

They spent the next few days in the town of Avaray in the western centre of the country, 20 miles from Blois. They began familiarising themselves with their new environment. Unlike Borrel, de Baissac had not seen a German uniform before. They wandered through the town looking at the soldiers, watching the crowded trains come and go from the station and picking up tips about identity cards and using ration tickets to buy food and clothes.

Even though they were under orders not to talk to each other about who they were or where they were going, Andrée told Lise that she had worked in a bakery on the avenue Kléber in Paris. De Baissac knew the shop, she used to buy her bread there before the war. They split up and Lise headed south-west to Poitiers to make contact with her brother. She had found Andrée 'Quick and determined, ready to face any situation. I liked her.'

Andrée went north by train to Paris. Her instructions were to go to the home of two sisters, Germaine and Madeleine Tambour, who knew where she was to stay. Suttill was scheduled to arrive at the next full moon, the night of 1/2 October, and was going to come in 'blind' without a reception committee. In the event that he could not make it the BBC were going to transmit a personal message saying that *Carmen envoy ses amities à Eugenie* – 'Carmen sends her regards to Eugenie'. They had a plan to meet in a cafe on the rue de Caumartin where he was going to wait for five minutes at noon every day.

On a foggy night Suttill and his radio operator, Jean Amps, parachuted into France. Suttill dislocated his knee on landing. He made his way to Paris where he completed the rendezvous with Andrée. The pair set off round northern France on a preliminary reconnaissance to meet the contacts they had been given. Some of these were supplied by Germaine Tambour, who had been secretary to André Girard (*Carte*) and his representative in Paris. Suttill's French was very good but his accent was strange. It was hoped he could pass as a Belgian. Borrel accompanied him everywhere, doing the talking where possible and physically helping him while his knee healed.

At El Alamein, a remote railway station in North Africa, on the evening of 23 October British and Commonwealth troops prepared to march across the minefields protecting Field Marshal Rommel's forces. The opening barrage began at 9.40 p.m. and for the next five and a half hours nearly half a million shells crashed into the German positions. Five days later, Rommel's army was in retreat.

By 26 October, Virginia Hall had heard nothing about the ticket she needed to get out of France using her cover as an American journalist. She signalled Nicolas Bodington asking for his help. He replied that she would need a visa and to send him her passport number. It took until 4 November to get the number to Baker Street. He then asked the *New York Post* to recall her officially. He thought it would be safest if the tickets and paperwork were sent to the consul in Lisbon to await her arrival.

The American consul in Lyon, William Leahy, warned her that the Americans were about to disembark 100,000 troops on the coast of North Africa, in an operation code-named *Torch*. He thought it was inevitable that the Germans would retaliate by abolishing the Free Zone in France. Hall was an ordinary citizen, without diplomatic status and well known to the Vichy authorities. With the German Army, the Gestapo and the Abwehr about to take control of Vichy it was, advised Leahy, time to go.

Hall abandoned her plans to spring the imprisoned agents including Brian Stonehouse and Denis Rake. She destroyed the documents, false identity cards and other incriminating evidence in her flat and gave the balance of her money to Robert Burdett, the senior SOE organiser in Lyon, warning him that she might disappear without being able to say goodbye. She signalled London telling them that 'Cuthbert', the nickname for her artificial leg, was being troublesome. London replied that she should execute him.

On the night of 17/18 November, a reception committee, which included three SOE agents – Francis Suttill, Andrée Borrel, and Yvonne Rudellat – flashed recognition signals to a bomber circling over their heads. Then parachutes blossomed in the moonlit sky, carrying containers full of stores. Resistance men were on them as soon as they hit the earth, collapsing the parachute canopies and heaving the long heavy cylinders onto horse-drawn carts. Soon the animals were plodding through the night to locations where the newly arrived equipment could be stored in secret. The drop was the first Suttill and his team had organised and was a complete success. Suttill sent a message to Baker Street saying that Borrel: 'Shared every danger ... Has a perfect understanding of security and an imperturbable calmness ... Everyone who has come into contact with her in her work agrees with myself that she is the best of us all ... Thank you very much for having sent her to me.'

In the same month, André Marsac, a division chief working for André Girard's *Carte* circuit, was ordered to take the file notes of 200 agents from Marseille to Paris. He set off by train. In his briefcase were the index cards, all written in uncoded, clear French.

He did not know that he was being followed. On the long journey north he fell asleep and did not wake when an Abwehr agent slipped into his compartment and silently stole the briefcase. That night it was opened at the Hôtel Lutetia, Paris, Abwehr headquarters. The contents were taken away to be read, recorded and cross-referenced.

Nancy Wake took a train from Marseille at the start of a long and tedious journey to visit Ian Garrow in his concentration camp at Meauzac. Her plan was to find the guard she had been told about, the one who could be bribed, who might be able to help get Garrow out. Watched by the inmates she walked up to the barbed wire surrounding the prison. Someone shouted and Garrow appeared, looking thin, grey and tired. No one knew about the friendly guard. Disappointed, she went back to Marseille, which was now full of German military personnel and vehicles.

Towards the end of November she was back in Meauzac. This time she succeeded in making contact with the guard in a bar, his price was 500,000 francs; he wanted 50,000 francs as a deposit and she had to find him a guard's uniform. Wake had only 10,000 francs on her and telephoned Henri, who telegraphed the money to her at the local post office.

The next day the commandant of the camp called her in and asked her why she was handling such large sums of money. Wake stared at him and said that although it might seem a lot to him it was nothing to her – she needed it to buy drinks for her friends. Then she wrote a blistering letter to the Post Office reprimanding them for revealing details of her private transactions. She heard no more from the commandant.

At the last minute the design of guard's uniforms was changed and everything was delayed while Nancy found a replacement. On 8 December the guard carried out his side of the bargain. He smuggled the uniform into the camp and hid it in a lavatory. Garrow put it on and as the guard was being changed, walked out of the camp where a car was waiting to take him to Toulouse. He was starving and weak and needed time to recover.

*

The same day, 8 December, Operation *Torch* began. An Allied force made up mainly of Americans landed at points on the North African coast from Casablanca to Algiers. Within seventy-two hours the invading troops were in control of 1300 miles of the African coastline. In France, as Leahy had predicted, the Germans retaliated by entering the Free Zone, moving in from the north and west. Virginia Hall met a trusted friend, a member of the Deuxième Bureau, a branch of Vichy intelligence, who advised her to get out of Lyon at once. Virginia said she had unfinished business she needed to do. Later that day she met her contact again. He told her that the German Army would be in the city within the next few hours, the last train to Perpignan was going to leave at 11 p.m. Hall went to her flat, packed her suitcase and left, locking the door behind her. She caught the Perpignan train with minutes to spare. German lorries and tanks entered Lyon and a few hours later the head of the Gestapo in Lyon, Klaus Barbie, arrived. Barbie was a 29-year-old psychopath, known to play the piano while his victims were being tortured. He said he would 'Do anything to get my hands on that Canadian bitch.' His intelligence had misinformed him about Virginia's nationality. A signal went out saying that Virginia Hall '. . . the woman with the wooden leg, is one of the most dangerous Allied agents in France. She must be found and destroyed at all costs.'

When Robert Alesch next went to Lyon he left a message for Dr Jean Rousset and visited Germaine Guérin. The next day the doctor was arrested and taken to prison in Dijon where he was tortured.

By the morning of 11 December Virginia Hall was in Perpignan, organising a guide to take her across the Pyrenees to Spain. She agreed to pay him 20,000 francs for his trouble and 60,000 francs for the journey. She had also agreed to pay the passage of two other escapers. That evening they were taken by lorry to a house near the foot of the massif du Canigou where they spent the night. They set off at dawn and climbed for the whole day. At nightfall they reached a hut over 4000 feet above sea level, Virginia was in agony, her skin rubbed raw by her false leg. The next day was harder and the path steeper and rockier. They climbed to a height of 8000 feet and in a place dominated by the mountain known as Pic de la Dona they reached the Spanish border where the guide left them. After another long march they arrived at the station where they were to catch the early-morning train to Barcelona. Before it arrived a Spanish patrol appeared and arrested them.

Hall tried to bluff it out, explaining that she was an American citizen. The police ignored her and drove the three fugitives to the prison in the ruined town of Figueres which had been bombed in the Spanish Civil War. The two men were sent on to the concentration camp at Miranda de Ebro.

In Figueres Prison the inmates were crowded into cold, damp, dirty cells. Hall's status as an American and her role as a journalist gave her some protection from the harsh treatment used on the other prisoners. She made friends with a prostitute who was about to be released and gave her a letter to take to the American consul who organised for her to be taken to the prison at Girona and then released on parole. Then she went to Barcelona where she waited while the consulate cabled the *New York Post* asking for their help.

The events of the last few weeks, especially the hard crossing of the Pyrenees, had taken their toll on Virginia Hall. She was weak and emaciated. On 4 December the owner of the paper wired 500 dollars for her immediate needs and finalised the details of the visa she needed to travel to England. The next day, Baker Street heard of her escape and sent a telegram congratulating her and telling her that they were going to repatriate her as soon as possible. She replied saying she wanted to get back into France and was wondering about a disguise.

By December, Déricourt had joined the SOE and was given the honorary commission of flying officer in the Admin and Special Duties Branch of the RAF. Later in the month he was taken to the airfield at Tempsford to meet some of the pilots who flew Lysanders into occupied France. Déricourt could not speak much English but he got on with the pilots and especially with Hugh Verity the newly appointed commander of A Flight. Verity could speak French and found Déricourt

> a pleasant fellow with rather wavy hair and regular features. He spoke only a few words of English but my French gave him somebody to chat to. Not that he was very talkative, rather the reverse ... Finding fields for us and laying on our operations was to be his main occupation when he got back to France. I liked him and he also made friends with Pick the squadron commander.

For the next three weeks he was taught the rudiments of working in the field and then went to the parachute school at Ringway. On 22 December with the code name *Gilbert* and carrying false papers in the name of 'Maurice Fabre' he sat in a car waiting to be driven across Tempsford airfield to the Hudson bomber, which was to fly him to France. He was wearing French clothes and in his pocket carried diamonds issued to him by Vera Atkins. He had told her that precious stones were more valuable in Paris than paper currency. Atkins thought he was lying and was going to sell the gems on the black market. Her objections were overruled. As Déricourt waited the weather closed in and the mission was postponed.

Noor Khan was bored. Since escaping from France in 1940 she had served in the Women's Auxiliary Air Force as a wireless operator. The gentle translator of *Jataka Tales* who loved writing for children did not find military life interesting. In an attempt to alleviate the tedium, she applied for a commission and unwittingly attracted the attention of SOE who thought that the bilingual radio specialist had '... interesting linguistic qualification which might make her of value for operational purposes'. She was invited to come for an interview with Selwyn Jepson at the Victoria Hotel in Northumberland Avenue. Jepson noted her 'Small still features, the dark quiet eyes, the soft voice and the fine spirit glowing in her.' He thought that 'In spite of a great gentleness of manner she had an intuitive sense of what might be in my mind for her to do.' He assessed that she was a careful, painstaking person who would 'have all the patience in the world', and told her that he was considering her for the role of an undercover wireless operator. Jepson went to great lengths to describe the dangers of the job and asked her if she fully understood what he was saying. He reported that: 'I had scarcely finished when she said with the same simplicity of manner which had characterised her from the outset of our talk, that she would like to undertake it.' Jepson made up his mind and 'with rather more of the bleak distress which I never failed to feel at this point of these interviews, I agreed to take her on.' Later she was enrolled as a FANY, signed the Official Secrets Act and disappeared from her Royal Air Force barracks, leaving only 'her blankets stacked neatly on the bedspring'.

1943: 'There are hard blows in prospect . . .'

In Casablanca, 1943 opened with a conference between Roosevelt and Churchill to discuss the date for the invasion of Europe. Churchill favoured operations in the Mediterranean or Norway and was uneasy about the prospect of invading France with too few men. In the end it was agreed that nearly 1 million troops were needed and this number could not be mustered in Britain until the following Christmas. A team called COSSAC was set up, named after the designation of its first leader, General Sir Frederick Morgan, chief of staff to the supreme allied commander. COSSAC's role was to plan the landings and to devise a deception scheme to make the Germans think it was going to take place in the Pas-de-Calais. The circuits of Resistance that SOE was struggling to set up in France were to be an integral element of D-Day planning.

Virginia Hall waited in Barcelona for nearly a month before she was able to get to Lisbon and board a boat for England. She arrived in London on 19 January 1943 and went straight to Orchard Court, the flat near the SOE headquarters where its agents were briefed and debriefed. It was famous for its black-tiled bathroom and was presided over by a butler called Park who had been a messenger for the Westminster Bank in Paris. At the flat she had a conference with Maurice Buckmaster, Nicolas Bodington and Vera Atkins. She had been in the field longer than any other agent. Her cover as a journalist had proved very effective and she had carried out almost every task she had been given. Without her there might be no circuits left in what had been the Free Zone. She was not only a mother to every agent who knew her and to many who did not but also the banker, guide and friend to the whole organisation in France. Later Buckmaster recommended her for an OBE. Hall herself was anxious for news of her comrades in France, especially in Lyon.

She did not know that Robert Alesch had returned to Lyon with instructions to find out where Virginia had gone and identify the remaining senior members of her circuit. One of his first victims was the brothel-keeper Mme Guérin who, thinking he was a trusted agent, gave him money and contacts. When she was arrested and taken to Paris for interrogation, Alesch spent several nights sleeping in her bed and took the opportunity to ransack her deserted house of furs, jewellery, china and money.

During the first weeks of the year, nearly 12,000 French police descended on Nancy Wake's hometown, Marseille. The force included 200 police inspectors from Paris, and squads of Gendarmerie. Their target was the Old Port, a maze of winding streets, narrow alleys, tumbledown buildings and passageways inhabited by prostitutes, pimps, gangsters, black-marketeers, people on the run from the Vichy police, refugees without identity papers and ordinary people whose families had been resident there for decades.

The huge force was led by René Bousquet, a collaborator who had been made general secretary of police. Heinrich Himmler described Bousquet as a 'precious collaborator in the framework of police collaboration'. The French police moved in at dawn on the morning of 22 January and for two days went from house to house checking identity papers, questioning and arresting people. Men, women and children were put onto lorries and driven into captivity. By the evening of 24 January 40,000 identities had been checked, 30,000 people had been thrown out of their homes, 6000 people had been arrested of whom 2000 were now in cattle trucks on their way to extermination camps. That night the Old Port stood empty. All the next day Nancy and her neighbours listened to the crump of high explosives as 1600 buildings were blown up. A pillar of dust hung over the city, obscuring the sun.

While the raids were in progress Nancy thought she could hear a strange clicking noise in the receiver of her telephone and when a man was caught going through the mailboxes at the entrance to her building she was certain she was being watched.

Nancy, Henri her husband, and other members of the Resistance decided that she must leave France immediately. She packed her bags and moved into another house while a route across the Pyrenees was arranged. Without her knowing, Henri cut the words LOVE FROM HENRI from a newspaper and left them under the clothes in her suitcase. As she left her home, she turned and waved at Henri shouting 'Back soon', loud enough for everyone to hear, including the police commissioner living opposite. She cried all the way to the station.

Far to the east in Russia, in the cellar of the ruins of Univermag, a department store in Stalingrad, General Friedrich Paulus, leader of the German 6th Army, signalled to his Führer: 'Troops without ammunition or food ... Effective command no longer possible ... Further defence senseless ... Army requests immediate permission to surrender in order to save lives of remaining troops.' Hitler's reply was 'Surrender Forbidden'. That night Goebbels broadcast on German radio: 'A thousand years hence, every German will speak with awe of Stalingrad and remember that it was there that Germany put the seal on her victory.'

In the city itself General Paulus sat on his camp bed in the corner of the cellar, tired, weary and dejected, in a 'state of near collapse'. On the 31 January his army surrendered. The last radio message to leave his headquarters read: 'The Russians are at the door of our bunker. We are destroying our equipment.' The transmission ended with the initials 'CL', the international code meaning 'This station will no longer transmit.' Dead, wounded and missing for both armies numbered nearly 2 million, around 800,000 of them Germans or their allies.

At the end of January a new uniform appeared on the streets of France: blue jacket, blue trousers, brown shirt and belt, topped by a blue beret. The men wearing it were Frenchmen, charged with counter-terrorism and often armed with captured British service revolvers or .303 rifles. The recruits had been promised exemption from deportation for work in Germany and were guaranteed full employment, adequate pay and plenty of rations. Their ranks were filled with thugs and petty criminals. They had powers to arrest, interrogate, torture and carry out mass executions. The new force was called the 'Milice française'. They were described by one SOE agent as the 'Scum of the jails, the most brutalised cream of the offal'. They were almost always local men who knew the area, the people and the dialect.

On 5 February, the combined commanders of the Allied forces were presented with a 'Most Secret' document: 'The Selection of Assault Areas in a Major Operation in North West Europe', a staff study examining the suitability of areas from the Hook of Holland to the Bay of Biscay for landing an invasion force. The report was sixteen pages of well-argued thinking about the invasion and covered the needs of the Allied armies, navies and air forces. The writers of the paper also considered the role of what they referred to as 'Patriots', local forces. They argued that 'in the operations being considered assistance from patriots may be of importance'. Unaware of the existence of SOE and lacking intelligence on the underground armies of the countries in question they went on to state that: 'In all areas, however, small parties dropped by air to rouse the populace and provide them with arms and explosives are likely to meet with considerable success.' The paper concluded by stating the most favourable place for landings would be in Normandy.

*

During the winter Nancy made three attempts to cross into
Spain but each time had to turn back because of the weather. She
was accompanied by Pat O'Leary, whose real name was Albert
Guérisse, a major in the Belgian Army and with Ian Garrow the
organiser of the Pat Line, the escape route out of France for downed
airmen and Resistance fighters on the run. After the third attempt
the train from Perpignan back to Toulouse was stopped by armed
police who arrested everyone. Nancy was interrogated for three
days. First she was accused of being a terrorist who had bombed a
cinema, next that she was a prostitute. In the end O'Leary bluffed
that she was his mistress and he was a member of the Milice. Nancy
was released. A few weeks later O'Leary was arrested, betrayed by
a double agent, and sent to a concentration camp.

Eventually Nancy tracked down an agent who could help her
across the mountains. She went to the address she had been given,
knocked on the door, which opened to reveal a suspicious man.
Nancy did not know the passwords but said 'I am Nancy Fiocca.
You are in charge of our guides. I work for O'Leary, so do you. I
want to go to Spain. I've had enough trouble getting here so don't
give me any crap.'

She was put in a group who were travelling at once. The guides
always took the highest and most difficult route and the crossing
usually took forty-eight hours. By the halfway mark everyone was
wet, tired and cold. An American collapsed and refused to go on.
Wake dragged the man to his feet and told him that he had a choice,
continue or be pushed over a cliff. Two hours later he collapsed
again. This time she pulled him along by his hair.

Weeks later, having travelled across Spain, Portugal and the Bay
of Biscay, Nancy lay in a tiny bed in the St James's Hotel, London,
alone.

The German invasion of the Free Zone caused the Allies to change
their policy about clandestine operations in France. Up to that
point aggressive acts of sabotage were discouraged or even forbidden. From the end of January SOE's new orders were to 'sabotage

the German war effort with every means possible'. There was a general feeling that the invasion of Europe would happen sometime in the coming year, 1943, and plans were made to introduce twenty new agents into France backed up by 1000 containers of stores. The transport problems went on. The pilots had asked to be received by reception committees and wanted prepared landing strips with lights and flashing recognition signals. They also wanted manpower to help disembark and embark passengers and unload and load cargo. This had not been happening and the RAF were becoming uncooperative. One SOE officer in London complained that 'a very great deal of time was wasted trying to convince the RAF to see the value of co-operation with the SOE ...'. Buckmaster put his faith in Henri Déricourt, his new air transport control officer, to sort things out.

Déricourt himself had been in France since the end of January. One of his first contacts had been SS *Sturmbannführer* Karl Bömelburg, the head of the French Gestapo. When they met, the two men were driven in a black Citroën through the Bois de Boulogne. Déricourt told Bömelburg about his trip to London and his new role as air controller for SOE, explaining that he was responsible for all the Lysander flights into and out of France. He added that England was a hotbed of Bolshevism, that the British themselves were on the brink of revolution and he was offering his services to the Nazis to stop the spread of Communism. They met again that day. At the end of the second meeting Déricourt was given the code name *Gilbert* and the number BOE/48 which meant he was Bömelburg's 48th agent. Déricourt moved into a two-room apartment on the third floor of 58 rue Pergolèse, right next door to Hugo Bleicher. The building was only ten minutes away from Bömelburg's Gestapo headquarters at 82–84 avenue Foch.

An early recruit to Déricourt's team was an old friend – Rémy Clément – who had been a pilot with Air France but was now grounded and bored. At first he was nervous of Déricourt's proposal, wary of the dangers of working with secret agents. Then he thought to himself that his friend was 'offering something I was craving for. To be involved with flying.' He became Déricourt's second in command.

Déricourt's first operation, code-named *Trainer*, took place on the night of 17/18 March in a field just outside Poitiers. He had four agents to get out and four to come in, an operation requiring two Lysanders. It was a freezing night, moonlight reflecting off the frost-covered field, code-named *B/19*. The first aircraft made a perfect landing, two people scrambled out, two climbed in and it was gone. The next plane was late. Déricourt passed the time talking to the new arrivals, handing round a flask of brandy to calm them. He soon found out who they were, where they were going and that they were all linked to Francis Suttill's circuit *Prosper*. After thirty minutes the second plane made a heavy landing on the frozen field. The undercarriage flexed hard on impact, the engine roared and flames began to play around the exhaust pipes and the engine cowling. The aircraft rolled to a halt, Déricourt heaved himself up the access ladder, thrust his face into the cockpit, grabbed what turned out to be an inflatable life jacket and stuffed it into the exhausts. The flames went out, the incoming passengers got out, the passengers for England climbed aboard and the plane took off. When Déricourt got back to Paris he made a report to Bömelburg telling him everything he had picked up in his chat with the agents.

By the end of the spring Suttill's *Prosper* network extended over most of northern France from the Ardennes to the Atlantic. When the invasion came he and his colleagues in London thought that he would be able to raise the equivalent of a division, nearly 20,000 men. Lack of radio operators and equipment continued to be a problem and even circuits not directly connected to *Prosper* relied on the circuit for radio contact with London. Suttill's base was the École nationale d'agriculture in Grignon to the west of Paris. In the spring of 1943, Déricourt got to know Suttill. They would sometimes lunch in the black-market cafe Chez Tutulle and Suttill drove him out to Grignon to meet other key members of his team, including Andrée Borrel and the radio operator Gilbert Norman.

Everyone trusted and liked Déricourt except Andrée Borrel, though she could not work out why.

One day in March, *Carte* agent André Marsac, whose briefcase had been stolen while he slept on a train, entered a cafe off the Champs-Elysées. He was accompanied by two people, his elegant assistant Lucienne, and a Russian. He was not aware that watching him were Hugo Bleicher and several other Abwehr agents or that the woman he was to meet was a German double agent. An hour later Marsac and Lucienne were in Fresnes Prison, a huge, unpleasant-looking warehouse-like building that could hold more than 1500 prisoners. Captured agents and Resistance people were often tortured and sometimes died there.

For the next few days Bleicher interrogated Marsac and by pretending that he was disillusioned with Hitler and wanted to go over to the Allies persuaded him that he was going to organise an escape and that Marsac and Lucienne were going to London. Marsac fell for it and introduced Bleicher to his assistant Roger Bardet, a tall, slim, wiry man in his late twenties. At the meeting Bleicher was given details of twenty important agents. Within days most of them were in prison and the *Carte* circuit ceased to exist. The only survivor was Roger Bardet who became a double agent working for the Abwehr. Bleicher continued working on André Marsac, hoping to turn him too.

One of the most important addresses for the *Prosper* network was 32 avenue de Suffren, the home of the two sisters Germaine and Madeleine Tambour who had worked for the *Carte* network. They allowed their apartment to be used both as a rendezvous and as a letter drop. Another flat in the same building was also used and at least ten key members of the *Prosper* network were regular visitors to the building, including Francis Suttill, Gilbert Norman and Andrée Borrel. Thanks to the information captured in Marsac's briefcase the German's knew about the building and the Tambour sisters.

Andrée and Francis came to spend most of their time in each other's company. They were often to be found at the Hot Club, a place for jazz enthusiasts. Inside the club, hidden up a narrow flight of stairs, was a small room that could be bolted from the inside. Only members of the underground knew about it or were allowed anywhere near it. In this room the two agents trained recruits to use weapons, including Bren and Sten guns. The demonstration weapons were hidden in the base of a heavy bookcase. One of the owners of the club was an expert in radio communications and had installed an aerial disguised as a clothes line. Like the Tambour sisters' flat the Hot Club was heavily used as a letter drop. When they weren't working, Borrel and Suttill, plus the radio operator Gilbert Norman, often ate together in the same restaurant, played cards in the same place and sometimes spoke in English, an enormous risk.

On Thursday 22 April, Bleicher and his men raided the Tambours' apartment and arrested the sisters. SS *Sturmbannführer* Hans Josef Kieffer, one of the most senior German intelligence officers in France, was furious – it was one of his men who had stolen the briefcase and he thought the two women should be prisoners of the SS not the Abwehr. Bleicher was very wary of Kieffer; he knew he was a Gestapo-trained policeman of the 'old type'. He was ambitious, spent all his waking hours at his desk and had very little room for humane feelings. Bleicher said, 'He had only one standard, success at any cost.'

On the day of the arrest, Armel Guerne, second in command of the *Prosper* circuit, was on his bicycle near the École nationale d'agriculture. He spent the daylight hours identifying places to hide food and medical supplies and examining a field to see whether it could be used as a landing zone for gliders. He arrived home at six in the evening and heard the news about the sisters. He knew that Madeleine Tambour could not stand up to interrogation and was likely to give away Suttill's identity. He went straight to the Tambour apartment, gambling that the Germans were no longer there.

When he arrived at the building he asked the concierge to check there were no German security men in the flat. Then he entered and searched it, trying to burn anything that referred to *Prosper* or *Carte*. What he could not destroy on the spot he took to a cellar in a neighbouring building to dispose of later.

When Francis Suttill heard what had happened he immediately cancelled all the current passwords and letter drops before telling London that the Tambours' address was not to be used again. Then he asked London for money to use as a bribe to release the sisters. London replied: 'We are not the Salvation Army.' Even so, money was raised and Suttill asked Jean Worms, a businessman and dealer, to start negotiations.

Worms had two contacts in the Gestapo. Suttill gave permission to offer them 250,000 francs. The bribe was accepted and a date arranged to hand over the two sisters at a place near the Château de Vincennes. At the appointed time a black Citroën appeared, while hiding in the shadows was the *Prosper* reception committee. The car stopped, the doors opened and the women got out, not the sisters but two heavily made-up, late-middle-aged prostitutes.

Worms and Suttill made another offer, this time 2 million francs. Kieffer agreed, even though he did not have the sisters, having failed to get the Abwehr to turn them over to the Gestapo. He set up a rendezvous in a cafe near Porte Maillot and said he wanted Francis Suttill and Gilbert Norman to receive the sisters in person.

On the day of the pick-up Suttill and Norman sat in the cafe. Again they were protected by men hidden near them, ready to open fire if anything went wrong. The black Citroën appeared, everybody tensed. The car stopped and a window wound down to reveal a Gestapo agent with a Leica. He photographed Suttill and Norman and the car accelerated away. The bewildered reception committee dispersed. Later Kieffer showed Bömelburg the pictures, telling him he was certain that one of the two men was the head of the *Prosper* circuit.

Hundreds of miles to the south, in Cairo, Christine Granville was finding life 'unbearable'. She wrote: 'There are about 90,000 officers here trying to have fun. You cannot imagine the way in which nobody here realises the atrocities going on in the occupied countries ... I am in despair.'

One acquaintance said: 'Men found her terribly attractive ...
but women would be rather fed up that she had such an effect ...'
One officer reported that 'She had the most extraordinary grace
and casual chic. When she came in a room even staff officers would
leap to their feet to offer her a chair.' A woman friend thought that
'Christine was solitary'. She hated parties and rarely accepted an
invitation. She arrived at one party looking hunched like a drowned
rat but had a 'mesmeric power of switching on her personality' with
a blend of 'vivacity, flirtatiousness, charm and sheer personality,
like a searchlight'.

From time to time she was asked what she thought of a certain
Polish officer or secret agent. About one man who was described
to her as being 'Tall, athletic and good looking with charming
manners' she advised, 'His brother has been for many years in a
lunatic asylum ... He might do worse than join him.'

Eventually she was offered office work at SOE Cairo's headquarters at Rustum Buildings. She refused and a friend wrote on her
behalf saying that she was 'Not the type who can abide office work'
and that she wanted 'Work with risk'. Christine herself offered to
do 'any kind of duty except office work, preferably near the front'.

Towards the end of April, Christine got news of what had been
happening in Warsaw. On 19 April, German troops had entered
the Ghetto to eliminate the 60,000 people who had not already
died from starvation, summary execution, disease or deportation.
The troops were led by Jürgen Stroop and were surprised to be
met by armed and organised fighters who put up much greater
opposition than anticipated. Even so, by 16 May the Ghetto was
a smoking ruin and the last vestiges of resistance had been wiped
out. Stroop personally detonated the explosives that destroyed the
Great Synagogue of Warsaw, writing:

What a marvelous sight it was. A fantastic piece of theatre. My
staff and I stood at a distance. I held the electrical device which
would detonate all the charges simultaneously ... I glanced
over at my brave officers and men, tired and dirty, silhouetted

against the glow of the burning buildings. After prolonging the suspense for a moment, I shouted: 'Heil Hitler' and pressed the button. With a thunderous, deafening bang and a rainbow burst of colours, the fiery explosion soared toward the clouds, an unforgettable tribute to our triumph over the Jews. The Warsaw Ghetto was no more.

Christine knew that her mother had been forced to move into the Ghetto. She never mentioned her again.

Noor Khan's SOE training got off to a bad start. She lacked confidence, hated physical exercise, was clumsy with explosives and frightened of weapons. But she worked hard to overcome her deficiencies and by the end of the first part of her course a training officer wrote: 'She is a person for whom I have the greatest admiration. Completely self-effacing and un-selfish ... extremely modest, even humble and shy, always thought everyone better than herself ... extremely conscientious'. She was given five days' leave, most of which she spent with her family. Then she was sent on to Group B, a signals training centre based at Thame Park in Oxfordshire, for the next phase of her training.

SOE was beginning to understand that radio operators were the most essential part of the system. Colin Gubbins said that without them the whole organisation would be 'groping in the dark'. Their life expectancy in the field was six weeks.

Noor was trained to use the 'Type B Mark 2' wireless, known as the B2. The set was fitted into a small suitcase holding the transmitter, receiver, battery, mains adaptor and Morse key. It came with 100 feet of aerial and 10 feet of earthing wire. Deploying the long aerial so that it did not give away the position of the wireless was always a problem. A feature of the set was that it could be converted from mains to battery power at the flick of a switch. When the Gestapo were homing in on a transmitter they could turn off the power to a block of buildings they suspected. If the transmission stopped they knew they were in the right place. By switching to battery the operator could keep transmitting, a two-edged sword because the Germans could keep tracking the set. The wireless had a range of about 500 miles and weighed 33 pounds. It was manufactured at the Bontex Knitting Mills on the North Circular Road near Wembley in London.

Noor had already been taught Morse by the RAF so she concentrated on increasing her speed of transmission. By the end of the course she was the fastest student, able to send at eighteen words per minute and receive at twenty-two. The students were instructed to build in checks that told London they had been captured and were working under duress. There were two checks: a bluff check that the enemy could be told about and a true check that was kept secret. A transmission arriving with the bluff check but without the true check was a signal that something was wrong.

When she was not crouched over her wireless set, Noor put in extra hours in the gym to improve her fitness. Her instructors worried that Khan's sensitive nature and vivid imagination might compromise her in the field. One instructor noted: 'I suggest that care be taken that she is not given any task that might set up a mental conflict with her idealism. This might render her unstable from our point of view.'

One night Noor was dragged out of her bed and into a room that appeared to be full of Gestapo officers. Bright lights were shone at her and she was made to stand while men shouted at her, trying to insult and humiliate her. At one point she was made to stand on a table. Khan was so frightened that she could hardly speak and by the end she was ashen, trembling and terrified. A witness found it 'almost unbearable'.

For her final practical exercise Noor was sent to Bristol where her tasks were to establish contacts, set up live and dead letterboxes and find a place from which she could safely transmit. She posed as a writer researching a book on the war and was in Bristol to see how children reacted to air raids. The police had been warned of her presence and when they arrested and interrogated her they reported that she made 'stupid' mistakes, giving away more than was being asked. One instructor found her behaviour during the long exercise exasperating. She had told a policeman that she was being trained as an agent and asked him if he would like to see her wireless set. After her interrogation a police superintendent had said, 'If this girl's an agent, I'm Winston Churchill.'

The verdict on the Bristol scheme came from an officer who said that she had worked hard but 'must learn to be more discreet'. One instructor at Beaulieu called Khan 'the potty princess' and said that her encryption techniques were 'completely unpredictable'. He added, 'Do you know what the bastard [father] taught her? That the worse sin she could commit was to lie about anything.' Noor's final report read that while 'She cannot be considered a fully trained operator ... she is quite capable of handling her set and passing messages.' The instructors worried that she was 'easily flustered when difficulties cropped up, especially if they were of a technical nature, and it is doubtful if she will ever be able to fully overcome this'.

Colonel Frank Spooner, head of the school at Beaulieu wrote: '... she is not overburdened with brains, but has worked hard and shown keenness, apart from some dislike of the security side of the course. She has an unstable and temperamental personality and it is very doubtful whether she is really suited to work in the field.' Buckmaster scribbled on Spooner's report: 'We don't want them overburdened with brains', 'makes me cross' and 'Nonsense'.

In Paris the amount of signals needing to be sent to London began to overwhelm the operators. One was helping out by sending messages for several circuits, a very dangerous practice and a breach of security. As part of the solution Buckmaster asked Noor if she was prepared to go to Paris and work as radio operator for a *Prosper* sub-circuit, *Cinema*. She agreed, even though she had not finished her training.

A fellow trainee, Yvonne Cormeau, considered that Khan was a 'Splendid, vague, dreamy creature, far too conspicuous – twice seen never forgotten' and argued that she should not be sent into France. Two trainees wrote to Vera Atkins saying that they thought Khan was not suitable to be sent into the field. Atkins took her to lunch, showed her the letters and gave her a chance to pull out, reminding her of the consequences of breaking down in the field and letting down her comrades. Khan insisted that she was the right woman for the job, she was going, come what may.

Buckmaster went to see Leo Marks, who was in charge of cryptography. He told him about 'That bastard Spooner' and called the instructors who had given her bad reports 'a mob of second raters'. Marks was scheduled to brief Khan on her code system and under pressure from Buckmaster agreed to give her a three-hour lesson rather that the usual one hour.

When Marks met Noor for the first time he said, 'As soon as I glimpsed the slender figure seated at a desk in the Orchard Court briefing room I knew that the only thing likely to be detached was one (if not both) of my eyeballs. No one had mentioned Noor's extraordinary beauty.' He tested her and found her work to be very erratic. She either made a lot of mistakes and became tearful at her own inadequacies or she worked faster and more accurately than any trainee he had come across.

Marks realised that her inability to lie was a profound and potentially deadly part of her psychology. To solve the problem he told her that if she made mistakes encrypting her messages it was as though she was lying, which shocked her. Then he talked about the monkeys crossing a bridge in one of her *Jataka Tales*. At the mention of her work Noor looked at him with an intensity that reduced him 'to chutney'. He said the monkeys were the letters and if the letters were wrong, they were lies that would cause the animals to fall off the bridge and be shot. Noor suddenly understood what he meant. As a final test he gave her three long messages to encrypt and bring to him the next day. She passed with flying colours and Marks was forced to declare her fit for service in the field. Before she left he told her that if she was captured she must include an eighteen letter 'transposition code' in her transmission. This would be a signal to him that she had been arrested and was working under duress.

*

Déricourt was now having regular meetings with Bömelburg in an apartment on the boulevard Malesherbes. The flat was one of two that Bömelburg had set up for the Déricourt briefings; they were bugged and empty except for a few pieces of furniture and a telephone. Bömelburg told Déricourt that in future he wanted to know about arrivals and departures in advance. He promised that he would not arrest the agents as they arrived, partly because he did not want to rouse suspicions in Baker Street. From then on, whenever new agents were due to arrive, the two men met in the flat where Bömelburg made notes while Déricourt told him the scheduled date and time of arrival, the coordinates of the landing field, the number of agents coming in and the number leaving for England. The agents themselves never knew they were in danger of being watched and followed from the moment they landed on French soil.

Noor Khan spent her last days in England at Orchard Court, finalising the details of her mission and waiting for the next full moon. Vera Atkins wrote her cover story using elements from Noor's real life. Her cover name was *Jeanne-Marie Renier*. She had a degree in child psychology from the Sorbonne and her character specialised in child psychology. Noor's code name was *Madeleine*.

Noor was issued with money, a false identity, ration and clothing coupons. These were produced by Section XIV based on the estate of Lord Aldenham in Essex. The section included men who had spent time in prison for forgery. Many of the copies were based on documents provided by agents returning from the field. Some documents were even supplied by the Germans as part of the double bluff they were playing on Baker Street through Déricourt.

Noor's clothes were made by a Jewish refugee from Vienna, Claudia Pulver. In her workshop in Margaret Street, London she meticulously unpicked hundreds of articles of clothing brought from all over Europe and copied them, making it impossible to tell them from the real thing. She worked in minute detail, knowing that a wrongly sewn-on button, the wrong stitching on underwear or a strangely turned cuff could betray an agent's origins. She fitted Noor with a simple wardrobe, suitable for a children's nurse without much money.

For emergencies Noor was issued with four sorts of pill. A knockout drop to slip into an enemy's drink; benzedrine tablets to combat exhaustion brought on by long hours under strain; a pill to simulate stomach disorders, something which might help to avoid or break up an interrogation, and a suicide pill in a rubber coating that looked like a raisin.

Noor was instructed that she was only to send and receive messages for the *Cinema* circuit and she must encode them herself. She was ordered to '... be extremely careful with the filing of your messages ...'

Towards the end of her stay Noor visited a friend, Jean Overton Fuller, who thought she must be in love, she looked so beautiful. Khan told her that: 'Everything I ever wanted has come at once.' The two spent the night talking and Khan asked Fuller to read her palm. The next day, after breakfast, Noor hugged Fuller and kissed her goodbye. She returned to Orchard Court where she was collected by Vera Atkins who drove her to RAF Tangmere in an open-top staff car christened 'The Hearse'. Noor was the first female radio operator to be inserted into occupied France. She was given the address of a safe house, which she could use if anything went wrong. It was 32 Avenue de Suffren, the apartment where the Tambour sisters had lived and been arrested several weeks before and the further use of which had been forbidden by Francis Suttill.

On the night of the 15/16 June, two Canadians, Frank Pickersgill and Ken Macalister were inserted into the Loire Valley in France by parachute. They carried with them messages and radio equipment. They were met by Pierre Culioli and Yvonne Rudellat. Culioli had been a regular French Army officer and was now the organiser of a sub-circuit of Suttill's vast *Prosper* network. Rudellat had been operational for nearly a year, training agents and taking part in acts of sabotage. The two were successfully masquerading as husband and wife. The Canadians' first destination was Paris but Culioli noticed that their false papers were wrong, the Germans had changed the system, requiring photographs to be attached to the cards with rivets rather than staples. He told the new arrivals to lie low while he went to Paris to get the right documentation.

The next night, 16/17 June, a reception committee led by Déricourt and his second in command Rémy Clément waited in the small field near Angers, scanning the sky, straining to hear the noise of approaching aircraft. With them were five passengers waiting to be flown to England. Lying on the ground were the bicycles that had transported everyone to the site. The noise of aircraft engines was suddenly heard. Déricourt shouted: *'Allez allez.'* Three of the reception committee took up positions carrying torches, which they shone into the sky. From the air the lights outlined a long 'L', an improvised runway. Another agent flashed the recognition signal in Morse to the aircraft now circling overhead. A Lysander dropped out of the darkness, suddenly loud and huge. It came down fast, and bounced across the grass, the engine noise changing pitch as the aircraft thundered down the field, slowed to a stop, turned and taxied back. Déricourt could see the face of the pilot, lit by the glow from his instruments; behind him were two silhouetted figures. The side hatch opened and some of the reception committee ran forward, huddling under the broad wing to help the first passenger, Cecily Lefort, onto the ground. The second passenger, Noor Khan, wearing a green oilskin coat, handed down two suitcases and then clambered out herself. Noor and Cecily were pulled half running to where Déricourt stood, overseeing the operation. The Lysander accelerated away and lifted off into the darkness. Déricourt shook hands with the new arrivals. Rémy Clément wheeled a bicycle over and gave it to Noor, telling her to follow him. The second plane had landed and was taxiing towards them, the noise of the engine and wind from the propeller dominating everything. Noor lent her bike against a tree, knelt down and buried the pistol she had been carrying. Clément waited, now astride his own bike. The second Lysander deposited its two passengers, accelerated away and climbed into the air. The group began to disperse. Cecily Lefort and Diana Rowden disappeared into the night. Clément nodded to

Khan, a questioning look on his face. She nodded back and then they too were bicycling into the dark leaving Déricourt alone in the suddenly silent and deserted moonlit field. Everything had gone according to plan exactly as it had said on the schedule he had given to the Gestapo who paid him £5000 for every agent he betrayed.

Noor and Clément rode on in silence through the night heading for the station at Angers where Noor was to catch a train to Paris. Once on board she was on her own. Her destination was 40 rue Erlanger, where her contact lived. When she arrived she was to say: *'Je viens de la part de votre ami Antoine pour des nouvelles au sujet de la Société en Bâtiment.'* ('I have come on behalf of your friend Antoine for news of the Building Society.') If he answered: *'L'affaire est en cours'* ('The business is underway'), she knew she was in the right place.

By the evening Noor stood outside the flat on the eighth floor of the building, holding a bunch of flowers she had bought as a present for the old lady she thought was her contact. The door opened to reveal a young man, the 34-year-old Henri Garry, head of the *Cinema* circuit. Noor was tongue-tied and forgot to say the pass-phrase. Garry asked her in and she met his fiancée, Marguerite Nadaud. Noor did not know what to say or do and waited for the old lady to appear. Henri offered her a cigarette, Marguerite went to make what passed for coffee in wartime Paris and eventually Noor blurted out the coded phrase. Henri gave the correct reply. Noor explained she had not eaten since leaving England because she had no idea how to use her forged ration coupons and so had opted not to buy anything, getting by on a bottle of Vichy water. Marguerite began to cook her a meal. Noor felt safe in the small friendly flat and talked about her mother. She revealed how difficult it had been to leave her and how worried she was that her mother had no idea where she was or what she was up to. Seeing that she was upset and exhausted, Marguerite and Henri asked if she would like to stay in the apartment while she found her feet. She accepted.

For the next two days she travelled about Paris with France Antelme, the head of another circuit, *Bricklayer*. After a couple of days he radioed Baker Street, telling them that Noor had arrived safely and was 'happy and all right'. Antelme introduced her to another radio operator, Gilbert Norman. They discovered that Norman, who was a couple of years younger than Noor, had been to the same school. Noor's wireless had not yet arrived and she used Norman's set to make her first transmission to London, setting a record – none of her comrades had got on air so quickly. In Baker Street, Buckmaster was pleased that the agent he had taken such a chance on was proving herself.

On Sunday 20 June, Gilbert Norman took Noor out to Grignon, to the College of Agriculture, where she met the director and his family plus the head of the new medical section, Professor Balachowsky, and his wife.

Francis Suttill had just been parachuted back into France after spending several days in London. He arrived seeming distracted and looking tired and drawn. When he discovered that Khan had been given the Tambours' address as a safe house he sent an angry signal to Baker Street:

> ... in spite of the fact that it is cancelled since February (cancellation confirmed personally by me in May visit). Please take disciplinary action. Had 'Madeleine' [Noor Khan] gone there yesterday afternoon she would have coincided with one of the Gestapo's periodic visits to the flat! ... I hope I have made myself clear. It is now 0100 hours 19th June and I have slept 7 hours since 0500 hours 15th June.

In spite of this the group had a relaxed lunch, all the friends and families safe and secure from the war and the dangers of their work.

During the day Noor helped to make tea for everybody. She carried it in on a tray and began to pour, putting the milk in first. Madame Balachowsky quietly pointed out that in France it was usual to put the milk in last. Noor's way was English and could betray her if she did it in front of the wrong people. Later on Professor

Balachowsky appeared carrying Noor's exercise book containing all her security codes. He told her that by leaving the book around she had endangered not only herself but anyone who saw it. He told her to be more careful, she must trust no one, not even him. Her closest ally might turn out to be a double agent about to betray her. She must behave as though she was under constant surveillance by the Germans, suspicious of everyone, trusting no one. Suttill decided that until her transmitter arrived, Noor was to work at Grignon, and live in comparative safety with the director, his family and the Balachowskys. She was to pretend to be one of the students.

The Canadians Pickersgill and Macalister had to wait until 21 June before Pierre Culioli and Yvonne Rudellat returned with new identity papers and thought it was safe to take them by car to Beaugency on the Loire where they planned to catch the train north to Paris. Culioli wrapped the crystals and messages in a small, fake Red Cross parcel and put it in the glove compartment. Outside Dhuizon they were waved through a roadblock; ahead the town was full of German vehicles and soldiers. They were stopped a second time and the Canadians were told to get out of the car, two soldiers took their place, and Culioli was ordered to drive to the Mairie where he and Yvonne were questioned and released. The Canadians had been taken into the building under guard. Yvonne and Culioli waited for them outside in the car. Suddenly a soldier appeared on the steps, shouting for them to come back inside. Culioli put his foot hard on the throttle and screeched off, trying to escape. He was immediately followed as he raced down the road and ran into a German patrol that opened fire. Bullets shattered the windscreen and Yvonne fell sideways onto Culioli's lap, blood pouring from wounds in her head and shoulder. Culioli tried to drive the car into a wall, hoping to kill himself but it bounced off into a field and stopped. The impact flung him out of the car. A bullet tore into his leg, he fell and was pounced on by soldiers. The Germans searched the car and found the package, which they opened discovering the crystals wrapped up with a label saying 'Pour Archambaud', Gilbert Norman's code name. A sheet of paper had instructions on how to use the crystals. They found messages, one addressed 'Pour Prosper' which was Francis Suttill and another 'Pour Mairie Louise', Andrée Borrel. In the boot they found the suitcase with Macalister's radio. A vehicle arrived to take the wounded agents to a local Luftwaffe hospital. Yvonne Rudellat was unconscious.

Unaware of the disaster that had overtaken Culioli, Francis Suttill sat tired, depressed and agitated in a cafe near the Gare d'Austerlitz. He was waiting for Macalister, Pickering and the now incarcerated Culioli. His workload and the strain of living under-cover were grinding him down and he was worried that the morale of the Resistance would plummet if the Allies did not invade in the next few months. When the Canadians arrived he was to hand them over to Armel Guerne who was responsible for making sure they travelled safely to establish the new circuit in the Ardennes. It became clear they were not going to appear so Suttill left the station and returned the next day. He spent another morning in the cafe and when by noon nobody had appeared he called it a day and had lunch with Andrée Borrel and Armel Guerne at Guerne's flat.

The next morning he returned to the café for a third time but still nobody appeared. He went back to Guerne's flat for lunch with the same group. Gilbert Norman joined them. Suttill was very agitated and declared that if the invasion did not come soon the Resistance would give up in despair and they would all be arrested. He spec-ulated wildly about the possibility of calling for an uprising in an attempt to force the Allies to cross the Channel.

All the while, Culioli, with his badly wounded and untreated leg, lay handcuffed to a bed in a German infirmary near the railway station at Blois. He was beaten and interrogated but revealed noth-ing. Then his briefcase was examined by the Gestapo who found records with detailed information about members of the Resistance all over northern France. Among them were files on Borrel and Norman complete with addresses. Culioli was sent by car to Paris for further interrogation at the avenue Foch.

Francis Suttill stayed the night in the house of Madame Renée Guépin. She was worried that he looked so exhausted and asked him what was wrong. He replied, 'It's not my health, it's much worse. I'm not allowed to tell you the trouble that weighs on my mind.' Then he said, 'There are hard blows in prospect and it is from London that it is coming.'

NACHT UND NEBEL

The next night, 23 June 1943, Andrée Borrel and Gilbert Norman stayed at the apartment of Maud and Nicho Laurent. They had travelled there separately, Borrel by Metro and Norman by bike, both arriving just after midnight. Nicho and Maud got ready for bed while Norman and Borrel worked at a table covered in false identity cards, coupons and the forged seals of almost every German *Kommandantur* in France. Andrée Borrel's attaché case was on the floor. The doorbell rang and Norman shouted to Nicho, telling him to answer it. Irritated that Norman was expecting visitors after curfew, Nicho went downstairs to the kitchen, a room that led into the garden. After a pause, Maud, now in a night slip, heard him shouting: 'Maud get dressed!' Suddenly twelve men stormed up the stairs waving revolvers and shouting. Maud screamed in anger, Andrée tried to escape, the men lashed out with their fists. Minutes later all four were bundled into cars and driven away for interrogation at the avenue Foch. When they arrived everything was in turmoil, all the lights on, officers and men milling about. Then Culioli arrived and was hauled out of the car, sweating and gasping in agony from the wound in his leg and the beating he had taken during his interrogation at Blois. He too was dragged into the building and taken up to a cell.

Later that night, cars arrived at the Hôtel Mazagran in a

run-down area near the Porte Saint-Denis. Armed men piled out and hammered on the door, waking the terrified proprietress, Madame Fèvre, asking for Francis Suttill using one of his code names – *François Desprées*. They examined the visitors' register and saw that Suttill was in room 15 and had been staying there for five days. Madame Fèvre said she had not seen him for a while. Soon the hotel was dark, silent and full of armed men.

The following morning, Suttill caught the seven o'clock train for Paris. Madame Guépin saw him off. He said goodbye to her and walked away, then stopped and came back, embraced her again and repeated his farewell. He did this a second time before boarding the train. He arrived at the Gare Saint-Lazare at nine o'clock and made his way to the Gare d'Austerlitz where he had an appointment with Déricourt. On arrival he was told that the two Canadians had still not appeared. He discussed Déricourt's Lysander schedule, agreed it, and then headed for his secret address, the Hôtel Mazagran.

He arrived to find the small hotel deserted and no sign of Madame Fèvre. He walked up the stairs, put his key in the lock and pushed open the door. Fists smashed into his face, he staggered and fell to the ground, helpless against the boots that thudded into his abdomen and ribs and broke his arm. He was dragged to his feet, handcuffed and led bleeding and shaking down the stairs. Madame Fèvre glimpsed Suttill being pushed into the back of a Citroën. Doors slammed and the cars drove off.

While the arrests were being made, Noor Khan was at Grignon, waiting for Gilbert Norman. For the past few days they had worked together. She transmitted his messages while he helped her to refine her radio and coding skills. She waited most of the next day until finally Professor Balachowsky appeared. He told her that someone had phoned from Paris with the news that nearly twenty senior *Prosper* agents had been arrested, including Andrée Borrel and Francis Suttill. As far as the caller knew Gilbert Norman was still at liberty. Noor immediately signalled London with the information. After the transmission she unplugged the radio, wound in the aerial, closed the case and, with Balachowsky's help, took it into the garden where she buried it, along with the code books. Then she went to the station, heading for Paris.

In the avenue Foch, Sturmbannführer Hans Josef Kieffer had given orders that Suttill and Norman were to be kept without sleep and interrogated day and night, for the next forty-eight hours. He wanted the answer to just two questions: 'What is your name?' and 'What have you been doing?' The two prisoners were held in separate cells and questioned by four men working in relays. An interpreter was present, Ernst Vogt, a short-sighted, colour-blind, sometime legal assistant. Andrée Borrel was also questioned and stayed silent. In her case were found documents with the names and addresses of more *Prosper* agents.

In Paris, Noor made contact with Henri Garry at his flat and they both went in search of France Antelme, not finding him until 9.15 in the evening. He ordered Henri to go into hiding and sent Noor Khan back to Grignon to talk to Professor Balachowsky. He wanted to know who had made the telephone call and what had really been said. Then he went to earth, staying with a friend. Very quickly, warnings went to the surviving organisers of *Prosper*: lie low.

After forty-eight hours neither Suttill nor Norman had given anything away. Kieffer decided the time had come to intervene. He showed Suttill photographs of SOE training centres and appeared to know all about the Ringway parachute school and the head-quarters of the Free French in Duke Street, even naming some of the staff. Most alarming of all, Kieffer had copies of the signals Suttill had sent to London and letters he had written. The SOE men were devastated. Then Kieffer made Suttill an offer: if he revealed where the arms and stores were being kept, the Resistance workers responsible for them would be arrested but not harmed. At first Suttill did not answer, then he asked Vogt, the translator, if his chief could be trusted. Vogt replied, 'Yes ... I know Mr. Kieffer. You can trust Mr. Kieffer.' Suttill agreed to the deal. Gilbert Norman was brought in and Suttill told him what had happened.

On 27 June, Noor returned to the Balachowskys sent by

Antelme. The professor told her to go away and to pretend that she knew nothing about him. He also warned her not to go back to Henri Garry's flat without telephoning first. If an unfamiliar voice answered saying he was a friend of Garry's then she was to assume that the Gestapo were in the flat.

The same day Antelme went to the cafe, Chez Touret, where Francis Suttill and Andrée Borrel used to meet and which they used as a letterbox. There he met Armel Guerne who told him that the mysterious telephone message had come from an elderly woman doctor, Madame Helmer, who also acted as a letterbox for Andrée Borrel. Next he went to Nicho and Maud Laurent's apartment where Norman stayed. Maud and Nicho's quarters were in chaos, while Norman's room was tidy with a tie hanging on a hanger and a bicycle leaning against the wall.

Antelme took Noor to a safe house at 1 place Malesherbes and hid with her there for the next two weeks. In hiding they became very close. Before he left he put her in touch with Henri Déricourt who needed a radio operator. With Déricourt to direct and protect her, Antelme was sure she would be safe.

On 7 July, in the avenue Foch, wireless expert Dr Goetz sat in front of a radio transmitter preparing to impersonate Gilbert Norman. His set had been fitted with the radio crystals captured in Pierre Culioli's car and his staff had used the captured materials to work out Norman's codes, his transmission schedule and security checks. Goetz was nervous, Norman had a very distinctive Morse style, fast and fluent. Sturmbannführer Kieffer kept visiting the room to check on progress, adding to the tension.

In London, Vera Atkins waited in the wireless room as she did every day. Fixed on one wall of the room was a blackboard onto which was chalked the name of any agent in the process of transmitting. There had been no transmissions from France for more than two weeks. Then a clerk went to the board and wrote *Butcher*, Gilbert Norman's code name. When the decoded message arrived it read: 'Prosper captured'. It was checked and noted that the transmitting hand had been stilted, and the secret security check had been left out. The Records officer, Captain Penelope Torr, suggested that Norman might have been captured, tortured and given away his codes and crystals. Buckmaster said, 'He'd rather have shot himself.' Torr pointed out that Norman had sent 149 messages, all faultless; she questioned why he should suddenly start making mistakes. Buckmaster dismissed the idea that Norman had been turned and ordered that a reply be sent pointing out the error of the security check.

In the radio room at the avenue Foch, Kieffer and Goetz waited to see if their trick had worked. Then a signal came in: 'You have forgotten your double security check. Be more careful in future.' Goetz took it to Norman's cell and read it to him. The 27-year-old former accountant heard Buckmaster's signal in amazement and anger. In the days that followed London continued to communicate with the wireless operator they thought was Gilbert Norman, asking questions about the capture and whereabouts of Francis Suttill. German wireless men were given the replies to transmit, all the questions were answered but only in the vaguest terms.

Penelope Torr went on worrying whether the sender really was Norman and eventually produced a report, pointing out that the wireless technicians who had listened to the Morse sent by 'Norman' considered it to be 'Unusual, hesitant, – quite easily the work of a flustered man doing his transmission under protest.' Buckmaster ignored the report and ordered that they were to go on trying to find out what had happened to Suttill. Vera Atkins agreed with him. Torr backed down; she was frightened of Atkins who she found sarcastic and intimidating. In France the number of arrests linked to Suttill's disappearance had risen to more than 400. In Berlin Hitler thought that the destruction of the *Prosper* organisation was a serious setback for Anglo-American plans to liberate France.

On the night of 9/10 July the winds over Sicily were blowing at speeds of more than 40 mph. Into them were flying the aircraft and gliders carrying the first elements of the forces taking part in the invasion of the island, Operation *Husky*. The troops were blown all over the island and many died when their gliders crashed into the sea. The next morning the shipborne element struggled through high seas to the beaches. In spite of the weather and some strong opposition, when the sun sank over the Mediterranean seven Allied assault divisions were ashore and the important port of Syracuse was in their hands.

News of the invasion spread round the world, raising the spirits of the French Resistance who began to believe that the liberating armies were going to arrive before the end of the year. In London Nicolas Bodington asked Buckmaster for permission to go to Paris and find out for himself what had happened to *Prosper*. This was against all the rules. Bodington was the second in command of F Section and knew all its secrets. If he was caught and broken under torture the results could be catastrophic. Buckmaster gave permission for him to go. In the avenue Foch the Germans picked up a message for Gilbert Norman telling him that Bodington was coming and asking him to fix up a safe house for Bodington to rendezvous. The signal that Bodington had arrived safely was *N'oubliez pas de renvoyer l'ascenseur* (Don't forget to send the lift back). Bodington landed on the night of 22/23 July, accompanied by his radio operator Jack Agazarian. They were received by Déricourt. Within a week, Agazarian, but not Bodington, had been arrested and tortured.

Noor was now almost alone in Paris. She had three contacts she met several times a week on a bench in the Tuileries. The first was a radio expert, Robert Guiles, who serviced her transmitter whenever it went wrong. The second was a barrister and the third was a businessman who the Germans thought was a Nazi sympathiser. After Agazarian's arrest Noor became Bodington's radio operator, often staying overnight with him. She introduced him to those bits of the *Prosper* network that had not been destroyed and to Robert Guiles, who had a list of people who could help SOE in the east of France.

Bodington helped her move to a new flat, on the boulevard

Richard Wallace overlooking the Bois de Boulogne. Many of the other apartments were lived in by officers of the SS. The number of arrested radio operators had grown to six and Noor's workload grew as she took on the transmissions of the arrested signallers. Antelme was called to London and added to her workload asking her to relay messages and to collect large sums of money. To evade the detector vans Noor often changed the place she transmitted from, and so was constantly on the move, her tiny figure weighed down by the thirty-pound suitcase concealing the wireless. Sometimes she transmitted from a car, driven by one of her contacts. The technique was to find somewhere in the country, off the beaten track, deploy the seventy-foot aerial, transmit as quickly as possible, pack up and drive off. This generally meant she had to carry the encrypted signals with her. One of the agents Noor contacted was a 21-year-old sculptor, Octave Simon, organiser of the *Satirist* circuit. She had lunch with him and then they began to walk together towards his home. At some point on the way she realised that they were being followed and made a dash for it. They escaped capture by seconds.

Before he returned to England on the night of 15/16 August, Bodington bought a cafe in the place Saint-Michel as a contact point for agents and escaping prisoners of war. More agents returned to London on the night of 19/20 leaving Noor the only British agent still in action in the Paris area.

Once home Bodington reported that: 'The entire Prosper Organisation is destroyed ... no element should be touched ... Prosper [Francis Suttill] should be considered dead.' Of the group in the Ardennes that Pickersgill and Macalister had been sent to organise he wrote: 'No one has the slightest knowledge of the Ardennes group, which must be considered lost.'

He also reported the disturbing information he had received in Paris from the agent Henri Frager who had been talking to an anti-Nazi Abwehr agent calling himself 'Colonel Henri'. Colonel Henri had told him that they knew all about Bodington's presence in Paris and had decided not to arrest him but to follow him and see where he led them. Even more worrying was the fact that Colonel Henri had warned him about Déricourt, saying that he had been 'compromised'. Frager himself thought the Gestapo had access to the reports he was sending to London and now thought that Déricourt was a traitor. Bodington told Buckmaster that the stories were 'obviously untrue'.

Later Buckmaster received a memorandum from one of his superiors arguing that 'The constant tapping of couriers' gave the Germans much more valuable information than the arrest of single agents or even whole groups. This is exactly what Bleicher thought in Paris. While the Gestapo wanted to arrest people as soon as they were identified, he preferred to let the agents roam free, leading him deeper and deeper into their circuits. He was especially interested in the mail that couriers generated. Maurice Buckmaster replied to the memo from his superior: 'I cannot agree . . . the courier that might have been seen by the enemy is of little practical value.'

While Bodington was away the war moved on. On 11 August the Germans began a full-scale withdrawal from Sicily and by the 18th the island was in Allied hands. On 3 September Allied forces set out across the Strait of Messina heading for Salerno on the toe of Italy.

In Paris Noor Khan had no idea that the head of the Gestapo in France, Karl Bömelburg was amassing a lot of information about her. In his files were interceptions of signals she had transmitted and photographs of letters she had given to Déricourt to send to London. One signal read:

> From Madeleine – Ops – Please arrange everyday scheds also using 3407 – if sched is missed possible recontact at 1800GMT same day – Please send another 3408 crystal. Someday if possible please send white mac FANY style. Thanks a lot. Its grand working with you. The best moments I have had yet. Kindly send one more Mark11 as one is U/S– am trying to repair. Madeleine.

One of the photographs was a letter to Vera: 'Dear Miss Atkins, (excuse pencil) your bird has brought me luck. I remember you so often. You cheered me up sweetly before I left – lots of things have happened and I haven't been able to settle down properly. Still my contacts have started to be regular and I am awfully happy ...' It ended 'Lots of love, Yours Nora'. Bömelburg also had copies of letters to Noor's mother and brother.

Noor's attempts to disguise herself were dramatic but not designed to make her anonymous or help her fade into the background. Her efforts included dying her hair red and wearing sunglasses. She had several close calls. An old friend from before the war recognised her and called out her name. Unwisely, not knowing if the woman could be trusted, Noor took her into an alley and told her what was going on. The pair agreed to meet a few days later. When Noor arrived for the meeting she had turned blond and was still wearing the sunglasses. One afternoon she arrived on the doorstep of her old music teacher Henriette Renié and asked if she had a room, again revealing what she was up to. Henriette was horrified and warned her that she might be shot. Noor confessed that this had been the fate of more than one of her comrades, inadvertently revealing that there were other SOE agents in Paris.

One afternoon she was crossing the place de l'Étoile. The roads were deserted except for a few cyclists, pedestrians and official German cars. Bicycle taxis were parked against the kerbs and a huge white sign with red lettering announced an 'International' exhibition, 'Bolshevism Contre l'Europe'. She carried the heavy case in which was concealed her transmitter. Walking towards her she saw Alexis Danan, with whom she had once planned to start *Bel Age*, a children's newspaper. For a second she caught his eye, trying to signal that he was not to approach her. He understood and they passed each other like strangers. Noor disappeared towards the Arc de Triomphe. She returned to the same place on two other occasions, Danan was there and she passed him, unsmiling but looking into his face with 'Magnificent surprised eyes'.

She also called on Dr Jourdan and his wife who had treated her for appendicitis when she was a child. The doctor had planted a rose in his garden and called it Noor Inayat. Rashly Noor used it to set out her aerial. At one point she returned to the area where she had lived with her family before the war. The area was full of soldiers and the house itself had been occupied. Even so she found a room with a friend and spent some days living and transmitting in an apartment block full of German officers.

At another location a German officer found her winding in her aerial and, not realising what she was doing, helped her. Once when she was travelling on the Metro with her suitcase, two German soldiers asked her what was in it and she opened it, telling them it was a 'cinematograph projector' showing them the crystals which she claimed were the projector lights. In all she transmitted over 120 messages and worked organising aircraft pick-ups, parachute drops and the distribution of false identity cards, food and clothing coupons. She said to a friend, 'It doesn't matter, they can do what they like with me. I don't mind. I shan't tell them anything.'

Noor's endless dance with the wireless detector vans and enemy agents put her under huge strain. Her schedule called for her to transmit at 1500 hrs every afternoon and receive at 1730 hrs. Sometimes she missed her transmission times and London was never certain that she had been able to listen to their messages to her.

Wherever Noor went she carried the exercise book in which she wrote all her codes and a transcript of all the messages she sent to London. In her mind she was carrying out to the letter the instruction from London to be 'very careful in filing your messages', which she took to mean keeping a record of them. In one safe house she left her exercise books open on the kitchen table. Madame Peineau, who owned the house, gave her a lecture on security and thought she looked exhausted.

Through Déricourt's Lysander service she received some sardines from her mother, but would not eat them as they were too precious a reminder of her home.

Towards the end of August, Noor's friend and comrade Henri Garry moved back to Paris. With him he brought his sister, Renée, a large, overweight, blond-haired woman, about thirty years old. Noor moved in with them and took on the task of transmitting his requests for arms, ammunition, plastic explosives and detonators.

At the avenue Foch, Kieffer came up with a new twist in the radio game he was playing with the SOE in Baker Street. Buckmaster received a signal that seemed to come from the Canadians Macalister and Pickersgill asking for a contact to be arranged in Paris. The two had been missing for weeks and were actually in Fresnes Prison being tortured. Bodington had already reported them as 'lost'. Buckmaster sent Noor 'message no 6' ordering her to go to the Café Colisée to meet the two agents and told personnel in Baker Street that:

> If Nurse [Noor] does not take message no 6 on her QRX at 17.30 today please will you ensure that it is sent on the first possible occasion as it is extremely urgent. It will be remembered that she will be listening at 1500 hours GMT daily but the message is so important that I particularly want to get it to her before 1500 hrs tomorrow 16 August.

Another instruction, sent the same day, said: 'Please will you listen every day at 1500hrs for Nurse [Khan],' Buckmaster wrote in pencil, 'until further notice.'

Noor went to the Colisée on the Champs-Elysées, and made contact with the cloakroom attendant using the correct password. Then she was taken to meet the two 'Canadian' agents, actually two Gestapo agents. The one who did all the talking was Karl-Horst Holdorf; blond with blue eyes, he spoke in an American accent and before the war had worked as a steward for an American shipping company. He told Noor that he and his colleague were setting up a circuit in northern France and wanted to get in touch with a M. Desprez. The other Gestapo man, whose name was Joseph Placke, was more silent, nodding and occasionally saying things in bad French. Noor knew about M. Desprez; he owned a factory and she had heard about him from Robert Guiles her radio expert. She told the American that she could help and would be in touch when she had made some arrangements. Noor was walking into a trap and now the Germans even knew what she looked like.

Meanwhile the war on the Eastern Front was going badly. On 8 September, Hitler flew to the headquarters of Field Marshal Erich von Manstein at Zaporizhia in the Ukraine. Manstein told him that the Soviets outnumbered his Army Group South two to one in men and equipment. Fieldmarshal Gerd von Rundstedt had already complained that the Eastern Front was being neglected because of the campaigns in North Africa and Italy. After the meeting Hitler flew home to the Wolf's Lair, his headquarters in Poland. On the way he learned that the BBC had announced the surrender of the Italians to the Allies. That night he announced Operation *Axis*, the occupation of Italy. Very quickly German troops entered Rome.

On the night of 22/23 September a new female agent prepared to parachute into France. On board a Halifax bomber, converted for long-range work, Pearl Witherington was trying to sleep curled up in a borrowed sleeping bag. She was wearing a heavy jumpsuit, a padded helmet and her ankles were supported by thick bandage bindings. Underneath the protective clothing she wore a brown tweed suit and a lambswool jumper, a suitable outfit for her cover as a secretary for a French cosmetics manufacturer. She carried 750,000 francs sewn into the hem of her skirt. Before setting off, one of her fillings had been replaced with gold, which she thought made her look like a prostitute. She had declined to accept the suicide pill but carried a Colt .32 pistol.

   On her course she had been judged to be extremely good at handling explosives and wanted to specialise in them. The training staff found her to be brave with strong leadership potential and a pleasure to teach. Her commandant disagreed, saying: '. . . she has not the personality to act as a leader, nor is she temperamentally suited to work alone.'

Pearl woke in alarm as the plane bucked in the sky, flak from high velocity 88mm anti-aircraft guns exploding beneath it. The dispatcher smiled at her and shouted, 'Don't worry ... we're used to it!' Then he opened the jump hatch, a round hole in the floor; it was time for her to crawl forward and sit on the edge. The pilot circled looking for the signals from the reception committee, three still lights showing the landing direction and a winking Morse recognition symbol.

Above Pearl's head a light flashed green, the dispatcher gave her a thumbs up, the red light came on and Pearl pushed herself into space, her legs straight, her ankles together and her arms pressed to her sides, holding the trousers of her jumpsuit. She was attached to the plane by a static line that unravelled as she fell. There was a jerk as the line reached full extension and pulled open the parachute.

The noise of the plane slowly died away, the ground rushed up and she landed in some bushes, struggling to collapse the canopy, stumbling and falling in the dark.

She tried to get her bearings, taking off her outer jump clothes and folding them in a neat pile. Ahead of her she saw a flat strip, which she thought must be the runway but then realised it was water. Her mouth was dry and she felt an overwhelming need to drink something. She carried a heavy satchel in which was a flask; she pulled it out and took a gulp, it was full of rum that made her gag and choke. She heard somebody whistle, two descending notes which she repeated. Two men appeared. One asked her where her luggage had landed and she told him she had no idea, it had taken all her concentration to land safely herself. The men led her away to a barn where she climbed a ladder onto a pile of hay, lay down fully clothed and fell asleep. Beneath her were twenty tons of supplies including ammunition and high explosives.

Witherington's orders were to work as a courier for Maurice Southgate, organiser of the *Stationer* circuit. She had known him since they were both at school together in Paris and Southgate knew Pearl's fiancé Henri Cornioley. The last time Pearl had heard of Henri was three years before when he was a prisoner of war. On her second day in France she made a rendezvous with Southgate who took her to the Hôtel Le Faisan in Châteauroux. To her intense delight she found Henri waiting for her, 'jittering like mad as if he were the one to have parachuted'. Henri escorted her to Limoges and left her in another hotel, himself leaving immediately for Paris. Pearl had no nightclothes with her and that night slept in her petticoat, waking to discover that she had shared the bed with an army of fleas.

Noor Khan arranged for radio expert Robert Guiles to meet the two agents who she thought were Macalister and Pickersgill at the place de l'Étoile on 25 September at 2.30. At the meeting the two Germans told Guiles about a 'traveller', 'Jacques', who had arrived from London and asked if he wanted to meet him. Guiles said he did and they agreed to rendezvous a week later. Later, when Guiles asked Noor how she knew the two men she explained she did not know them but that London had instructed her to contact them. Neither Noor Khan nor Robert Guiles knew that the man they thought was 'Jacques' was another imposter. The real Jacques was an SOE agent who had been arrested on the day of his arrival. London thought they were communicating with him and were unaware that they were talking to a German radio operator.

The day before the meeting another agent, this time genuine, rang Guiles and asked if he knew about the 'traveller' from London. Guiles told him he not only knew about the traveller but was going to meet him and invited him to come along.

Noor made the arrangements but was not to be part of the rendezvous. 'Jacques' would be wearing a tailcoat, a beige khaki raincoat, a maroon trilby hat and carrying a newspaper. Just after 2.00 p.m., outside the Trocadéro, Guiles plus the genuine agent and the German agent masquerading as Pickersgill waited for 'Jacques'. He appeared and as they all shook hands eight French police officers appeared with revolvers and arrested Guiles and the genuine agent. They were both handcuffed and driven in separate cars to the avenue Foch.

Noor was unaware of this, but as the days went by, wondered where Guiles was. She asked a colleague, Viennot, what she should do, telling him that she thought he could have been arrested. Viennot suggested she telephone the vanished agent's apartment, which she did. When the telephone rang Guiles was waiting; standing over him were two Gestapo men with guns who had told him that if Noor rang he was to arrange a meeting with her. Noor asked him if everything was all right and said everyone was worried about him. Guiles told her not to worry and arranged to meet her at the corner of the avenue Mac-Mahon and rue de Tilsitt on 1 October at 10 a.m. The call ended, Noor thought her friend sounded vague and off balance. When they attended the meeting, Viennot went ahead, leaving Noor near the Arc de Triomphe. As he approached the rendezvous he could see Guiles sitting alone. Then he noticed there were six other men hovering nearby. Suspecting they were Gestapo he went back to Noor and they aborted the plan. A few minutes later they watched as, in the distance, Guiles was escorted to a car and driven off.

Noor once more changed addresses and her appearance. With Viennot's help she bought a blue suit, a polo-neck jumper and a navy-blue hat, changing these clothes with her English-style macintosh and grey dress. She dyed her hair brunette; it had become coarse and brittle from so many changes of colour. It was Viennot's turn to warn her it was dangerous to carry the exercise book with her codes and asked her to destroy it. She refused, telling him that her orders from London were to file everything. She said she kept the book with her because it was more dangerous to leave it behind where it might be found by a collaborator. Later, in front of Madame Prénat, whose house she was using to transmit, Noor broke down, covered her face with her hands and cried, sobbing, 'I wish I was with my mother.'

In London, Violette Szabo had almost completed her training, which had been interrupted when she badly sprained an ankle in parachute training. She was considered by one instructor as

'... temperamentally unsuitable for this work. I consider that owing to her too fatalistic outlook in life ... she lacks the ruse, stability and the finesse which is required ... when operating in the field she might endanger the lives of others working with her.' Earlier in her course Vera Atkins had other worries and wrote:

You have probably not yet met this woman who is a new and fairly promising trainee. She has a one year old child and is very anxious to know, at once, what pension arrangements would be made for her in the event of her going to the field ... Provision for her child is such a primary consideration for her that I am sure she feels unsettled about her training and future until this question has been dealt with ... I wish we could make more precise assurance to our women agents with children.

Another report described her as: 'Marvellous, vivacious, a lovely person but volatile, you had to watch her, she was careless.' In spite of this she was sent to complete her training at Beaulieu, the SOE finishing school.

At Gestapo headquarters on the avenue Foch, Hans Josef Kieffer received a telephone call from a woman calling herself Renée. She claimed to have something very interesting to tell him and wanted him to send a French-speaking officer to the gardens behind the Trocadéro. He would recognise her because she was going to wear a flower and carry a magazine under her arm. The woman instructed that the contact was to approach her and say 'André' to which she would answer 'Renée'. Kieffer put the telephone down and ordered his senior interpreter Ernst Vogt to make the contact. An armed plain-clothes man was to follow him at a distance.

In the Trocadéro gardens Vogt saw an overweight, fair-haired woman holding a magazine. He went up to her, they exchanged the code words and she began to talk. Renée said she knew the name and whereabouts of an SOE agent code-named 'Madeleine' who was the radio operator for the *Cinema* circuit. He could have this

information for 100,000 francs. This was a bargain; Vogt knew
that the going rate for the betrayal of an SOE officer was nearer
1 million francs. He agreed and she gave him an address, 98 rue
de la Faisanderie where Noor was staying with a woman called
Solange.

The next day, knowing that Noor and Solange were both out,
Renée took Vogt to the address. She led him up the stairs and
showed him where the key was kept. She let them both in and
showed Vogt Noor's transmitter and her code books in the bedside
drawer.

Not long afterwards Vogt took another agent, Pierre Cartaud,
to the flat, opened the door with the key, let Cartaud in and left,
locking the door behind him. Cartaud was one of Kieffer's most
trusted and admired men. He had started in the Resistance but had
been captured and turned. He was an excitable man and could be
violent. Vogt went back to his office leaving two other men to watch
the main door to the building.

Noor appeared, walking towards the *boulangerie* next door to
her apartment building. The two agents began to follow her. She
went into the bakery, chatted for a moment with the owner then
left, heading in the direction of a nearby church. The two men
hurried after her, preparing to grab her. Something made Noor
turn round, the men slowed, their faces hidden under their hats.
Realising something was wrong Noor ducked round a corner and
disappeared into a warren of small streets. The Gestapo men followed her, turned the same corner and to their anger found she had
vanished. They broke into a run, trying to guess where she might
have gone. After a long search they gave up and went back to the
avenue Foch.

In the flat Cartaud heard footsteps on the stairs outside and a
key rattling in the lock. He crossed to the door and pressed himself
against the wall. Noor pushed the door open and stepped into her
room, which was just as she had left it. She took a pace forward,
the door slammed shut and the huge figure of Cartaud grabbed her
from behind. She burst free and flew at him, screaming, pulling

his hair and clawing at his face trying to blind him. She bit his finger, tearing the flesh. He pulled clear of her, blood running down his hand. He tried grabbing her wrists to handcuff her, but failed. Eventually he managed to throw her yelling and hissing onto the sofa, pulled out his gun and told her to shut up and be still or he would shoot her. Noor spat at him. Cartaud edged towards the telephone keeping the gun trained on her, then lifted the receiver and dialled Kieffer's number. The officer listened to the panting agent's plea for assistance and heard Noor shouting in the background. He told Vogt to get back to the rue de la Faisanderie and to take three men with him. Vogt and his crew drew up near Noor's apartment, and walked quietly towards the building, trying not to draw attention to themselves. Inside they ran up the stairs to Noor's room and found the door ajar. Pushing it open they discovered the small woman sitting upright on the sofa, snarling at Cartaud who was on the other side of the room with his gun trained on her. Blood dripped from his hand onto the front of his trousers. Noor began to scream in anger, calling them 'filthy Boches' and raging against the luck of being caught just before she was due to fly back to England. Vogt thought the young woman looked dangerous, like a cornered tigress. The big men overwhelmed her, handcuffed her and took her downstairs to the car, which whisked her into captivity. Cartaud and Vogt recovered the exercise book in which Noor wrote down all her messages and the case with the wireless set hidden in it. They made sure that the flat was tidy, closed and locked the door, left the key in its hiding place and went back to the avenue Foch, hoping that no one had seen what had happened.

Hans Josef Kieffer was in a state of excitement as he waited for the arrival of his latest prisoner. One of his men was amazed that such a small woman, with the air of an innocent child, could be so important. Inside the building Noor was frogmarched across the splendid hall and up the marble staircase heading for Vogt's office on the fifth floor. They forced her to sit in a chair, shaking with rage and anger, while Vogt asked again and again who she was, who were her accomplices and what was she doing in Paris. She answered, spitting at him, her eyes glittering with fury, 'You know who I am and what I am doing. You have my radio set, I will tell you nothing. I have only one thing to ask you, have me shot as quickly as possible.' Vogt told her he was not going to shoot her and continued to question her. She refused to speak and after an hour Vogt gave up, deciding it was time to lock her in one of the seven tiny cells along the corridor, converted from the old servant's quarters. He said he would talk to her more in the afternoon and led her to a cell. He was about to leave her in the charge of the guards when she demanded to have a bath. Vogt shrugged and agreed. To keep an eye on her the guards put a brick down to stop the door closing. Noor screamed at them in another fit of fury calling them pigs and telling them she was not going to undress in front of their filthy eyes. She got her way. As soon as the door was shut she opened the bathroom window and pulled herself through the narrow opening. Below was a drop of five floors with only a flimsy gutter to stand on. The roof sloped away above her head and she held on to the tiles to keep her balance. To her right was a dormer window, which if she could reach it she could swing up onto and crawl over the roof to freedom. She began to move slowly, concentrating hard.

Vogt decided to check up on what was happening. He found the guards outside the bathroom door. There was no sound but the running water. Vogt went into the lavatory next door and looked out of the window. He found himself staring at Noor as she edged along the gutter towards his window. She was oblivious to his presence. Vogt let her get almost all the way to him and then very quietly, so as not to startle her, he spoke to her, using the code name he knew her by: 'Madeleine, don't be silly. You will kill yourself. Think of your mother. Give me your hand.' Noor stared at him for a second before grasping his outstretched hand and allowing herself to be hauled in through the window. Guards surrounded the defeated woman and marched her sobbing to one of the seven cells where they left her alone. The corridor was filled with the noise of her howling, lamenting that she was a coward not to have thrown herself off the roof and killed herself.

It was not just the guards and Vogt who heard her. Three other cells were occupied. One by a French officer named Léon Faye, another by Gilbert Norman who had been arrested with Andrée Borrel and the third by SOE agent John Starr.

In an attempt to calm Noor down, Vogt went to Norman's cell and asked him to come and talk to his captured comrade. She was amazed and angry to see him. He did not look as though he had been tortured and seemed calm. He told her that the Germans knew a lot about SOE and that her suicide would have been pointless because their mission was over, they had been defeated. Norman was taken back to his own cell. A guard brought food for Noor's lunch but she refused to eat it.

In the silence of the afternoon Noor began to examine her cell. The ceiling was high and in the middle of it was a square opening barred with iron rods. Above the opening she could see a window. Her bed, covered in a clean grey blanket, could be folded against the wall. There was no other furniture.

In the evening Noor was taken back to Vogt's office. He had ordered supper for her, along with tea and cigarettes. She refused to eat the food but drank the tea and smoked one cigarette after another. Vogt showed her photographs of the reports she had sent to England. He also had copies of her coded messages neatly decrypted by his own staff. He asked her about Orchard Court, mentioning Buckmaster and other people in Baker Street. He talked about Beaulieu where she had done some of her training, even pronouncing it in the English way, 'Bewley'. He showed her photographs of the letters she had sent to her mother; the sight of them made her cry. Finally she said to him, 'You know everything, you must have an agent in London.' Vogt nodded and said, 'Perhaps.' The interview ended at midnight. Vogt said, 'Well, I am going to bed now. I shall take you to your cell and advise you to do the same. I hope you will sleep well and reflect about everything before we meet again.' Then he led her along the corridor, a guard pushed her into her cell and locked the door, leaving her alone in the dark. In the cell opposite John Starr heard her begin to sob. Her crying went on until dawn.

The next day her interrogation began again. Vogt pointed out that some of the people she was in touch with were innocent bystanders who had just done her the odd favour. She was making it impossible for him to distinguish between real agents and simple friends. If she kept silent he would have to arrest everybody she was in contact with. He promised her that if she told them who the agents were the others would come to no harm. Noor pretended to cooperate, giving away disjointed, meaningless bits of information. After two days' questioning the only information Vogt had extracted from her was that she was a lieutenant in the WAAF.

Next Vogt summoned the wireless specialist Dr Goetz who took her down to his office and questioned her about her radio equipment, her codes and her training. He asked where she transmitted from and told her that she had been very hard to track down. Noor sat in silence, refusing to be drawn. After two hours Goetz lost his temper and took her back up to Vogt. As he handed her back he said, 'She is impossible! I have never met a woman like her!'

Vogt took over again. He changed tack, talking to her about anything that came into his head, about the war, her work or her family. At one point in the afternoon Kieffer came in. Noor looked at him and said, 'To you I will tell nothing – even less than to him. I don't trust you. You are false and are trying to set a trap for me. I can read it in your eyes.' Kieffer stormed out, demanding why Vogt didn't hit her. Later Vogt asked her why she had antagonised his boss. She replied that it didn't matter to her, she didn't care.

Dr Goetz began to transmit, pretending to be Noor. He had her wireless set and her crystals. Using the exercise books found in her room his men had been able to work out her security checks and her code. Best of all they had been listening to her transmit almost since she arrived and knew her style. Goetz invented a phony circuit for Noor and told the Abwehr radio staff to refer to it as *Diana*.

An early signal that seemed to come from Noor warned: '*My*

Cachette unsafe. New Address Belliard Hundred and fifty seven rue Vercingetorix Paris, Password de la part de monsieur de Rual. This perfectly safe. Goodbye.' The message contained her bluff security check but not her true check. Leo Marks, in charge of cryptography, read the message, went to Buckmaster and said that he thought Noor had been blown and was a prisoner.

On 2 October a signal appeared on Buckmaster's desk. It had been sent the day before from an agent called Jacques Weil, a trusted radio operator who had escaped to Switzerland when *Prosper* collapsed. The message read

Cipher tel from Berne Desp 13.57.1.10.43. Rec. 1820 2.10.43.

Immediate

Following from Jacques

SONJA? RETURNED FROM PARIS 25TH REPORTS ERNEST MAURICE AND MADELEINE HAD SERIOUS ACCIDENT AND IN HOSPITAL? MAURICE IS BARDE. MADELEINE [NOOR KHAN] W/T OPERATOR . . .

AM TRYING TO GET GENUINE INFORMATION VIA SONJA . . .

Buckmaster replied saying: *Have had apparently genuine messages from Madeleine since 25th and therefore regard Sonja's news with some doubt. Can you give us estimate Sonja's reliability?*

Sonja was Weil's fiancée and was still in Paris working as a courier for several different agents. Because *Sonja* had been locally recruited Buckmaster did not trust her. He ignored the message and went on believing that Noor was safe and still transmitting.

The radio operator Cecily Lefort, who had been inserted on the same Lysander as Noor, was now working as a wireless operator for Francis Cammaerts, commander of the huge *Jockey* circuit,

The women recruited by SOE came from all walks of life

Andrée Borrel
Shop assistant

Christine Granville
Aristocrat

Virginia Hall
Consular service clerk

Noor Inayat Khan
Writer

Violette Szabo
Shop assistant/Mother

Nancy Wake
Journalist

Pearl Witherington
Senior secretary

The leaders of 'F' Section were not professional soldiers

Col. Maurice Buckmaster
Commander
Senior manager
Ford Motor Co.

Flight Officer Vera Atkins
Intelligence officer
Oil company
representative

Major Nicolas Bodington
Second in command
Freelance journalist

The German opposition

Feldwebel (Senior NCO) Hugo Bleicher
Abwehr officer
A Salesman in civilian life

Sturmbannführer Karl Bömelburg
Head of Gestapo, France

Henri Déricourt
Air movements officer

Mathilde Carré
'The Cat'

**Paris playground for German
soldiers**

Female agents were trained in the same skills as the men

The accent was on physical fitness

Weapons training

Wireless operators
were in great demand

The ability to kill at close
quarters was essential

Life in the field

Agents were sent into France at night by parachute or Lysander

The Lysander was a strong reconnaissance aircraft that could land and take off from small fields

Virginia Hall operating a radio powered by bicycle generator

Christine Granville on the remains of a blown-up bridge

Nancy Wake's Maquis assembling for attack on Gestapo HQ, Montluçon

Ravensbrück Concentration Camp: destination for many captured female agents including Violette Szabo

Four agents were burnt alive in an oven like this

Women were worked to death in the bitter cold

SOE and the Resistance helped bring Allied victory from D-Day to the end of the war

Liberation of Paris

German officers under guard in the Hôtel de Ville

After 1442 days of occupation, Paris was free

Hundreds of thousands of people turned out to greet General de Gaulle

The liberators arrive

Allied tanks outside the Hôtel de Ville

The names of the women of 'F' Section who never came home are recorded on the SOE memorial at Valençay in France

Yolande Beekman
Denise Bloch
Andrée Borrel
Muriel Byck
Madeleine Damerment
Noor Inayat Khan
Cecily Lefort

Vera Leigh
Eliane Plewman
Lilian Rolfe
Diana Rowden
Yvonne Rudellat
Violette Szabo

covering an area as big as Wales, nearly 8000 square miles. Cammaerts found Cecily to be lost in the shadow world of the Resistance. She was not suited to the loneliness and isolation of being a radio operator. Cammaerts thought she was a pessimist who looked on every new day as a threat that might bring her arrest. He wanted to send her home, but could not afford to lose a radio operator.

On 10 September, Cecily went to a house she had been warned to avoid. The Germans were watching the property and pounced, hammering on the door. In the garden were two other agents who heard the noise and bolted to safety leaving Cecily alone in the house. She hid in the cellar but was found, arrested and sent to Lyon for interrogation by the Gestapo.

As a result Cammaerts had to move his headquarters and tried to work out a plan to rescue Cecily, which proved to be impossible. Cammaerts moved his circuit to Seyne-les-Alpes. *Jockey* was the most important circuit in the south of France, controlling the only route across the Alps into Italy. Baker Street began to worry that they had another *Prosper* on their hands.

While Noor braved her interrogation in the avenue Foch, Virginia Hall was in Spain working as an organiser. Like Christine Granville in Cairo she was bored, frustrated and felt that her talents were being wasted. Worse, she had no word of what had happened to her friends and comrades in Lyon. In September she had written to Buckmaster saying that she wanted to go back into the field. She had been united with two of her 'boys' who had been captured and escaped. They were preparing to go back in and wanted her as their wireless operator. She asked Buckmaster to give her a chance and let her train on the wireless. He replied a month later, calling her 'Doodles'. He said, 'I know you could learn the radio in no time; I know the boys would love to have you in the field; I know all about the things you could do and it is only because I honestly believe that the Gestapo would also know it in about a fortnight that I say no, dearest Doodles, no.' Instead he offered her the chance to return to England as a briefing officer. She could use her experience to make sure that agents going into the field were prepared for the dangers they faced and she would be invaluable helping to debrief returning agents. He offered a carrot – she might be able to go back into action after D-Day. He didn't promise anything but said it was a possibility.

In July, Christine Granville had found a friend, Captain Patrick Howarth, an officer in the Intelligence Corps who spoke fluent Polish. He had been briefed about Christine in London and warned to avoid her. He was introduced to her and quickly decided that 'she was a very remarkable woman'. He first saw her 'Stretching cat like in the Gezira sun' wearing a dark-brown jacket, a light- brown skirt [and] 'brilliant, brown, mobile arresting eyes'. Recognising her potential, and realising that she would hate working in an office, he decided to help her. He arranged for her to be recruited as a FANY and then, in October, to attend a wireless telegraphy course. She was promised that once trained she would be sent to Turkey. She quickly learnt Morse but hated the rest of the course, often loudly declaring that it was not possible, she could not get the hang of it. Even though the Turkey scheme was cancelled she persevered and eventually could send at fifteen words a minute.

In the apartment on the rue de la Faisanderie, which she had shared with Noor Khan, Solange heard a quiet knock on the door. She opened it to find Pierre Cartaud, the man who had arrested Noor. He politely asked if he might come in as he had some news of an old friend. He pulled a sheet of paper from his pocket and said it was from *Madeleine*. Before he handed it over he reassured her that he was with the Resistance and was acting as a liaison agent for *Madeleine* because, for reasons he would rather not go into, she could not come herself. Solange read the letter and recognised the handwriting as *Madeleine*'s. It was a request for some clean clothes and a few bits of make-up, which it was all right to give to 'the bearer' of the message. Solange wrapped the items in paper and gave them to 'the bearer'. He politely wished her good day and left.

One evening Vogt asked Noor to have supper with him in his

office. This time they got on well and even managed to make the odd joke. Vogt told her that she was a clever, lovely girl and that her mission was a complete waste of her life. She told him she did not care and that she would do it all over again if she could. Then he told her that almost all her fellow agents were in prison and that Section F was finished, so her sacrifice was in vain. Noor answered, staring him in the eyes, her voice high and piping, a contrast to her interrogator's low, calm tones. She said, 'It does not matter, it makes no difference, I have served my country, that is my recompense.'

One of the three prisoners on Noor's corridor was John Starr, who had been a poster artist, and when Kieffer discovered that he could draw he had asked him to make maps and documents. Starr cooperated, justifying his actions with the thought that he might discover useful intelligence or find an opportunity to escape. As well as drawing, Starr helped Kieffer with radio transmissions to London and entertained the guards with caricatures and even birthday cards. As a result he spent a lot of time in the guardroom, hunched over the table with his paper and pens. He had known about Noor since the day she arrived. Pierre Cartaud had described the arrest and shown him the livid wound where Noor had bitten his finger. Noor was sometimes escorted into the guardroom to borrow a book, a petite figure dressed in dark trousers, a grey polo-neck jumper and plimsoles. Whenever she crossed his line of vision Starr thought she appeared poised and self-controlled, like a student, serious about her work, her hair light brown with curious red highlights. Sometimes he caught her eye and once or twice they had exchanged words.

During the cold nights he heard her crying, the muffled sound of her sobs unreal in the confined world of the fifth floor. One afternoon Noor sat on her bed writing. She heard footsteps, a scuffling noise and something rolling on the floor. Then more scuffling and a small square of folded paper slid under her door. The noise of the feet went away to be replaced by the sound of the guards talking to each other.

She bent down, picked up the paper, sat on the uncomfortable iron bed, unfolded it and read, 'Cheer up. You're not alone. Perhaps we shall find a way to get out of here.' Then there was a little sketch of the corridor and the lavatory with an arrow pointing at the basin.

The next day Starr visited the lavatory. He felt under the basin, which was low and dark. His fingers found a square of paper wedged into the small gap where the ceramic sink met the wall. It was from Noor, the small paper filled with tiny writing. She told him how pleased she was to make contact and said that she was already in touch with the Frenchman in the cell next door to hers, communicating by tapping on the pipes in Morse. Noor did not know that his name was Leon Faye and he was a colonel who had been arrested in the great sweep of the Free Zone, Operation *Donar*.

Starr had an idea that if they could remove one of the bars from the square holes in their ceilings they could climb up and escape through the dormer window. His was easy because the bars were held in place with metal clips screwed into wood. The bars in the other two cells were fixed with cement.

Over the next few days Starr managed to steal a screwdriver. Then he kept moving his bed round his cell until it was underneath the bars. At first the guards were suspicious of what he was up to, but eventually they gave up worrying. Once or twice Kieffer went in to check that nothing suspicious was going on. After a while everything calmed down. Starr unscrewed a metal clip holding one of the bars and let it rest on the frame. Then he left the screwdriver in the lavatory for Noor. Over the next few nights Noor and Faye chiselled away at the mortar holding the bars in place. Noor was the smallest of the three and had to balance on the edge of her folded bed, reaching forward, her arms aching above her head. One night she fell, crashing to the ground. Feet ran up the corridor and her cell door was flung open; the guard wanted to know what the noise was about. She told him she had tried to hang herself from the bars in the ceiling. He shook his head and went away.

The work took days. By tapping in Morse code Noor and Faye could tell each other when the screwdriver was back in the lavatory. The damage to the ceilings became more and more apparent. At first they used bread to hide the holes but this was too white. Noor thought she could darken it with make-up and asked Vogt if Pierre Cartaud could go back to Solange and get face powder, lipstick and scent. Vogt agreed and sent Cartaud off.

When Cartaud called on Solange the second time, he found she had guests, one of whom he recognised as the agent code-named *Phono*. Solange introduced him to the couple who she said were Henri Garry and his fiancée, Marguerite. She reassured them that Cartaud was on their side and carrying out tasks on behalf of their friend *Jeanne-Marie*, another of Noor's code names. Marguerite and Solange went into the bedroom to gather the odds and ends that Noor had asked for. Cartaud and Henri smoked and talked. Henri said he was expecting to be taken off to England soon and that he had hoped there would be a message from *Jeanne-Marie* telling him when. He added that they were staying with Solange because there had been arrests and they were worried that their own apartment was being watched. They finished their cigarettes and Cartaud left. Then Solange left for the parfumerie where she was the manager, hoping she was not late, leaving Henri and Marguerite quietly pottering in the flat, planning their day. Later there was a knock at the door and they opened it to find Cartaud back again, with him were Ernst Vogt and three other men with guns. By lunchtime Henri and his fiancée were in cells on the fifth floor of the avenue Foch.

Eventually the three escapers were ready. They knew when they got to the roof they would be five storeys up with no idea how to get down. The idea was to use blankets to make ropes and they decided to carry the blankets round their shoulders, not cutting them up into strips until they knew how much length they were going to need. In the days spent dealing with the bars Starr had managed to pick up a cosh.

Night fell and Starr spent as long as he could drawing in the guardroom to hide the noise of the others as they heaved themselves through the openings they had made and up through the windows onto the roof. Then he went to the bathroom and washed, whistling tunelessly. He shouted to the guard that he was going to bed. He heard the rattle of keys as his cell door was locked and then the lights went out.

Minutes later he was on the roof; Faye was waiting but there was no sign of Noor. She was still inside her cell, wrestling with the last bits of plaster, trying to free the bar. Above her she could see the other two signalling for her to hurry up. Faye leant back down through the window; with arms stretched he could just reach Noor's bars. He took the screwdriver from her and began to scrape at the cement. Dust and grit fell on Noor. She moved towards the wall and while she waited for Faye to finish she scratched a V for Victory and a Royal Air Force roundel on it. Two hours later the metal came free and Faye hauled Noor up, hugging and kissing her as she struggled onto the roof where Starr also squeezed her in his arms, kissing her in relief.

In the moonlight they could see they were in the middle of a series of steep sloping roofs. Ahead was a parapet and a sort of balustrade. From there they could lower themselves onto a flat area far below and then scramble to safety. Noor led the way, edging along narrow stone ledges, easily the most nimble. At the parapet they tore the blankets into strips, tied them together and began to slide down. At that moment the air-raid sirens sounded, anti-aircraft guns barked, searchlights swept the sky and bombers droned overhead.

In the building the guards on the fifth floor discovered the empty cells and went into action. Telephones rang, whistles blew and alarms wailed. All over the building soldiers began clattering down stairs, pulling on their jackets and grabbing rifles. Steel-helmeted men appeared in the street carrying powerful torches, and surrounded the building, staring up at the dark roofs while others clambered out of windows with more torches.

Starr had all the notes he had made in the prison and hid them in flower pots, dropping his cosh. They crawled across the lower roofs trying to keep out of the way of the torches, more and more of whom were appearing as the guards entered the surrounding buildings. Then they reached a window and broke it, the sound of falling glass drowned out by the noise of the air raid. They climbed in and found themselves in a darkened apartment; they had no idea if anybody lived there. Then they crept to the front door, opened it and found stairs that seemed to lead to the street. They made their way down, expecting at any moment to meet the occupants or for a light to turn on. On the ground floor, they crept across the hall and slowly opened the front door. Ahead of them was a brick wall. It was new, too high to climb and had turned the street into a cul-de-sac. At the other end of the street, on the avenue Foch, they could see troops moving about using lorry headlights for illumination. Faye whispered that they should creep to the open end of the road and make a run for it. With Faye leading, they walked in single file pressing themselves against the walls, heading towards the soldiers and the light. Faye suddenly made a dash and was fired on by automatic weapons. Noor and Starr watched from the dark side of the street as uniformed men ran at him, knocked him over and hit him with their rifle butts, kicking him with their boots. Faye curled into a ball, trying to avoid the blows. Starr pulled at Noor's sleeve dragging her back to the open front door and up the stairs to the safety of the apartment. Inside they sat on a sofa. Noor was crying. They realised that someone was standing on the stairs looking in at them. She called, 'What's going on? Are you thieves?' Noor replied in a loud whisper, 'We're not thieves. We're escaped prisoners.' Then soldiers burst in through the front door, grabbing the two escapers and dragging them down to the street, back to the entrance to number 84, punching and kicking them as they went.

Kieffer strode about, shouting in anger. The fugitives were dragged through the door and he screamed: 'You are all three going to be shot. Take them upstairs to the fourth floor and line them up against the wall.' After a short pause Kieffer reappeared. Faye said,

'I have only done my duty,' and a guard hit him hard in the mouth. The prisoners were searched. Starr had a photograph of Kieffer. The intelligence chief said, 'What are you taking my photograph away for?' Starr replied, 'A little souvenir.' The tension in the room eased. Kieffer stared at them for a long time and then ordered his men to take them back to their cells, saying he would see them later.

The night went on, Noor sat in her cell alone, still crying. Kieffer came in and asked her to sign a declaration that she would make no further attempts to escape. If she gave her parole he could continue to keep her in the avenue Foch and in relative comfort. She refused, saying it was her duty to try to get back to England to continue the fight. Kieffer said in that case she forced him to take the most extreme measures. Later she heard him ask Faye the same question; he too refused. When his turn came Starr agreed and gave his word that he would not repeat the escape attempt.

Kieffer sent an immediate telegram to Berlin, declining to take any further responsibility for Noor or Faye. He pointed out that the avenue Foch was not a prison and requested she be transferred to Germany.

The next day, in the late afternoon, Noor arrived at Pforzheim in south-west Germany. She was led into a filthy cream-coloured cell. The only furniture was an iron bed, which she was made to sit on while first her feet were cuffed together, then her hands, and then a chain run between the two cuffs and locked in place. The chain was too short for her to be able to move properly. The 72-year-old governor was informed the prisoner was very dangerous and to be kept chained in solitary confinement. All communication with her was forbidden. The governor had never known a prisoner be treated so harshly.

Her classification as a prisoner was *Nacht und Nebel – Rückkehr Unerwünscht* (Night and Fog, Return Not Required). The terms of such imprisonment had been defined by Field Marshal Keitel:

Efficient and enduring intimidation can only be achieved either by capital punishment or by measures by which the relatives of the criminals do not know the fate of the criminal ... The prisoners are, in future, to be transported to Germany secretly, and further treatment of the offenders will take place here; these measures will have a deterrent effect because: A. The prisoners will vanish without a trace. B. No information may be given as to their whereabouts or their fate.

Prisoners sentenced under the decree were termed *Vernebelt* – transformed into mist.

Meanwhile at his new hideout, Francis Cammaerts received a signal telling him to: GO TO PARIS NOVEMBER 12 STOP MEET BISTRO PLACE CLICHY SUNDAY MORNING MAN WITH FIGARO NEWSPAPER.

At the rendezvous the 'man with Figaro newspaper' told him that he was to go by train to Angers where he would be met and taken to an airstrip. A Lysander would take him from there to London. The pick-up went like clockwork and was organised by Henri Déricourt. Cammaerts noted that the security was perfect.

In London, Henri Frager had just returned from France determined to prove that Déricourt was a dangerous double agent and that Gilbert Norman had been turned and was now a traitor. He was interrogated at great length about his conversation with Colonel Henri (Hugo Bleicher). He repeated everything he had said to Bodington in August. He confirmed that Bleicher had told him the Gestapo were running a radio pretending to be Gilbert Norman so tricking London into thinking the agent was alive and well. He repeated his assertion that the Germans had other SOE radios and were using them to feed false information to London. He went on insisting that Déricourt was a double agent. At the end of his report the interrogating officer wrote that he was satisfied that Frager was '... attempting to the best of his ability to tell the truth and that he is genuine'. The interrogation report was read by MI5, Maurice Buckmaster and Nicolas Bodington.

*

Nancy Wake was looking for ways to get back into the war. She had rented a flat in St James's and redecorated it, hoping to be reunited, as planned, with her husband, Henri. In anticipation of his arrival she bought him pyjamas, slippers and a dressing gown plus a bottle of brandy and a bottle of wine but he remained in France. She saw a lot of Ian Garrow, now returned and recovered from his ordeal. Nancy had a nightmare that Henri was dead.

She decided to see if the Free French would use her as an agent and got an interview with Colonel *Passy*, the code name for one of de Gaulle's most senior intelligence officers. At the interview she was flattered to discover that the French knew who she was and admired the work she had been doing in the Resistance. Even so, *Passy* told her it was unlikely that he would be able to offer her a role.

Depressed and confused she went back to her flat. The next day she received a telephone call from an officer in British Intelligence demanding to know what she had been doing at General de Gaulle's headquarters. She replied she did not know what he was talking about, she hadn't been anywhere near the French. The officer persisted, telling her when she had arrived, when she left, what she was wearing and where she had gone afterwards.

Nancy realised that the British were spying on the French because they did not trust de Gaulle. The general himself did not trust the British and persisted with the belief that it was France and Frenchmen who would beat the Germans. She understood why *Passy* did not have the slightest intention of hiring her.

Encouraged by Garrow and several other of her friends she volunteered for a job working in the canteen at Combined Operations Headquarters, just round the corner from her flat. The canteen was stuffed with gushing well-connected women talking about 'Darling Dickie' (Lord Louis Mountbatten, the mastermind behind the disastrous Dieppe raid) and 'Darling Bob' (Major General Robert Laycock, Mountbatten's replacement). She hated it.

It was not long before Nancy's name crossed the desk of Selwyn Jepson and she was invited to attend an interview with the SOE.

She was accepted for training as an agent in the field, 'Commencing immediately'. She was ordered to report to Welbeck House on 8 December but was not to bring any kit as she was going to be in London for a bit. She arrived drunk. The first impression she made on her instructors was summed up by one who said, 'Not a very "distingué" type of person but very likeable, extremely good natured, and willing ... Seems to take life as a big joke ... she is perhaps handicapped by her physical fitness.' Vera Atkins described her as 'a real Australian bombshell. Tremendous vitality, flashing eyes. Everything she did, she did well.'

Her training proper was to begin in the new year.

On 28 November 1943, in the Russian Embassy in Tehran, Stalin, Roosevelt and Churchill met to discuss the future of the world. A few weeks earlier the British had reluctantly agreed that the invasion of Europe, Operation *Overlord*, was the 'main object' for 1944. Churchill raged against 'This bloody second front' and said that Operation *Overlord* should be thrown 'Overboard'. What he wanted was an invasion from the south, what he had taken to calling 'the soft underbelly of Europe'.

At the conference Roosevelt was the first to speak. Not giving Churchill a chance to interrupt, he outlined the plans for *Overlord* and asked Stalin to reply. The Russian leader confirmed that *Overlord* must be 'The basic operation for 1944' and went on to ask Churchill 'if the Prime Minister and the British staffs really believe in Overlord'. Churchill was forced to concede it was Great Britain's 'stern duty to hurl across the Channel against the Germans with every sinew of our strength'. Stalin demanded to know when the invasion was to take place and who would command it. He was assured that the date was 'sometime in May' but the commander was yet to be appointed.

The high spot of the conference was a dinner held on 29 November, which was Churchill's birthday. Flanked by Russian and British honour guards Churchill stood before Stalin, holding a four-foot-long sword sheathed in Persian lambskin dyed crimson.

The prime minister proclaimed, 'I am commanded to present this sword of honour as a token of homage from the British people.' Stalin took it and kissed the sheath, before handing it to Roosevelt, who grasped the gold and rock crystal handle and unsheathed the blade, along which was written the inscription 'To the Steel-Hearted Citizens of Stalingrad'. The president announced: 'Truly they had hearts of steel.' The sword was resheathed and handed with reverence to one of Stalin's oldest comrades, Voroshilov, a loyal general who had not expected to be involved in the ceremony. He fumbled and the sword slipped from its scabbard, heading for the floor.

On 7 December, President Roosevelt announced that Dwight Eisenhower was going to lead the invasion of Europe.

Around Christmas, Baker Street became suspicious about the messages coming from Noor's set. Vera Atkins decided to investigate. She asked a series of questions about Noor's family. In Paris, Goetz read the questions and asked for an agent to be sent to Germany to interrogate the prisoner and get the answers. In the meantime he used her letters and what little he had learned about her from other prisoners to work out some of the answers himself. Noor refused to cooperate. Goetz had no choice but to transmit his own answers. Vera Atkins read them and pronounced herself satisfied that they were genuine and that Noor was still at liberty.

In Germany, in Pforzheim Prison, 'the highly dangerous prisoner' Noor Khan spent her time in solitary confinement, chained hand and foot. Three times a day she was served a slop made from boiled potato peelings or old cabbage leaves. Her chains prevented her from feeding or cleaning herself. Once a week she was brought a change of clothes and was washed. Apart from these visits the door of her cell never opened. The long, lonely, slow days dragged on into months, the only sound the noise of the feet of the guards patrolling the corridor outside, or the noise of the spyhole opening as they checked that she was still alive. Noor exercised by shuffling round her tiny prison, the chains and heavy metal shackles biting into her skin, bruising her arms and legs. All communication with her was forbidden. The chief warden alone took pity on her. Sometimes he visited, sat on her hard bed and listened as she told him about her Sufi background, her father and her family. Leo Marks, the only member of SOE who suspected she had been captured, was ignored.

'The life that I have ...'

By the beginning of 1944 the planning for Operation *Overlord*, D-Day, was in full swing. It was confirmed that the invasion fleet would cross the Channel at its widest point, heading for Normandy's wide, open beaches. One admiral described it as 'The largest and most complicated operation ever undertaken.' The king of England, George V, wrote in his diary about the invasion, 'The more one looks into it the more alarming it becomes in its vastness.' Floating concrete structures known as Mulberries were constructed, ready to be towed across the Channel where they were to be sunk forming instant harbours to speed the unloading of men, millions of tons of equipment and supplies across the sands. Concrete ramps were built on British seafronts down which heavy vehicles could rumble onto landing craft. An ingenious major general named Hobart came up with a range of vehicles made to help the troops storm the beaches. His ideas included amphibious tanks nicknamed 'Donald Ducks', flame-throwing tanks called 'Crocodiles' and flail-tanks with spinning chains designed to thrash the beach and detonate mines. All over the south of England huge quantities of stores were piled along miles of country roads. One observer saw a train, which he described as the largest he had ever seen, 'passing slowly by, packed with tanks'.

The Germans knew the invasion was coming but had no idea

where. Von Rundstedt told Hitler that he thought there were three possible targets, the Channel coast, the south of France or the Bay of Biscay. His predictions were intercepted, decoded at Bletchley Park and circulated to senior Allied commanders. Rommel was put in charge of the 'Atlantic Wall' and said that the state of the defences looked 'very black', guessing that the site for the invasion would be the Pas de Calais. To confuse the Germans, the Allies came up with a deception plan called *Fortitude*, part of which was aimed at making the Germans think the invasion would come exactly where Rommel predicted, to encourage him to keep his troops there, well to the east of the real invasion in Normandy.

Phantom armies were created, tens of thousands of men who existed only on paper and over the radio waves. The swashbuckling General Patton was put in charge of the nonexistent '1st United States Army Group', with its headquarters at Dover. An important element in the deception was Mathilde Carré's ex-lover Roman Czerniawski. After his arrest in Paris he had gone over to the Germans and been sent to England as a spy. He was discovered and rather than be executed had become a double agent, code-named *Brutus*. Czerniawski reported to the Germans that the 49th English Infantry Division was massed in Norfolk with its headquarters at Beccles. Had they been able to check they would have found only empty fields.

All over England, Allied men and women used their minds and muscles to prepare for the coming struggle. Through the months of preparation the invasion began to claim its victims. Men died, training with live ammunition, drowning in exercises with the amphibious tanks or in many other accidents caused by the ferocity of the programme. Supreme Allied Commander, General Eisenhower, inspected a parade of officer cadets who within a few months would be in battle. He told them 'you young men have this war to win'. He emphasised they were going to be decisive in the coming battle to crush 'that enemy of ours'. Then he wished them luck and said he would like to meet them all again, 'somewhere east of the Rhine'.

In France, the Resistance knew they were on the brink of

liberation. In the north, fields were identified that could take glider-born landings and parachute drops. Supplies of arms, ammunition and explosives poured from the sky. SOE teams were ordered that when the great day came they were to sabotage anything that might hamper or demoralise the Germans. Targets included airfields, tele-phone exchanges and communication facilities of any sort.

SOE in general, and F Section in particular, continued to be distrusted by the upper levels of the Secret Intelligence Service and the Royal Air Force, who saw the organisation as a waste of time. F Section's fight for resources was helped by the presence in London of Michel Brault, the lawyer who had been introduced into the system by Mathilde Carré in the early days of the war.

After the destruction of *Interallié* Brault had fled to the Rhône Valley where he worked for a Resistance organisation called *Combat*. For several months he had been the quartermaster for almost all the underground organisations in France. Through his efforts, supplies of food, clothing and medicines had reached the men spending the winter hiding out in the mountains of France. Many of these were young men between the ages of twenty and twenty-three who had fled to avoid being sent to do compulsory work in Germany under a law known as Service du travail obligatoire. About 200,000 men had vanished of whom about a quarter had joined the Resistance. They lived rough and had become known as the Maquis, a Sicilian word meaning scrub. Brault was one of the most knowledgeable men in France about what the guerrillas needed and eventually he was summoned for interview by Winston Churchill. As a result the prime minister called a semi-official 'meeting of ministers' at which he talked about some of the things he had discussed with Brault, describing an underground army ready to help the invasion, a force of 'brave and resistant men who could cause the most acute embarrassment to the enemy'. He went on to say: 'It was right that we should do all in our power to foster and stimulate so valuable an aid to Allied strategy.'

Guerrilla attacks against the Germans, especially in south-eastern France, began to increase. Von Rundstedt complained that 'The life of the German troops in southern France was seriously menaced and became a doubtful proposition.' The Wehrmacht began to retaliate, rounding up and shooting hostages, burning farms and villages, techniques they had used in Russia.

On 24 January 1944, Violette Szabo made her will. In it she stated that: 'I bequeath unto my daughter ... All of which I die possessed.' Vera Atkins was a witness to the simple instrument. Szabo named her mother as her executor. The beneficiary was her daughter Tania, not quite two years old.

It came as a shock to Maurice Buckmaster when Virginia Hall told him that she wanted to transfer to the Office of Strategic Services, the OSS, the American version of the SOE. In the months since she left France she had, at her own expense, trained as a radio operator. She had also pulled strings to get an interview with the London Branch of OSS. Her experience in the field had impressed them and they wanted her to join as soon as possible. On 10 March she signed a contract with OSS agreeing to 'Proceed to any place to which she may be directed, whether within or outside the ... United States ... to keep forever secret this employment ... and assume absolutely all risks incident to this employment.' The contract ended by pointing out that in the field she would be on her own; if she was caught she would be disowned. Her salary was $336 per month and her job was to act as a radio operator.

Once in the field her orders were to help organise the underground armies, establish three radio centres, find places to receive and hide drops of arms, explosives and equipment and to sabotage the German war effort wherever she could.

Buckmaster had other problems; he was under pressure from MI5 to do something about Henri Déricourt and the accusations made against him by Henri Frager. They were worried that the Déricourt situation might jeopardise the secrecy of the plans for D-Day. A meeting was held at which Buckmaster protested that his man was innocent and that to pull him out would wreck what F Section was doing in France. He was adamant that the strain of working in the field had deranged Frager. He described him as 'Extremely passionate and emotionally unhinged' and said that he had made up the whole story. Bodington agreed with his chief. Buckmaster went on to say that the story was part of a German plot to discredit one of his best agents. He also claimed that Déricourt's record was impeccable and that no agent had even been compromised, let alone arrested as a result of his activities. A memo was circulated in MI5 recording that 'In spite of the most disquieting reports received about [Déricourt] "F" Section officers are united in their belief that he is innocent.'

In the end Buckmaster agreed to bring Déricourt back to England and to keep him there for the duration of the war. Before he was recalled Déricourt had dinner in the flat of Gestapo chief Karl Bömelburg. The only other guest was Dr Goetz, the radio expert. They talked about Déricourt's new orders and plotted how he might go on being useful once in London.

On the evening of 22 March, aboard a Royal Navy motor launch, Virginia Hall met the agent with whom she was to travel to France. His name was Henri L. Laussucq, code-named *Aramis*. As they talked he let on that in civilian life he was a painter and that he was sixty-two years old, which made him one of the oldest OSS agents. Virginia said very little about herself except that in 1936, in Turkey, she had fallen from a horse and as a result had lost part of her leg.

As the vessel crossed the Channel Virginia changed her appearance, transforming herself into a tired old woman in her seventies – dowdy with a mass of lank, dark hair. She looked nothing like the pictures of her circulated months before by the Gestapo in Lyon.

They transferred to a small dinghy and were rowed ashore. As he tried to climb out Laussucq stumbled and fell, gashing his leg on the sharp rocks. Then they trudged off, Virginia carrying the suitcase with the thirty-pound radio hidden inside. Between them they had 1.5 million francs. They were heading for Brest and a train to Paris.

After arriving at the Gare Montparnasse on 22 March they went straight to rue de Babylone to an apartment owned by an old friend of Virginia's, Mme Long. She had stayed there before and valued the fact that Mme Long did not ask questions. The American artist talked about his background and the fact that although this was his first mission he thought he had what it took to make a success of it. Once he was out of the house Mme Long said that she did not want him to stay in the house ever again. The less she knew about things the better and *Aramis* was too talkative and indiscreet.

The next day they went on their way, Hall weighed down by the radio and held back by Laussucq, whose gashed leg was giving him trouble. They reached Saint-Sébastien, 200 miles from Paris, and stayed in a hotel where the owner was a supporter of the Resistance. The next day they were taken to a primitive building without water or electricity just outside a small hamlet. The place was lived in by a farmer and his old mother. Virginia decided to use this as her base. It was remote enough for her to deploy the aerial without it being spotted. Then she told Laussucq to go back to Paris and carry on with the rest of the mission. He was to come back once a week with the messages he needed to send to London.

Hall settled down, cooking for the farmer and his mother on an open fire and helping lead the cows out to graze. She sent her first radio message ten days later saying that she had a good temporary base and that Laussucq had returned to Paris. A fortnight later he began to make his weekly visits. He was not a strong man and each trip wore him out. He could not carry bags or parcels and after every trip he spent several days in bed, exhausted. Virginia advised him to stop coming himself and to send a courier. He became indignant and rejected any advice Virginia tried to give him.

Filthy, and weighed down by her chains, Noor Khan had been in solitary confinement for nearly five months. A group of three women prisoners arrived. One of these, Yolande Lagrave, a political prisoner, was put into cell number 12 opposite Noor who was in cell number 1. Yolande had no idea who Noor was and never saw her, but could hear her cries as she was regularly beaten by the guards.

The pitiful rations were distributed in metal bowls, which were collected after each meal period. In an attempt to communicate with
the woman in cell number 1 Yolande scratched a message on the
base of her bowl that read: 'There are three French girls here'. That
evening a message came back, scratched on another bowl: 'You are
not alone, you have a friend in cell 1'. The next message read: 'Think
of me, I am very unhappy'.

In London, Maurice Buckmaster was writing a recommendation
for Noor to be awarded the George Medal, the highest award for
gallantry available to a civilian. What he wrote bore no relation to
the truth: 'In July [1943] she was involved in a shooting match at
Grignon but managed to escape. She was therefore instructed to
return to England. She however pleaded to be allowed to lie low
for a month. At the end of that time she reported that she felt her
security re-established as a result of the arrangements she had made.'
Buckmaster was referring to the signal the Germans had sent on
Noor's radio: *My Cachette unsafe. New Address Belliard Hundred
and fifty seven rue Vercingetorix Paris, Password de la part de monsieur de Rual. This perfectly safe. Goodbye.* Buckmaster went on:

> This officer's devotion to duty enabled contact with this country to
> be maintained and as a result it was possible to re-inforce and re-
> construct the group and today it is in perfect order . . . it is unique
> in the annals of this organisation for a circuit to be so completely
> disintegrated and yet to be rebuilt because, regardless of personal
> danger, this young woman remained at her post, at times alone,
> and always under threat of arrest.

Buckmaster ended by writing that on top of all this Noor had helped
the escape of thirty Allied airmen 'shot down in France'.

Not far away from Buckmaster's desk was filed the signal from
Sonja reporting that Noor had been badly injured and was in hospital, meaning she had been arrested. Lord Selborne at the Ministry
of Economic Warfare added his weight, writing a few days later
recommending Noor for an MBE and writing that she had played a

'big part in maintaining a group in France which without her courageous leadership would have been permanently destroyed'. In Paris,
Goetz went on transmitting, pretending to be *Madeleine*, Noor's
code name, asking for money, supplies and agents.

On 8 April, Virginia Hall was visited by a newly arrived parachutist,
Elisée Allard, one of a team of three sent to destroy railway systems
in the run-up to D-Day. He asked her to let London know that the
three of them had arrived safely and told her they had left a large
sum of money with the owner of a cafe ready to be picked up by one
of Maurice Southgate's couriers.

When Maurice Southgate heard about the money he sent Pearl
Witherington to collect it, saying: 'Some parachutists have arrived.
They have money for the network; go and collect it. Go to La Chatre.
There's no password, we don't know anybody there and nobody
knows you. Just in case there's a problem you can say that Robert
sent you. Sort it out.'

The rendezvous La Châtre was a grocery store with a bistro
attached. Pearl went in and said good morning to the woman behind
the counter, asking her if the owner was in. The woman replied that
he was away for the day. Pearl said, 'I really need to see him. Money
has arrived on behalf of Robert. He sent me. I've come to collect it
for our network.' The woman would not budge. She said that the
owner, who was her husband, was not in, and she had no idea what
Pearl was talking about. 'You can come back tomorrow.' Pearl tried
to say that she could not come back the next day because there were
only three trains a week and the next one was not until the day after.
The woman shrugged and Pearl left.

Two days later she came back. The woman behind the counter
looked at her, expressionless. A man appeared from a side door
and ordered her to follow him. He went up a spiral staircase to a
room where she was told to sit down. The room had two doors,
one of which he closed and the other he left slightly ajar. He began
to ask her questions that she could not answer. She knew that if he
thought she was a member of the Milice or a collaborator he would

kill her. On the other hand he could be a member of the Gestapo or the Milice trying to trap her; she had no way of knowing. Finally she took a chance and asked him, 'Do you know Octave?' 'No,' he replied. Pearl told him, 'Octave is M. Chantraine.' The man stared at her, impassive. Pearl blurted, 'I was parachuted onto his farm on September 23.' He said, 'Ah, yes.' The side door opened and five men trooped in and shook her hand. They had been waiting, positioned to kill her. Before the interview her interrogator had been convinced that she was on the other side. He had everything ready to strangle her and get rid of her body; instead he gave her the money that Allard and his comrades had left with him.

Later Virginia Hall learned that Allard and the two other newly arrived agents had been betrayed and arrested. Other arrests followed and she worried that someone, possibly Allard, would break under torture and reveal where she was and what she looked like. She sent a signal to London saying 'The wolves are at the door' and disappeared on the train to Paris, leaving no address. She was back to square one.

Nancy Wake spent the first three days of her training at Welbeck House in London, nicknamed 'The Flat'. She was examined by a New Zealand psychiatrist who asked her to tell him what she saw when he dropped ink on blotting paper. Her answer was 'ink spots'. The doctor became agitated and tried to get her to see a pattern or an animal. Nancy told him that he was wasting her time and that he ought to go back to New Zealand.

On the day she was due to go to Scotland to start her training proper, a friend took her to lunch at a restaurant in Jermyn Street. She drank a lot and returned to the flat in the early evening, ready to leave for Scotland. She found one of the instructors having a row with a French student who was also bound for Scotland. The row grew, Selwyn Jepson became involved and he accused Wake of drinking. She swore at him and he sacked her on the spot, telling her to go home and get ready to hand in her FANY uniform. She spent the evening plotting how she could make another attempt to join the Free French and the next day got hold of two friends who were on General de Gaulle's staff. By the afternoon she had been reinstated but had no idea why or how. After that she referred to Jepson as 'that creep Selwyn Jepson'. When he was around she tried to be on her best behaviour saying that she pretended to be 'Miss Prim and Proper'. Later she insisted that she had not been drunk. One supervising officer said that her 'abnormal cheerfulness' might be mistaken for drunkenness.

Nancy turned out to be good at most things on the course and especially enjoyed using explosives. She was a 'very good and fast' shot and enjoyed being taught what she described as 'silent killing'. She hated parachute training. Her reports noted that she took the training seriously but was nervous and always hesitated before jumping. She found it especially hard to learn the correct technique for exiting through the hole in the fuselage floor. She looked down, threw her arms about and leant forward. She had a tendency to land on her feet with her legs apart, which was dangerous. At the end of one jump she fell over and knocked herself out. What really frightened her was jumping from a balloon. She persevered and eventually became a parachutist third class.

Another student on the explosives course was Violette Szabo, who was limping after her accident in parachute training. About Szabo Nancy said, 'Not only was she very beautiful but she was great fun. We never lost an opportunity to get up to some mischief at the school.' The two women shared a room and the high spot of their mischief-making was to debag one of the instructors and hoist his trousers up the flagpole. Szabo and Wake became close friends and when that part of the course finished saw a lot of each other in London.

Nancy's final training scheme was to go to Chester and contact a Mr Davies, the manager of a tobacco company. She had to see if she could enrol him in the Resistance but must do so without compromising him. Her other task was to infiltrate an engineering firm and find out whether it, or its products, could be sabotaged.

The scheme ended when a plain-clothes police officer visited her hotel. He called her room and asked her to come to the lobby. She refused, telling him to come up to her. The inspector questioned her at length and in depth. Nancy did not waver from her story. When the man left he wished her luck in finding a house. Nancy had no idea whether he knew she was on an exercise or whether he thought she was a genuine enemy agent.

The report on Nancy's scheme said: 'She came triumphantly out of this with full marks. Her cover story, which was well thought out and plausible, stood up intact to a thorough questioning ... this was a very good scheme ... both her contact and the police were very impressed.' Overall she did well on the course and her final report read: 'I have the very favourable opinion of this student. Excellent character, good mixer, keen and reliable. Off parade she enjoys life in her own way, drinks and swears like a trooper.' Another instructor added, '... has the power of leading men'.

While Nancy was finishing her course, her friend, Violette Szabo, was in London, receiving last-minute instructions in coding from Leo Marks. When he first saw her he said that: 'A dark haired slip of mischief rose from behind the desk which Noor had once occupied ... she had a cockney accent which added to her impishness.' Szabo was having trouble with her encrypting. When she apologised for wasting his time, Marks, mesmerised by her looks, told her that he had all the time in the world, the whole day if necessary. He realised that her problem lay with the French nursery rhyme that she was using as the basis for her encryption and decided to give her another one, something he had written for his girlfriend who had died before Christmas in an air crash in Canada. His plan worked and Szabo gave him a chess set she had won at the fairground.

On 5 April, Szabo took off from Tempsford airfield in a US B24 bomber. She was travelling with other agents but once they had arrived she was to go on her own to Rouen. In her pocket was an identity card that described her as Corinne Reine Leroy, a 23-year-old commercial secretary. In her SOE report she was described as 'self confident, plucky and persistent, not easily rattled'. Before she left she had told her mother, 'If I can't get a job when I am demobilised, I can always be a burglar.' She dropped into the silence of the night, floating down onto a field near Cherbourg. In her mind was the code poem that Marks had given her to memorise.

> The life that I have
> Is all that I have
> And the life that I have
> Is yours.
>
> The love that I have
> Of the life that I have
> Is yours and yours and yours.
>
> A sleep I shall have
> A rest I shall have
> Yet death will be but a pause.
>
> For the peace of my years
> In the long green grass
> Will be yours and yours and yours.

Violette's mission was to find out what had happened to a circuit in the north of France called *Salesman*. A month earlier a garbled signal had reached Baker Street:

Tor 1028 12th March 1944
Bluff check omitted True Check Omitted

73 seven three stop

FOLLOWING NEW FROM ROUEN STOP XLAUDEMALREAUX DISAPPEARED BILGIVED ARRESTED BY GESTAPO STOP RADIO OPERATOR ARRESTED STOP IF CLETENT STILL WITH YOU DO NOT SEND HIM STOP DOFTOR ARRESTES STOP EIGHTEEN TONS ARMS REMOVED BY POLICE STOP BELIEVE THIS DUE

ARRESTATION OF SEFTION FHEIF WHO GAVE ASRESSSES.
ADIEU.

'CLETENT' was *Clement* the code name for Philippe Liewer, the head
of the *Salesman* circuit based in Le Havre. When the signal arrived
Liewer was in London making an intelligence report. The message
was a warning that the Gestapo had arrested one of Liewer's section
chiefs who had given away addresses and the location of an ammunition dump. The agents had been arrested and the ammunition
seized. The sender advised Baker Street not to send *Clement* back
to France, but nevertheless he had returned. By 6 April Violette was
in Paris from where Liewer sent her straight to Rouen.

As her train pulled into the battered Gare de Rouen-Rive-Droite,
she could see the ancient cathedral blackened by soot, damaged and
surrounded by bombsites. The city was full of German soldiers who
knew that when the invasion came it was likely that Rouen would
be in the path of the advancing Allied armies. Over the next three
weeks she visited the contacts she had memorised. She avoided talking to strangers in case her cockney-accented French alerted Gestapo
officers or the Milice. She was shocked to see posters with photographs of Philippe Liewer offering a large reward for his capture. She
ripped one down and scrunched it into her handbag, not knowing
how she would explain it away if she was stopped and searched.

She found out that *Salesman* had been penetrated when one of
its agents was arrested with incriminating documents. The second
in command was among those being interrogated by the Gestapo;
it was discovered that he had been beaten almost to death by his
inquisitors but said nothing. Nearly 100 other agents were in the
cells or had already been deported to Germany.

The fate of *Salesman*'s agents in Le Havre was difficult for Violette
to ascertain. The port was in a forbidden zone and security very
tight. She concluded that the circuit had been destroyed beyond
repair. On 27 April she took a train back to Paris to rendezvous with
Philippe Liewer in time to be picked up by a Lysander on 30 April.

For the next two days Violette wandered round the capital, which had been under occupation for four years. The streets were nearly empty except for official German cars, velo taxis, a sort of rickshaw drawn by a bicycle. Civilian cars were usually noisy, dirty *gazogènes*, fuelled by gas produced from burning wood, the thick fumes hanging in the air behind them. German soldiers traipsed around the city photographing each other in front of the tourist spots and drinking in the bars and cafes. Most French people walked, their wooden clogs clattering on the pavements.

Violette carried 100,000 francs to cover her expenses and to pay people. At 14 rue Royale she discovered the showroom of the couturier Edward Molyneux who had dressed Marlene Dietrich, Greta Garbo and Gertrude Lawrence. Just along the road at number 3 shiny staff cars deposited high-ranking German officers, often accompanied by their French mistresses, at the fashionable restaurant Maxim's. In Molyneux she spent nearly 40,000 francs on three dresses, one in black crêpe with a lace neckline, another in red tartan and the third a floral pattern printed on silk. For good measure she bought a yellow sweater, called a 'golf'. She finished her shopping spree with a pair of red floral earrings, some perfume for herself and her mother and a little dress for her daughter Tania. She had never before owned such expensive clothes.

On the night of 29/30 April, Violette was extracted from France in a Lysander. She wore her headphones plugged into the intercom, the only way she could communicate with the pilot in front of her. Suddenly the plane was caught in the beam of a searchlight. Shells exploded all round while the pilot struggled to escape the light. Violette screamed and the intercom went dead. A shell exploded directly underneath the aircraft and she began to panic, frightened by the explosions and the silence in her headphones. They flew on with Violette disorientated and isolated in the back of the plane, staring at the pilot's silhouette. After nearly sixty minutes she felt the aircraft descending. As it touched down at Tempsford it lurched to one side and slewed round, one of the wing tips scraping along the runway throwing up dust and mud until it slowed and stopped. The pilot, Bob Large, climbed out and saw that one of his tyres was in shreds, hit by shrapnel from anti-aircraft fire. In the dark Violette screamed at him in French, which was so fast and colloquial that he could not understand what she was saying. He calmed her down, a car arrived to pick her up and she realised what had happened. She suddenly smiled at Large and said '*Vous êtes pilote?*', kissed him and was gone. Later he learned that she had been so shaken by the flak and the landing that she thought her pilot was dead and the man trying to help her out of the aircraft was a German soldier about to arrest her.

Nancy had been assigned to an agent called John Farmer to work as his courier. Denis Rake, who had escaped from prison and made his way back to England, was designated to be their radio operator. While a prisoner he had been interrogated and tortured, receiving a bad injury to his foot making it impossible for him to use a parachute. Arrangements had been made for him to be taken out by Lysander about two weeks after Wake and Farmer arrived. Their job was to make contact with Maurice Southgate, leader of the *Stationer* network.

The briefing officer said that Southgate, code-named *Hector*, was in touch with a Maquis leader calling himself 'Colonel Gaspard'. It was thought he led a group of about 20,000 men, of whom only 5000 were armed. Southgate said that 'Gaspard' had approached him 'on his knees' asking for equipment. Their first job was to find out whether 'Gaspard' was loyal to de Gaulle or the Communists. If he was for de Gaulle they were to organise the supply of arms, equipment and clothing and help turn 'Gaspard's' men into a guerrilla army. The officer finished by saying that they were likely to see 'a good deal of active fighting'.

The night before they were due to leave Wake threw a party in a night club in Park Lane, the Astor. The revels went on until the early hours. At four o'clock in the morning Nancy and her friends could be seen doing parachute rolls up Piccadilly on the way to her flat. They fooled about, drunk and heading for the unknown, singing 'The Battle Hymn of the Republic', changing the words to 'Gory gory, what a hell of a way to die'.

The next day, 29 April, Nancy and John Farmer were driven to

RAF Tempsford where a US Air Force B24 Liberator bomber was waiting for them. In the hours before take-off Nancy pulled baggy overalls over her camel-hair coat. In a canvas pack she carried nearly 1 million francs, a change of clothes, two satin embroidered nightdresses and a red Chanel lipstick. She was armed with two revolvers and stitched into the lining of her coat was a suicide pill. She also carried a small silver compact given to her by Maurice Buckmaster with the words '*Je te souhaite une bonne merde*', a very correct French way of saying 'Good luck'.

Once airborne Nancy began to feel very sick. The dispatcher shouted to her, 'We've never had a woman before!' and grinned. Nancy asked him, when the time came, to give her a shove to get her out of the plane. He gave her a thumbs up.

On the approach to the drop zone the pilot brought the plane down to 600 feet and slowed to about 120 mph, following the landmarks. Soon he could see the signal torches.

In the cold fuselage the dispatcher opened the hatch known as the 'Joe Hole' because the agents were nicknamed 'Joes'. John Farmer crawled over to it, swinging his legs into space, sitting on the rim, his static line waving above him, clipped to a steel hawser. The green light came on, Farmer pushed himself forward, arms by his sides. He disappeared into space. The plane banked, circling round for the second agent. It was Nancy's turn. She looked at the dispatcher who shouted, 'If you're afraid we can take you back!' Nancy said, 'All I want to do is get out of this bloody plane!' Then the red light came on, the dispatcher gave her a shove and she too disappeared.

She landed in the pitch-dark, the big canopy ballooned and collapsed and Nancy struggled to release the harness. She drew her service revolver and waited, ready to fire. Like many people after a parachute insertion she felt very thirsty, dehydrated by the tension and the unpressurised aircraft. After a while she heard voices, someone called in French and she was back in the war.

Nancy and John Farmer spent the next two days in the village of Cosne-d'Allier waiting for Southgate. Farmer worried that their presence would attract the Germans and did not want to hang around any longer than necessary. Southgate arrived to find Nancy standing, naked, in a tin basin of water washing her body and talking to Farmer. Beside her lay her pistol.

Later Southgate took Farmer into Montluçon, to meet Pearl Witherington and to see what life under the Occupation was like. It was the 1st of May, a sunny day, and Pearl, Henri and a French agent were picnicking outside the town.

Southgate made a last-minute change of plan and decided to go alone to meet a new radio operator, René Mathieu. Leaving Farmer he headed for the house where the operator was staying not noticing a Citroën parked at the end of the road. He knocked on the door, which opened to reveal half-a-dozen men, their guns pointing at him, and armed men appeared in the road behind him.

A distraught man on a bicycle interrupted Pearl's picnic with news of the arrest of Southgate and the radio operator. The picnickers vanished into the woods. Trucks rumbled into the town dropping off soldiers with equipment to set up roadblocks as they began to sweep the area looking for agents. Later a signal reached Baker Street – *Hector is unwell* – which decrypted as *Maurice Southgate has been arrested*. Once it was dark, Pearl, Henri and other members of the circuit escaped, heading for a chateau called Les Souches where they planned to make a new base.

By now Southgate lay unconscious in a Gestapo prison cell. Before being beaten, his wallet, watch and personal possessions had been stolen. A few hours later the radio operator, Mathieu, was dragged into the cell, his back streaming with blood, massive bruises disfiguring his face. He was handcuffed to Southgate and the two men spent the night trying to make up a cover story, muffling their voices by hiding under a ragged blanket.

The next day Southgate was pulled into the interrogation room and shown a false identity card in his own name and another one for Pearl. Then he was beaten with a stick on his back and legs, the interpreter calling him a swine and a son of a bitch.

The burnt *Stationer* network was divided into two and Pearl Witherington was given command of the northern part, which was named *Wrestler*. Her responsibilities covered the triangle formed by the towns of Valençay, Issoudun and Châteauroux and she made her headquarters at Château Les Souches. She was the only female SOE agent to lead a network. Buckmaster promoted her to WAAF section officer. Her code name was *Pauline* after a doll she had once owned. Her fiancé, Henri, became her second in command.

In London Buckmaster sent a request asking for Violette Szabo to be promoted. He wrote that she had '. . . just returned from a special mission in the field which although of short duration was of considerable importance. She has fulfilled the mission extremely well and I should like it very much to be recognised by making her an Ensign in the F.A.N.Y.s.' After this Szabo had little to do except wait for her next mission. She passed the time seeing her family and daughter Tania. Sometimes she took the little girl to meet her colleagues in Baker Street. She also saw a lot of Bob Maloubier, another agent just returned from France. They played records together. One favourite was the Mills Brothers singing 'I'll Be Around'.

Across the Mediterranean, the planners at SOE Cairo came up with a scheme to drop Christine Granville back into Hungary to organise large-scale sabotage work. One officer thought that while it was 'an operation involving the greatest risks and only a slight chance of success' Christine had the 'right personal qualities to stand at least a chance of survival' and that she 'is a person of quite outstanding courage with exceptional charm'. Another officer thought that dropping her 'blind' into Hungary was 'little short of homicide'. The head of the Balkan Section in Cairo intervened, saying that while he considered Christine to be a 'Polish lady of considerable beauty and great courage . . . as brave as a lion' he did not want to send her on 'a suicide mission' and cancelled the operation.

He signalled London reporting his decision and saying that if 'you have some other project in mind, for example FRANCE please let us know soonest'.

*

By now Virginia had cut all contact with Laussucq, who was bewildered and upset by her hostility towards him. After spending a short time hiding in Paris, Virginia moved to Cosne-Cours-sur-Loire where she stayed for a while with a colonel in the Gendarmerie and his wife. Ever wary of being discovered, she soon moved on and stayed for short periods with farming families, still disguising herself as a peasant woman. She continued to collect military intelligence. None of the young soldiers heading north in military convoys had any idea that the hunched old woman delivering milk was an American agent, and that she was keeping notes about their convoys, the number of vehicles, the time they appeared and the direction they were heading. In the evenings she transmitted her notes to London along with requests for supplies to be sent – batteries, chargers, clothes, money and bandages.

From America Virginia's mother wrote asking about her daughter. The reply read:

> from a security point of view there is little I am permitted to tell you … [but your daughter] is doing an important and time-consuming job which has necessitated a transfer from London … We are in constant touch with your daughter, and are immediately informed of any change in her status. I shall be happy to communicate whatever news of her to you.

Nancy Wake and John Farmer were in trouble. With Maurice Southgate a prisoner of the Gestapo it was difficult to make contact with 'Colonel Gaspard'. The wireless operator Denis Rake had been inserted by Lysander as planned but ran into an old boyfriend, Alex, an air-liaison officer, who claimed to know how to find Nancy. The pair set off in Alex's black Citroën, a type identical to those used by the Gestapo. Alex drove wearing the uniform of the Milice and carrying a German pass in his pocket. They travelled from safe house to safe house and eventually discovered where Nancy was hiding. Before contacting her, Alex and Rake thought it would be nice to have a romantic couple of days together. They stopped at a small village on a river, swam, drank, sunbathed, slept and made love. Rake described it as a 'drowsy fantasy'.

Nancy and Farmer eventually made contact with 'Colonel Gaspard', who turned out to be Colonel Emile Coulaudon, regional commander of the French Forces of the Interior (FFI), the name that de Gaulle had recently given to describe all Resistance groups in France. Coulaudon, a powerful, strong-willed former businessman was not at all pleased to meet the two agents, especially as they had no radio operator with them. He denied knowing Southgate and said that he did not expect any help from the SOE. Things were made worse by the discovery that there was another Allied group in the area called *Freelance* who were also trying to work with Coulaudon. After a week things calmed down and Farmer gave him a peace offering of 2 million francs and a list of targets to attack on D-Day.

Nancy disliked Coulaudon and was suspicious of his men. One evening a group of them gathered in the chateau's large kitchen, drinking and smoking. Nancy could hear them talking about her, speculating that she carried a lot of money and wondering how they could kill her and rob her. Coulaudon suggested that it was time to move on to another Maquis group. Nancy agreed.

Nancy's new Maquis leader was called Henri Fournier, who impressed her with the way he ran his small army. He had funded his group with a lot of his own money. Like Nancy he did not get on with Coulaudon.

Denis Rake's romantic idyll ended and he was driven by a member of the Resistance to the chateau. The journey was long, tiring and dangerous. When he arrived he found Nancy sitting on the low wall of a cemetery near an isolated hotel where she was hiding out. He greeted her, calling her 'Gertie', his nickname for her, asking if she was looking for a site for her grave. Then he cheerfully apologised for his late arrival and lied to her about why it had taken him so long to make contact.

*

At the beginning of May, Christine Granville was given a tempo-
rary commission in the RAF and ordered to report to the SOE base
in Algeria, code-named *Massingham*, to train before being sent to
France. She went to her farewell party wearing her new uniform.
Vodka flowed accompanied by cucumber sandwiches, and a fellow
SOE officer said, 'I do not think I ever saw her look happier.'

The commanding officer of *Massingham* found Christine too flamboyant and argued that 'her courage was best restrained until nearer
the time of liberation'. She gained her parachute wings and spent
hours firing weapons. Her technique was to close her eyes because
she claimed, 'I could never bring myself to shoot anyone.' She was
good at handling explosives but hated the noise when they went off.
The enforced period of training did not suit her – she wanted to be in
action in time for D-Day. One night, after supper, she took General
Stawell, the regional head of SOE, into the sand dunes to argue her
case. By the time they emerged she had got her way.

On the night of 22 May, Pearl Witherington waited in the dark in
a field near her headquarters. Round her were gathered a reception
committee. Three torches with red lights stretched away from her.
Standing close by was her radio operator struggling with the ultra-
high frequency transmitter, the S Phone, strapped to his body. He
was trying to make contact with a bomber that had been circling
overhead for nearly three-quarters of an hour. In the cold, noisy
fuselage of the aircraft another radio operator strained to pick up
the voice signal from the ground but could hear only static. The pilot
continued to circle, talking into the intercom, worried that the red
signal lights should have been white. He told his crew that he was
considering aborting the mission. The dispatcher relayed this to the
agent whose name was René Dussaq, code name *Anselm*. Dussaq
saw that the Joe Hole in the plane was already open; he moved forward, swung his legs into space and jumped.

Seconds later he was on the ground, blown nearly four miles off
course. He then went to find Pearl's Maquis and three hours later
made contact. As he walked, lorries full of German soldiers were

driving into the night to investigate what the Allied plane had been doing. By dawn Dussaq was in a wood, hiding with thirty-three young underground fighters. The German lorries arrived, disgorging soldiers who surrounded the wood and opened fire. Dussaq scrambled into a ravine, shouting in French for the youths to follow him, leaving the Germans firing at each other from the edges of the wood, killing and wounding their own comrades.

Dussaq spent the night in a hotel in Châteauroux. The next day a police inspector came to his room demanding to see his papers and ordering him to come to police headquarters. Downstairs was a Gestapo agent and three gendarmes. Dussaq knew that if he shot the inspector the noise would alert the others. Instead he told the policeman in a low voice that if he persisted he would kill him. During his training it had been noted that Dussaq was 'a dirty fighter ... conversant with the commando type of close combat fighting'. The inspector backed away and left the room. Dussaq dived through a window and escaped.

Nancy Wake had received an order from London to pick up a newly arrived agent from Montluçon. She had no idea how to do this. With Southgate's arrest almost all the details of safe houses, contacts and passwords had been lost. She knew there was a contact in Montluçon, a woman called Mme Renard, who had once worked for an embassy in Paris and who had a reputation for making cakes. Nancy did not know where she lived. A member of the group said that his wife lived in Montluçon and she might be able to help track down Mme Renard.

Nancy set off at night in a petrol-driven car with her bicycle tied to the roof. The driver stopped at every village on the way to check that the roads ahead were clear of German patrols. On the edge of Montluçon they pulled off the road and hid the car in a copse. Nancy then got on the bike, leaving the driver to guard the car. She rode with great care, watching for roadblocks and listening for the tramp of a patrol. From the wall of the town the face of Pearl Witherington stared from posters offering a reward for her arrest. When Nancy reached the house she knocked quietly on the door and a woman let her in. The woman had never heard of Mme Renard. Then Nancy asked if there was anyone in the town who had worked for an embassy before the war. The woman nodded, yes she did know of such a woman. Armed with another address Nancy set off again into the silent streets.

Someone who could have been Mme Renard opened the door and listened in silence as Nancy tried to explain who she was and what she wanted. The woman continued to stare not uttering a word. Nancy thought that she could smell baking and blurted out the truth. The atmosphere relaxed, the woman led her into the kitchen and quietly called a name. A cupboard door opened and Nancy took in the man who had been described in a report as 'an exceptionally attractive young man'. Just under six feet tall, wiry and immaculately dressed, holding a Colt .45 in his hand. It was her friend René Dussaq, linguist, parachutist, Hollywood stuntman and Olympic athlete. They had trained together in England. Dussaq flashed her a white-toothed smile, Nancy laughed and the pair embraced.

Dussaq's orders were to act as a weapons instructor to the Maquis and to make himself generally useful. One of his roles was to help hold landing grounds if parachutists were used in the impending invasion of southern France. He was an expert in all forms of small arms, including the bazooka, a new rocket-propelled American anti-tank weapon, much coveted by the Resistance. Nancy nicknamed Dussaq 'Bazooka'.

Dussaq did not like the fact that he was going to travel by car. He climbed into the back, holding the Colt in his hand, peering into the dark. Nancy got into the front, on her lap were two Sten guns and half-a-dozen grenades.

When the pair reached the Maquis camp high on the slopes of Mont Mouchet, Dussaq was introduced to the Maquis commanders and the agents John Farmer and Denis Rake. Dussaq soon realised that there were more than 7000 Maquis in the mountains, and that they were largely untrained and poorly armed men, some even without boots. He warned the commanders that it was against all the rules of guerrilla warfare to keep such a large force in one place.

He did not know it but the Allied high command agreed with him. In the excitement and frustrations of the run-up to D-Day the Resistance had developed conflicting ideas about what its role in the liberation was going to be. Some Resistance leaders, like Emile Coulaudon, saw it as their task to form small armies and engage in large-scale warfare. There were also the conflicts of political interest between groups loyal to de Gaulle and those in the highly organised Communist groups. The Allies had compounded the problem by issuing inconsistent and confusing orders to the French Forces of the Interior (FFI).

In an attempt to grasp the problem de Gaulle appointed General Marie-Pierre Koenig commander of the FFI and therefore of the Resistance fighters. On 21 May, SHAEF, the Supreme Headquarters Allied Expeditionary Force, issued a directive to those fighters who were preparing to band together in France. It read: 'In keeping with the basic tactics of guerrilla warfare, the FFI have been instructed not to create liberated areas or to get too involved in any military action from which they cannot break off at will. The policy is to form large numbers of small groups not larger than 100, each highly mobile and capable of dispersion if attacked.'

At the end of May the Germans attacked Coulaudon's Maquis on Mont Mouchet. Around 3000 infantry arrived on the mountain, backed up by the Luftwaffe, artillery and two motorised response units from the Feldgendarmerie in Paris. The fighting was fierce and confused. Two men appeared saying they wanted to join Coulaudon's Maquis. It was discovered that they were German agents trying to infiltrate the group. The men tried to escape and in the ensuing gun battle both were wounded and a Maquisard killed. One, known as Roger the Légionnaire, was hit three times in the chest but survived because he was wearing a bulletproof vest.

Under brutal interrogation, which included torture by fire, Roger confessed that he was a spy and his mission was to find and kill senior members of Coulaudon's group. He also knew about Nancy, 'the person who obtained the arms from London', although he did not know she was a woman or what she looked like. The two agents were shot and their mutilated bodies left in an unmarked grave on Mont Mouchet.

After twenty-four hours of fighting, the Maquis were forced to withdraw, heading for a plateau above the village of Chaudes-Aigues. Soon hundreds of young men, untrained and without equipment, were pouring into the village, eager to join the Maquis. Dussaq set about training the new arrivals. Large quantities of supplies arrived by air and night after night Nancy waited with the reception parties, fortifying herself against the cold by sucking bread soaked in plum brandy.

On 1 June, the BBC transmitted messages to the Resistance warning them that the invasion was now days away. Three days later messages were transmitted telling the Resistance to stand by, the invasion was about to happen. One was for Philippe de Vomécourt:

> *Les sanglots longs*
> *Des violons*
> *De l'automne.*

These were the opening lines of Verlaine's 'Chanson d'automne' and for de Vomécourt were the signal that his railway-line cutting teams should get ready.

D-Day

On the evening of 5 June 1944, Philippe de Vomécourt heard the next three lines of the Verlaine poem:

Blessent mon coeur
D'une langueur
monotone

The Allied invasion of Europe was underway. Hundreds of similar messages were streaming over the airwaves; the transmissions lasted for eight hours. At Les Souches, Pearl Witherington heard the first of four messages – *Quasimodo est une fête* – that were her group's orders to cut telephone cables, block roads, sabotage railway lines and harass the Germans.

A few days earlier American OSS Commander 'Gravy' Graveson had queried why SOE had given absolute priority to cutting telephone wires. He was told that the order had come over a year ago. Without telephone wires the Germans were forced to send Enigma encoded radio signals. The code breakers at Bletchley Park, who had cracked many of the Enigma cyphers, were able to listen in. This secret, Graveson was told, was known to a handful of senior people, which included the president and the prime minister. To reveal it would be an act of high treason.

German wireless operators reported an increase in the number of BBC personal messages. Warnings went out that the invasion might come in the next forty-eight hours. The armies ordered to defend the western wall of fortress Europe had often been told the invasion was about to happen. The warnings were ignored.

To help coordinate action between the Resistance and the Allied Command, the American OSS, the British SOE and the French BCRA (Bureau central de renseignements et d'action) had cooperated to form teams code-named Jedburghs. These were three-man groups – a commander, an executive officer and an NCO radio operator. They were to be dropped in uniform; their equipment included personal weapons, a wireless, one-time code pads and explosives. The first team, *Jedburgh Hugh*, parachuted in near Châteauroux on the night of 5/6 June, close to where the first SOE agents were dropped in 1941.

At dawn on 6 June, the invasion force began to disembark across the beaches of Normandy. By nightfall 160,000 Allied troops had landed and were holding on by their fingertips. During that first day 10,000 men had died or been injured in the process.

In the evening, at 6.00 p.m., General Charles de Gaulle went on air from the BBC, speaking to the French people. He told them: 'The supreme battle has begun ... For the sons of France wherever they may be, whatever they may be, the simple and sacred duty is to fight the enemy by every means at their command.'

The same day a message arrived for Colonel Buckmaster transmitted 'in clear' that could be read by anyone. It came from the Germans over the turned *Butler* circuit radio. It read:

> We thank you for the large deliveries of arms and ammunitions which you have been kind enough to send us. We also appreciate the many tips you have given us regarding your plans and intentions which we have carefully noted. In case you are concerned about the health of some of the visitors you have sent us you may rest assured that they will be treated with the consideration they deserve.

Leo Marks received the signal first and rang Buckmaster to warn him it was coming. Marks had suspected for a long time that the *Butler* circuit was blown but Buckmaster had thought otherwise and continued to use it. Buckmaster's response was 'They're trying to shake our confidence' and rang off.

Just before midnight the Germans read Buckmaster's reply:

Sorry to see your patience is exhausted and your nerves not as good as ours but if it is any consolation you will be put out of your misery in the near future. Please give us dropping grounds near Berlin for reception organiser and w/t.operator but be careful not to upset our Russian friends who take offence more quickly than we do. We shall deliver further communications personally.

The radio game was over.

Earlier in the same day, Field Marshal von Rundstedt telephoned his 7th Army Headquarters, part of Army Group B defending northern France. The beachheads, he ordered, must be cleared by nightfall at the latest. He was told that his orders were impossible to carry out.

Another force, Army Group G, was tasked with defending central and southern France. Soon its radio net was buzzing with messages about the actions of the Maquis, what the Germans called *Banditen* – terrorists. 'Impression growing that the *Maquis* are a strictly organised military force, and effective action against them possible only with mobile heavy weapons ...' The town of Tarbes was reported to be 'infested with guerillas ... Two trucks of 2nd SS Pz pioneer battalion attacked by guerillas in lorry with machine gun ... 2 SS killed, driver taken prisoner.'

The German 1st Army based in Bordeaux sent signals that whole departments of the Massif Central were in the control of the 'terrorists', towns were under siege and more attacks were expected at any moment. It said the town of Tulle had been under attack by mortars and artillery since the previous night.

By the beginning of June, Virginia Hall had succeeded in supplying the Maquis of Nièvre et Cher with arms and money. On 8 June she received orders from OSS to move to the Yssingeaux region to investigate a new Maquis group that claimed to be trained and waiting for equipment and orders. Once more she just disappeared, no one knew where she had gone or how to contact her.

News of the landings spread all over Europe, penetrating even the Nazi prisons. Agnès Humbert heard it from a Russian prisoner working with her in a forced labour camp. She had been moved there after a year working in a dye factory, her hands covered in blisters and nearly blind from the fumes. Noor Khan read about the invasion in a message scratched onto the bottom of her tin bowl.

By now 4000 young men had rallied to the huge Vercors plateau, 300 square miles of rock whose monstrous eastern edge towers 1000 feet over the town of Grenoble. The native inhabitants were farmers, foresters and shepherds. New arrivals were mostly young men. The Vercors was a natural fortress, cut by deep gorges, caves and one of the biggest forests in Europe, ideal for hiding an underground army. There were broad meadows where sheep, cows and goats grazed among cornfields, which were ideal for airborne landings. It was the Vercors that the Maquis planned to hold as a 'réduite', a fortress where they would fight for three weeks until, it was promised, Allied paratroopers, gliders and planes loaded with heavy weapons were going to descend from the sky to relieve them.

On 9 June, three days after D-Day, the towns and villages on the plateau declared themselves to be the Free Republic of Vercors. They erected a large sign that read 'Here begins the land of the free' and unfurled their flag outside the Mairie at Vassieux-en-Vercors. The banner bore a French tricolour emblazoned with the Cross of Lorraine, and a V, combining the symbol of the Free French with the symbol for victory and Vercors. At the same time, nearly thirty miles to the north of the plateau, the Germans were massing, supported by the Milice and bringing up heavy artillery. The men preparing to face them on the high plateau were in desperate need of supplies, especially ammunition. Like those at Mont Mouchet, many of them were unarmed and untrained.

On 10 June an order arrived from General Koenig, sent to FFI groups all over France, causing confusion and dismay: PUT MAXIMUM BRAKE ON GUERRILLA ACTION STOP CURRENTLY IMPOSSIBLE TO SUPPLY ARMS AND AMMO IN SUFFICIENT QUANTITIES STOP WHEREVER POSSIBLE BREAK OFF ATTACKS TO ALLOW REORG STOP AVOID LARGE SCALE GROUPINGS FORM SMALL ISOLATED GROUPS STOP.

Over to the south-west, Heinz Lammerding, commander of the 2nd SS Panzer Division Das Reich, had his own ideas about fighting the Maquis. For every German wounded three Maquis were to be hanged and for every German killed ten Maquis were to be hanged in public, which Lammerding saw as a more potent way of demoralising and humiliating the enemy than shooting. He was told that his commanding general 'heartily concurs'. Lammerding also proposed to round up 5000 hostages and send them to Germany.

A signal went out from Army Group G saying: 'The development of the gang situation in the Massif Central demands immediate and unhesitating action by major formations.' Lammerding's Das Reich was ready to move at a moment's notice. They were to head north for Normandy, through the Massif Central. Tracked vehicles and armoured formations normally move long distances by rail, or on low-loaders. Thanks to the Maquis and the Royal Air Force the rail lines north had been cut and many of the vehicles that the Germans had planned to requisition had mysteriously vanished.

Nevertheless, Lammerding's highly skilled planning staff set to work. Moving an armoured division is difficult, even with railways and low-loaders. The planners had to take into account that heavy armoured vehicles moved slowly and had to make frequent stops to refuel. Once near the battle zone the column was going to be vulnerable to air attack and restricted to moving in the short summer nights. The staff estimated that the move to Normandy was going to take ten days.

While Lammerding struggled with the problem of moving his tanks, Violette and three comrades spent the day playing cards and table tennis at Hassells Hall, the SOE despatch centre near RAF Harrington. They had been there for three days and had already made two unsuccessful attempts to parachute into France. The first had been aborted before take-off because of bad weather, the second because the reception committee had not shown up. Vera Atkins, who was there to see her off, was amazed at Violette's calm and how incredibly beautiful she looked in her blue-and-white flowered summer dress with the white marguerite earrings and clip she had bought in Paris only a few weeks before.

That night they were driven to the airfield where yet again they went through the departure routine. The USAF Liberator lumbered into the air on what they prayed would be the final attempt. The night was clear and the visibility good as they headed for the drop zone, a field near the village of Sussac about thirty miles to the south-east of Limoges. When the dispatcher opened the Joe Hole, Violette lurched around the narrow fuselage kissing the crew goodbye.

She was the second to jump, it was just after 1.45 a.m. in the morning. She was followed by a nineteen-year-old radio operator, Claude Guilet. Once the agents had left the plane the twelve cylindrical supply containers were released. Violette hit the ground, wincing at the pain in her injured ankle. She threw off her parachute harness and climbed out of her jumpsuit. She was led, limping, towards a big black car that had bounced onto the field. The other three joined her, climbed aboard and the car drove off through the reception committee busy manhandling the heavy containers onto lorries and horse-drawn carts.

The car pulled up outside a grocer's shop where the agents found cooked food waiting for them and beds with clean sheets. The next day they woke to find that Sussac was a small, quiet village in a gentle wooded valley near a lake. A ruined chapel stood on a small hill on the outskirts.

The drivers of the Das Reich division fired up their engines, filling the air with the smell of petrol and hot oil. Minutes later nearly 12,000 men in 2,600 vehicles – heavy tanks, self-propelled guns, armoured cars, flak units, half-tracks, armoured cars, staff cars, motorcycles, and support vehicles pulled away into the chill dawn light. They had been ordered to travel 100 metres apart and the drivers struggled to keep station, the lighter, faster vehicles constantly running up close behind the lumbering armoured machines.

Soon track pins began to shear, metal shrieked against metal; engines overheated and seized; engineers swore and toiled as the sun rose in the sky, burning off the early-morning mist. The column ground on, the tanks bellowing like elephants. Soldiers wondered what would happen when they met the 'strictly organised military force' that their commanders had told them to get ready for. Men scanned the sky, looking for the black dots that could mean death in the form of Allied fighter-bombers and tank-busters.

Outside the village of Groslac, a lookout heard an advancing column and fired his rifle. On the old bridge across the Dordogne fourteen men, armed with rifles, grenades and a single Bren, heard the shot. They wore makeshift uniforms or faded blue work clothes. They were the '3rd Section, Company Rémy, Ace of Hearts Maquis' and were there to hold up the advancing enemy. Under their berets they squinted down the road waiting for the leading elements to arrive.

The tanks clattered round the bend, the Bren and rifles opened up, and 3rd Section's world disintegrated in a storm of German heavy machine gun and cannon fire. The Hôtel Jardel standing between the defenders and the column was hit, and burst into flames, bits of the building falling onto the road. Black smoke billowed everywhere. Terrified villagers running for cover were scythed down. On the bridge a defender stood, rushed forward, and was torn to bits before he had gone a few yards. The fight went on for four hours before the survivors scrambled away, heading for the safety of the woods. The armoured column rolled on, troops turning their faces from the heat of the burning building, their eyes flicking over the bodies of the dead civilians. In the town of Tulle, Das Reich met more guerrilla activity. By nightfall ninety-nine citizens were hanging from the lamp posts.

One officer, a brigade commander called Major Helmut Kämpfe, had been captured by the Maquis, driving in his open Opel staff car towards his headquarters. Kämpfe was a tall, strong sportsman, very popular with his men. His car was found, the doors open with no sign of violence. A Schmeisser sub-machine gun with no magazine was discovered under it. The search for Kämpfe went on all night, a farmhouse was ransacked and two farmers shot. The Milice were summoned to help with the search. In the early morning roadblocks were set up all over the area. One stood at a crossroads in the village of Salon-la-Tour.

Violette was ordered to make contact with a Maquis leader, the 22-year-old Jacques Poirier, code-named *Nestor*. She was to set out the next day, 10 June. She spent the evening talking to Claude Guilet the radio operator. They sat in the house where Guilet had hidden his transmitter, talking about the war, the risks they were running and the danger they were in. Violette told Claude that life was a gamble and that the only way to live was to take chances, everything depended on the fall of the dice, the twist of the cards. Guilet had been in the field for three days, Szabo was a veteran of just over three weeks. She told him she had a big day coming up – over a hundred miles to cover – and walked back through the dark to her own billet to sleep.

At dawn a young Maquisard, Jean Dufour, had volunteered to drive her halfway to her rendezvous. She planned to go the rest of the way on a bike which two men were busy tying to the back of the car, a petrol-driven black Citroën. A woman asked her if she would like some flat shoes to replace the heels she was wearing. Violette refused. Then she asked Dufour for a Sten gun. At first he said that if they were stopped it would be safer to be unarmed. Violette insisted, she wanted the automatic weapon and ammunition. She got her way. With everything ready she climbed into the car. She wore a trim light suit with no stockings and carried her small suitcase and the Sten gun.

The villagers thought Violette looked beautiful, 'like a little doll'. The woman who had offered her the shoes thought she had a lot of guts. Dufour drove to a village where he picked up another

Maquisard, also called Jean. On the outskirts of Salon-la-Tour they passed under a railway bridge and drove up a slight hill. As they came over the crest they saw that dead ahead of them was one of the roadblocks set up to find Kämpfe. It was surrounded by uniformed men and an armoured car. A soldier waved at them, signalling for them to stop. Others stared in their direction, cocking their weapons, suspicious of the black petrol-driven car. Since D-Day French people had been forbidden to drive cars using petrol.

Dufour slammed on the brakes, the tyres screeched as the car slid to a halt, thirty yards from the roadblock. Immediately to their left were some old farm buildings leading to a yard. Dufour flung open his door, and lay on the ground firing his Sten gun. He saw that on her side of the car Violette had done the same. Then they both ran, covering each other with fire, weaving towards the buildings. By the roadblock a woman appeared, seemingly unaware of what was going on; a soldier aimed at her and fired. She fell, tossed around like a tiny rag doll. An armoured car rolled forward, firing its machine gun. Bullets whipped through the air, some slammed into the car, others ricocheted off the road and the walls of the buildings.

In the yard a little boy scurried up some stone steps and disappeared into a hayloft where he crouched watching Violette and Dufour climb over a gate into a field full of ripening corn. The boy's father appeared, a German officer grabbed him waving a Luger pistol screaming, 'Terrorist?' The terrified man put his hands in the air stuttering 'Français ... français.' Other soldiers skidded towards the gate, one carried a Spandau, the MG 42 light-machine gun, another lugged a box of ammunition, a belt of glinting brass cartridges round his neck.

Violette and Dufour zigzagged through the corn, sweating and shaking with the effort. Behind them the Spandau opened up, firing in five-round bursts, the cartridges chattering into the breech and ejecting into the air at 1200 rounds a minute. The gun leapt about on the wooden gate the gunner was using as a rest, the noise was deafening.

A round skimmed against Violette's left arm, cutting the skin as she headed for a wood at the edge of the field. Blood soaked her torn dress, her breath rasped in her throat and her heart thudded in her ears. Other automatic weapons opened up. Violette's injured ankle gave way and she fell, pain shooting up her leg. Dufour stopped, grabbed her arm and tried to pick her up and drag her with him. They reached the cover of some apple trees; running to their left was a railway line. Violette shook him off and told him to run, she was too exhausted to go on. Then she braced herself behind one of the apple trees, pulled back the bolt on the Sten gun and began to fire. By the gate a man fell, someone pulled him away, dragging him out of sight.

Violette fired in squeezed, three-round bursts, exactly as she had been taught. She had two magazines, each capable of holding thirty-two rounds but actually loaded with thirty to avoid putting the magazine spring under too much pressure, causing the misfires for which the gun was notorious. Soon her ammunition was gone, soldiers spilled into the field; she tried to run, her ankle gave way again and she fell. Hard male hands grabbed her, half-pulling half-carrying her, kicking and screaming across the field to the road where it went over a bridge. The armoured car appeared, a young officer got out, congratulated her on her fight and offered her a cigarette. She spat in his face screaming that she would smoke her own cigarettes. He told his men to take her away. They dragged her struggling up the road while she shouted at them to let go of her arms. Nearby, Dufour crouched, hidden by a pile of logs. Violette spent the night in a cell in Limoges. The next day, while her comrades tried to work out how to rescue her, she was transferred to cell 453 on the fourth floor of the grim Fresnes Prison in Paris. Nobody in her circuit had the slightest idea what had become of her. She was interrogated in the avenue Foch, by SS *Sturmbannführer* Kieffer.

In Violette's cell was another prisoner, Mme. G. Meunier. Violette told her cellmate about herself and her family saying over and over again, 'I know who has denounced us. He is a member of French section, he is at the moment in London, and he is the one who told the Germans about our real identity.'

*

The soldiers of Das Reich took their revenge for the kidnapping of Major Helmut Kämpfe on the village of Oradour-sur-Glane, machine-gunning the men, burning the women and children in a barn and dynamiting the buildings.

News of the massacre reached Baker Street on Sunday morning. Buckmaster was in the radio room with an assistant, Nancy Roberts. When he read the signal he kept saying to her that he could not believe the Germans would do anything so evil.

At Chaudes-Aigues Nancy Wake was exhausted from dealing with the parachute drops. She staggered down to the public baths, which were fed by the hot natural springs beneath the town. Afterwards she flopped into bed and closed her eyes. Minutes later the sound of automatic gunfire ripped through the night.

Unseen by the Maquis a large force of German troops was working its way across the area, supported by tanks, artillery, mortars, armoured cars and fighter-bombers. Chaudes-Aigues was on a main road leading north, which they needed to get reinforcements to the Normandy battlefield.

For a while there was chaos. 'Colonel Gaspard', Emile Coulaudon, refused to withdraw and wanted to fight to the last man and the last round. Nancy and the other agents packed all their equipment and possessions into cars. Rake sat hunched over his wireless, trying to contact London. It was outside his scheduled transmission time and he could not get a response. When in the end he got through he sent a signal from Farmer cancelling the rest of the drops and asking that Emile Coulaudon be ordered to withdraw.

All around the Germans were pressing on the position, held back by the Maquisards who fought with outstanding bravery. Under fire and very tired, Nancy drove to every position she could find, distributing arms and ammunition.

When she had finished she found Rake, still at his radio, waiting for orders from London. She was immobilised by the need to sleep, thirsty, hungry and with every bone in her body aching. She staggered to a farmhouse where she had been told it was safe for her to shelter, lay down and slept. She was woken up by a Resistance man who told her that the position was dangerous and might be overrun at any minute. She stumbled out, crashed down at the foot of a tree and went straight back to sleep, oblivious to the sound of gunfire.

In the morning orders came through Rake's set that Emile Coulaudon was to abandon his last-ditch stand and pull out. Nancy made Rake sign it to look as though the orders had come direct from General Koenig. The fighters of the Chaudes-Aigues Maquis, 7000 men, split up into small groups, between 50 and 150 in each and began to make their way through the German cordon.

Nancy left by car, over her head a Henschel ground-attack aeroplane appeared, firing its 7.92mm machine guns. She could see the pilot, his face hidden by his goggles and oxygen mask. Bullets impacted around her. Ahead a young Maquisard leapt out from the bushes waving for her to follow him. She jammed on her brakes and flung herself into a ditch beside the road. Then she ran, zigzagging from bush to bush following the young man. The plane flew on. The Maquisard told her that René Dussaq was waiting for her further down the road.

To get off the plateau they had to cross the River Truyère. All the bridges were in German hands but the Maquis had prepared other crossing points, hidden by trees. They had piled tons of local stone, making invisible causeways under the surface of the water and hidden them with tree trunks strapped to the top. When the first group reached the fords, men slithered down the banks and released the logs, which floated downstream. Using sticks and each other for support they crossed and escaped, heading for Coulaudon's new headquarters in Saint-Santin.

For days afterwards men arrived with stories of the long hike. René Dussaq went off looking for Denis Rake and John Farmer. He reappeared days later with Rake who had been wounded in the leg and lost his radio equipment and transmission codes. Nancy got Rake to bed and gave him a bottle of eau de cologne to use as an antiseptic. She said he drank it.

*

At Les Souches, the estate where Pearl Witherington had her head-quarters, Pearl's fiancé and second in command, Henri, had taken over the outbuildings to act as weapons stores and had ordered trees to be cut down to barricade roads. A man arrived on a bicycle; he had come from Paris. He said there were no other barricades on any of the roads to the capital. A German Fieseler Storch aircraft flew low overhead. A bugle sounded, a warning from the guard post on the main road. Pearl was the only one to hear it. She ran and found Henri. 'We're under attack,' she said. 'We can't be, it's Sunday,' Henri replied. Henri fired into the air, trying to establish whether it really was a German unit or a party of Maquisards. Somewhere in the distance a machine gun opened up. Pearl ran into one of the outbuildings and climbed a ladder into the attic where she had hidden a cocoa tin full of money and her bag. Next she grabbed her bicycle and pedalled towards some buildings where the latest drop of arms had been stashed. The guns were still covered in the grease they had been packed in for transport. Pearl loaded them anyway, her hands filthy from the oil. Then she began to put detonators in the hand grenades, unscrewing the base, sliding in the charge and then screwing the base back on. Each grenade took about ten seconds. The noise of firing had moved closer and she could hear men shouting in German and French. A Spandau machine gun was hammering away, answered by the slow rattle of a Bren.

A Resistance fighter crashed in, shouting to Pearl to leave at once, the Germans had left their lorries and were advancing in open order across the fields towards them. She dropped everything and ran to a farm about a mile away. The Germans followed, small figures running, crouched and firing. She scrambled into the farm building just as Henri shot at the closest pair of soldiers. One fell, the other stopped, dropped onto his stomach and aimed his rifle. A building was on fire, flames billowed out, silhouetting the soldiers who were now shouting and waving, trying to encircle the farm. Pearl ran into a wheat field, terrified that it would catch fire and burn her to death. Soldiers spotted her and fired. Bullets scythed into the wheat as she crawled away on her hands and knees. Out of sight she froze, hiding from the spotter plane, only moving if the wind blew the wheat about, threatening to expose her position. Smoke stung her eyes, the sun beat down, waves of heat washed over her from the flames. Lorries roared up and down the roads, men shouted. The Fieseler Storch plane drifted slowly overhead. Pearl curled up into a ball, trying not to be spotted. She was a long way from the farmhouse. As the sun set she buried her revolver, thinking it would be worse for her if she was captured with it.

The shouting died down, the lorries backed away and everywhere fell silent except for the loud crackling of the flames as the barn burned. Pearl stood up. She could see the farmer's wife and daughter trying to put out the fire. She waved, frightening the two women who ran back into the house.

Later she learnt that a small group of German soldiers, middle-aged men who did not want to die, had spent the day in the farm kitchen, eating eggs and avoiding the war. They shot up the furniture and burned down a cowshed. Over the next two days they returned and did more damage, burning houses, looting, wrecking more furniture and threatening to shoot people. Pearl found out the whole thing had been a premeditated attack on what the enemy thought was a big Maquis stronghold. Thirty-two French people lost their lives in the battle of which Les Souches was a small part.

On the afternoon of 14 June Virginia Hall and another woman who had accompanied her stood in front of a large stone building in the village of Le Chambon-sur-Lignon. Over their heads fluttered the French tricolour and the international flag of the Red Cross. The door was opened by a tall young man whose name was Auguste Bohny. Virginia told him that she was a Belgian journalist and had heard he was part of a Swiss organisation doing remarkable things for refugee French children and wondered if he would allow her to interview him. He agreed and they talked for an hour. Bohny revealed that among his charges were concealed Jewish children and there were others hidden all over the area. Virginia told him that she was English and she wanted to make contact with the local Maquis. Bohny said he could not help them, he was a foreign neutral and could not endanger his status. By now it was late, the women were tired after their long journey from Cosne-Cours-sur-Loire and he advised them to stay the night before returning. They agreed, disappointed that their mission was a failure.

As the night deepened three men appeared outside the refuge. One carried a sub-machine gun and a hand grenade; his name was Pierre Fayol and he was head of the Maquis in the Yssingeaux region. They had been summoned by a secret message from Auguste Bohny.

At three in the morning the men sat in Virginia's bedroom. Fayol told her that his men were short of arms and that they wanted to go to the help of the Maquis around Mont Mouchet. Virginia asked him whether he had identified places to receive parachute drops, did he have command of about forty men, and was he prepared to obey orders from the Allies? He answered yes to all three questions. He had a reconnaissance unit code-named *YP, Yssingeaux Parachutage* that had identified usable drop zones; he had the men and would obey any order that didn't contradict his own superiors. He asked Virginia what she wanted them to do. She replied, 'Sabotage.' Fayol said he needed arms, explosives and money. Virginia told him to pick her up at eight the next morning.

The next day a Citroën Deux Chevaux bounced along the roads across the Yssingeaux plateau. One of the three passengers was Virginia being taken on a recce of the landing sites. Between them they began to give the fields code names, Morse recognition symbols and BBC *messages personnels* phrases. The Yssingeaux plateau became *Shark*, with the recognition symbol 'L' for Love and the *message personnel* phrase *The shark has a tender nose*.

Later Virginia gave the Maquisards an advance of 152,000 francs, telling them it was 150,000. She waited while they counted, and was relieved when they pointed out her error. By 17 July Virginia was back at her headquarters in Nièvre sending a radio message to London saying that the Maquis of Le Chambon-sur-Lignon were to be trusted and that they consisted of 200 men and were able to call on a further 300 at short notice.

*

The battle of Les Souches had left Pearl Witherington's Maquis without weapons, ammunition or a radio. All she had was the 500,000 francs she had rescued from the cocoa tin under her bed. She and Henri made their headquarters in a farmhouse with no water and no lavatory. The farmer lived there with his wife and son and his grandfather. To find a radio she needed to make contact with Philippe de Vomécourt, brother of Pierre. Pearl set off on her bicycle, crossing the River Cher in her bare feet, the bike across her shoulders, complaining about 'some damned sharp stones'. Before she could make contact the Germans moved in on de Vomécourt. He and his men vanished, Pearl's search had been a waste of time.

Eventually de Vomécourt turned up at Pearl's headquarters dressed as a gamekeeper, saying that the Germans always respected a uniform. Pearl was back in touch with London and the result was a huge drop – Sten guns, plastic explosives, grenades, Bren guns and rifles tumbled out of the sky. It took two days hard work collecting and distributing the equipment. Pearl had no time even to wash.

In the Vercors, the Maquisards were standing by, ready to take on the German Army. An SOE agent sent an urgent request to London: REMIND YOU OF URGENCY TO PARACHUTE MEN AND ARMS REGION VERCORS STOP COULD RECEIVE AT LEAST ONE REGIMENT OF PARA TROOPS STOP ... ARMAMENT AT PRESENT INSUFFICIENT STOP CANNOT RESIST IF ATTACKED ... READY TO RECEIVE DAY AND NIGHT.

After several attempts a reply came: ... WILL DO OUR BEST TAKING INTO ACCOUNT LIMITED AIR TRANSPORT FACILITIES.

Another message arrived from the Allied commanders: SEND MEN HOME BECAUSE MOBILISED PREMATURELY. This had originated from the French general, Koenig. He knew that thousands of young men were flocking to the Maquis, untrained, unarmed and sometimes even without shoes. Koenig did not have the resources or the time to deal with the sudden influx of manpower. A greater worry was that the pre D-Day ideas of turning the Vercors and other areas into 'redoubts' made no sense. In his view the classic role of the guerrilla fighter was to sabotage and confuse the enemy, to appear from the shadows, strike and then vanish, leaving the pitched battles to trained troops.

Even so, a gigantic French flag flew from a peak overlooking Grenoble, its red, green and blue colours flapping proudly in the mountain breeze, declaring to the world the presence of a large, fixed Resistance stronghold.

In spite of the efforts of the Resistance and the RAF, the first vehicles of Das Reich began to arrive in Normandy on 15 June, exactly on time and on schedule. The only way to have stopped the heavy armoured division was by carpet-bombing it or engaging it in a set-piece battle with a similar force. Even so the guerrilla fighters had achieved a great deal; like wasps they had tormented Das Reich along every mile of its route to the battlefields of Normandy. The Maquis had succeeded in doing what the Allied planners wanted them to do: 'harassing the enemy', what a young Resistance leader described as 'messing things up', making the lives of the enemy soldiers a misery.

Without a radio, Nancy, like Pearl, was helpless. Rake thought there was a Free French operator twelve miles away on the other side of the mountain. Nancy borrowed a bicycle and laboured up the steep hill, sometimes riding and sometimes wheeling her bike. The other side was easier, downhill all the way. The bike's brakes did not work, she went too fast and fell off several times. She arrived to find that the operator had vanished, scared off by the presence of German activity.

Her next plan was to go to Châteauroux where Rake thought there was another operator. The town was 125 miles away. There was a car available but Laurent, her commander, would not let her use it because it was too risky, German roadblocks were everywhere and they did not have up-to-date identity papers. He didn't think she could make it to Châteauroux on a bicycle. Nancy told him she had no choice, they had no other way of contacting London and arranging supplies.

He gave in and mapped out a safe route using quiet side roads.

Men were sent to recce it, checking for roadblocks and German activity and a brand-new ladies' bicycle was bought on the black market. While the preparations were being made, Nancy asked a tailor in the nearby town of Aurillac to wash and mend her clothes, which were torn and dirty. He decided they were too damaged and offered to make a new outfit in twenty-four hours. Next she found a cobbler who agreed to supply a pair of strong shoes without the necessary coupons. While she was talking to the cobbler the tailor rang and warned her not to come back as there were Milice living next door to him and they had begun to ask about 'the woman in slacks'. To avoid the roadblocks Nancy escaped through the fields.

In her village there was a couple, the parents of the young man in whose house she was staying. She asked them if they could help her collect the new clothes. They produced a trunk stuffed with old clothes. Nancy chose a white piqué dress which she thought must have been fashionable before the First World War, a pair of old trousers and pair of worn-out boots. A farmer who was taking vegetables to the market offered to give her a lift.

The next day she put on the dress and the heavy boots. She scrubbed her face and pulled her hair back in an ugly bun. Then she climbed aboard the cart, surrounded by fruit. On her lap she held the farmer's old corduroy trousers.

The horse and cart plodded through the green rolling hills leading to the jagged, volcanic Cantal mountains, one of the loneliest and most isolated areas in France. They reached the wide bridge leading into Aurillac and were stopped at the first German checkpoint. The soldiers prodded at the fruit and lifted up the vegetables, checking for weapons and explosives. They asked the farmer a few questions and waved him on his way, ignoring his 'daughter'. The cart rumbled on, its iron-bound wheels crunching on the cobbles heading through the grey, shuttered-up streets towards the sharp spire of the church. They were stopped several more times and the same thing happened. When Nancy finally slouched into the tailors he did not recognise her; then he realised who she was and roared with laughter, getting her to try on the outfit he had worked all night to prepare. It was a good fit, but needed a few adjustments. In her oversize boots she clumped back to the market and her 'father', the poor man who was unlucky enough to have sired such a charmless and unmarriageable woman.

The next day the outfit was smuggled out of the town and was a perfect fit. Nancy set off on her bicycle and was accompanied as far as Montluçon by a Maquisard who wanted to visit his pregnant wife. The pair set off into the mountains, grinding up and down the lonely hills passing no one but the odd farmer moving his livestock. Coulaudon had sent word ahead to the villages warning the local Maquis that she was on her way, telling them to keep a look out for her and to warn her about German roadblocks, convoys and troop movements. When they had to travel on main roads Nancy and her companion pushed their bikes, ready to dive into the ditches at the first sign of approaching troops. In Montluçon, there was a Dunlop tyre plant, which the Germans had requisitioned and the town was full of inquisitive Gestapo officers and Abwehr agents. Just before the town they split up and Nancy rode north heading for the small market town of Saint-Amand-Montrond and then Issoudun before the final leg of her journey to Châteauroux. The country was softer and easier to negotiate. On the way she stopped at a bistro to see if she could pick up any information about the road ahead. She sat on her own eating, drinking wine and listening to the other customers talking. The gossip was that enemy activity in the area was comparatively quiet. That night, exhausted and aching, she slept in a barn and was woken by the sound of aircraft flying high overhead. In the distance she could hear the thud of anti-aircraft guns and the distant boom of high explosives rumbling across the fields.

The next day she reached Saint-Amand-Montrond, which was silent and empty, the shutters all closed. Two German patrols tramped by and ignored her. She found a cafe and stopped for coffee. The owner of the cafe was anxious and told her to be careful, a group of hostages had been rounded up and shot the night before and Bourges, with its beautiful twelfth-century cathedral, had been hit by an air raid.

Once more she set off, forcing her aching legs into action. On the horizon far to the right across flat land and sparkling marshes she could see the silhouette of Bourges Cathedral. The lonely figure on the bicycle pushed on through unknown territory, visible from miles away with nowhere to hide and no identity papers.

As she pedalled, lorries began to pass her packed with troops heading in the direction of Issoudun, which she could now see in the distance. As they whistled and cat-called her, she thought: 'I'd like to break their fucking necks.' At the River Théols she joined a queue of military vehicles waiting to cross by the two-arched bridge that led into the town.

Nancy found a black-market restaurant where she could eat and have a drink. Before she ordered her meal she did her best to clean herself up. Later she shared wine and brandy with the patron. She got him tight and pumped him for local information, anything that might help if she ran into trouble. Then she cycled round the markets buying anything that did not need coupons. She ended up with a string bag full of fruit and vegetables, which she carried in the basket of her bike, hoping that she looked like a housewife. Her whole body ached and her thighs were rubbed raw.

The main road to Châteauroux was packed with lorries carrying troops, blocking her way, forcing her to make a giant detour to approach the town by a minor road and even that had a roadblock checking vehicles leaving the town. She hesitated but a soldier waved her through. She pedalled on looking for the bistro where Denis Rake had said she might make contact with SOE elements.

She found it exactly where Rake had said it would be. Inside she approached the patron and asked for a coffee. She stood at the counter sipping the bitter mixture made from toasted barley and chicory, chatting, dropping identifying code words into her talk. He too chatted away, dropping in the correct response codes. Nancy's new contact directed her to an SOE safe house, telling her that was where the radio operator was to be found. When she arrived at the house they refused to help with the transmission – she did not know why.

Angry, depressed and aching all over, Nancy got on her bike and

peddled back in the direction of the bistro. On the way she encoun-
tered an underground fighter she had met a few weeks earlier. He
told her his radio operator had been shot and he was looking for a
Free French operator he had been told about. The owner of another
bistro warned them that the radio operator had gone and there were
security men in his house waiting to arrest anyone that called. By
now the Germans were surrounding whole streets and searching
houses. Nancy decided to get out of the town and headed into the
country, looking for a Maquis group that might help. Eventually
she found one and a message was sent to Buckmaster asking for the
urgent supply of a radio set to Nancy's group.

The journey back to camp at Saint-Santin took her twenty-four
agonising hours. She travelled by whatever road was fastest, knowing
that if she got off the bike she might never be able to get back on
it. If she needed to urinate, she urinated on the bike, which made
the damage to her thighs much worse; they were bleeding and felt
as though they were on fire. At Saint-Santin she was given a hero's
welcome but could not sit down, walk or stand up. She lay in bed
for days, her limbs locked, every movement agony. In seventy-two
hours she had travelled over 310 miles.

In the early hours of 19 July a new radio operator appeared from
the sky, a nineteen-year-old American marine called Roger Faucher,
code-named *François*. Strapped to his leg was his radio and tucked
inside his jumpsuit were his codes. Descending around him were
twelve containers of supplies. Nancy Wake was back in business.

On 6 July, Andrée Borrel sat in a large grey car. With her were the
driver, a member of the Gestapo and three other SOE agents: Vera
Leigh, Sonya Olschanezky and Diana Rowden. Vera Leigh was a
small woman who had once wanted to be a jockey. Before the war
she had been a dress designer and had run a fashion house in Paris.
She trained as a courier and had been flown to France in a Lysander
in May 1943. On landing she was received by Henri Déricourt
who briefed the Gestapo about her. She was arrested in Paris on
30 October 1943. Sonya Olschanezky had been recruited in France

and worked as a courier for the SOE although she had never been trained. It was Sonya who tried to warn Baker Street about the arrest of Noor Khan, to whom she bore a strong resemblance. Buckmaster had ignored the warning. She was captured in Paris in January 1944. The third woman travelling in the car, Diana Rowden, had arrived in France with Noor Khan, Cecily Lefort and Charles Skepper, all of whom had been arrested. Skepper was already dead having been tortured to the point where he was no longer recognisable. A few months earlier, in November 1943, Diana had been betrayed by a double agent and arrested.

The powerful car pulled up the steep track, through the pretty village of Natzweiler and past the Hôtel Struthof which had once been a small ski resort. A small, ugly, brick gas chamber had been added to the hotel. The car went higher up the hill, passing a low wall hiding a building with a swimming pool and then turned to the left. Ahead of them the women could see two huge watchtowers framing a pair of massive gates over which was a wooden arch covered in barbed wire with a sign reading 'Konzentrationslager Natzweiler Struthof'. The inmates called the construction 'Das Tor'. The four women had no idea what they were doing there. Soldiers pushed open the gates and the car drove on. Through the windscreen, spread below them in an ugly panorama, they could see the camp. Low wooden buildings built on stepped terraces cut in the mountainside. Below the buildings were more square structures above which rose a thin metal chimney.

The car passed under the eyes of grey, tired, starving, identical-looking men. Several were fellow SOE agents and many of them were categorised as *Nacht und Nebel* ('Night and Fog'), sent into the mountain mists, to be worked to death or murdered. They wore jackets with N+N stencilled on the back and each had over his heart a yellow badge on which was painted three black, concentric circles, a target. One of the men watching was Pat O'Leary, who Borrel had once worked with organising the escape route across the Alps for Allied airmen and agents. Vehicles hardly ever appeared in the camp and the prisoners wondered what it was doing, and who was inside it.

The car completed its impromptu drive past and had returned to the office buildings beside the main gates. The doors opened, the women stepped into the clear, mountain air and were led into one of the buildings where the senior SS administrators were busy organising a party in honour of Dr Plaza, the camp doctor, who was leaving the next day. They were told to sit on chairs in the corridor and wait.

In an adjacent room two officers began an argument about the paperwork regarding the women. One said there was a signal from Berlin ordering their execution that evening. The other argued that this could not be true. Orders for execution usually came by a secure teleprinter line or by handwritten letter. They then had an argument about whether the women's names should be entered into the camp records; one of the officers did not want to do this.

News of the women began to spread through the camp. A Polish prisoner who acted as an interpreter in the offices had seen them in the corridor and reported that they seemed fit and well dressed; he said they were very quiet and one was smoking a cigarette.

The women were ushered out of the building, back into the sunshine. An SS officer led them down the steep slope towards the chimney at the bottom of the camp. An NCO brought up the rear. The road was called the Lagerstrasse, the Camp Road, and it was the main thoroughfare of the complex. Every man who could find a place to watch stared at them. Rumours spread that they were there to start a *Puff*, a brothel, but others said they looked too classy. Another rumour spread that the girls were to be used as secretarial help in the camp offices.

By now the prisoners working in the granite quarry outside the camp were returning, marching under the guard of SS troops holding leashed, fierce dogs. To the right of their path a man was digging a ditch to lay pipes. His name was Brian Stonehouse and he was an SOE radio operator who had been captured in 1941 and who had survived two concentration camps including Mauthausen, 'the Bone Grinder'. Stonehouse was a fashion painter and as the women passed within a few feet of him he particularly noticed their clothes. In front carrying a fur coat went Andrée Borrel. Behind her in brown came Sonya Olschanezky, her handbag over her shoulder, a small brown suitcase in her hand. She was followed by Diana Rowden who wore a blue suit and had a Scottish ribbon in her hair. Finally Vera Leigh, dressed in brown like Sonya and carrying a handbag. The women walked in line and in silence with their heads slightly bowed. Stonehouse thought that they were a mirage, a miraculous apparition from 'the real world'.

In the officers' mess, the building with the swimming pool that the car had driven past earlier in the afternoon, the senior staff were arguing about how best to kill the women. One said that as the women were spies they should be hanged. The camp executioner, Peter Straub, objected. He thought that as the prisoners were British and French, hanging would cause too much of an outcry; it would be, he said, *ein grosses Theatre*. He insisted they find another way to kill them. This surprised his colleagues because he was good at his job and normally enjoyed the drama and spectacle of hangings.

It was the two camp doctors who came up with the solution: the women must be injected with a lethal solution of something. The only problem was that they did not know whether they had enough of any such substance in stock. A call was made to the dispensary near the crematorium and the orderly there was instructed to see how many capsules of Evipan were available. This was a sleep-inducing drug used in anaesthesia. It had a rapid but short-lasting effect. The orderly looked in the drug cabinet and reported that there was only enough for the normal requirements of the operating theatre. Next he was asked to check on the stocks of Phenol, a drug that has a toxic effect on the central nervous system causing shock, delirium, coma and rapid sudden collapse. It is also corrosive to the eyes and skin. Its use was widespread in the Third Reich as a cheap and efficient way to kill individuals. Mixed with oil it was used for experiments on children.

The orderly confirmed that he had 80 cc of the drug in the dispensary. Two of the medical staff were told to report to the crematorium with the Phenol, a 10 cc syringe and a selection of large-gauge needles.

At about 5.00 p.m. the four women arrived at the end of the road. In the distance the pine trees swayed in the gentle late-afternoon breeze. They were led round the back of a squat cement building, which was a prison block. They were marched inside and led into a room big enough to hold them all. It had a barred window. The door slammed shut and was locked.

In a hut close to the prison block, a prisoner who was a doctor began to call and whistle, very softly, so as not to alert the guards. A window in the block opened, and Andrée Borrel appeared, calling that her name was *Denise*. The doctor pulled cigarettes from his pocket and threw them across. Some fell to the ground and some went through the window. *Denise* told him that she was French and that some of the others were English.

In another hut word arrived for Pat O'Leary that the women were SOE agents and he should come to the doctor's hut if he possibly could. At about 7.00 p.m. he set off, scrambling through two accommodation huts, scuttling across the gap between, hunched against the bullets that would follow him if he was seen by the guards. He reached the hospital block which was next to the prison building. Through the window he could see the head and shoulders of a girl framed in a window of the prison block. He called: 'Hello, hello, are you English girls?' The reply came: 'Yes we are English and French.' He asked: 'Why are you here?' The face vanished and O'Leary shouted: 'I am a British officer.' He thought he recognised Andrée Borrel from two years before. Whispered word flashed down the block that the SS were coming; O'Leary knew that if he was caught talking to the women he would be shot.

An announcement came over the loudspeakers ordering all the inmates on pain of death to be in their barracks by 8.00 p.m. and to stay there. Prisoners were usually allowed to stay outside until 8.30 p.m. Another command came that the curtains were to be drawn and anyone caught looking out would be shot. A rumour spread that the women had been transferred from Fresnes Prison in Paris and were going to be executed that evening.

The executioner ordered the furnace stoker to make sure the

crematorium was lit and ready at maximum heat by 9.30 p.m. The male prisoners saw the SS heading down towards the prison block. Flames and sparks coming out of the chimney into the evening air told them that the crematorium furnace was burning.

In the kitchen a soldier collected four meals, thin soup and bread, and carried them down the steep camp road. At the block the rations were taken from him and carried to the women. Vera Leigh asked for a pillow. Movement in the camp died down. The sun had set, the guards in the watchtowers traversed their machine guns along the huts and up and down the main track. Sparks continued to fly out of the crematorium chimney.

At 9.00 p.m. the medical orderlies trudged up the long, steep track towards the gates, one carrying a dark-brown glass bottle with a glass stopper, the camp's supply of Phenol. The other carried the 10 cc syringe and the needles. At the top they found that the huge gates were open. Coming towards them was a party of officers including the two doctors, one in his SS uniform and the other in civilian clothes.

In the prison block the women were separated and each put in a small, dark cell, too small to be able to stand up. At the camp gates the party shuffled about. It was now nearly dark, one man carried an oil lamp, normally forbidden on the grounds of safety. The doctors and officers were nervous, reassuring each other, looking for safety in numbers. The camp adjutant spoke to the group, telling them that it was important to act quickly. They moved into the camp, the gates swung shut behind them and they walked down the hill, the oil lamp bobbing in front of them, the guards in the towers tracking them with their machine guns.

In the prison block the translator wanted to look at the women he had seen earlier in the day. He opened the steel observation window and peered in on the group. Behind him the executioner said, 'Pretty things, aren't they?' The stoker continued to work the furnace. Slowly the temperature gauge crept up. The executioner told the stoker to go back to his cell, then turned off the lights in the crematorium. The stoker lay on his bed pretending to sleep.

The main party arrived and assembled in a room that contained beds. One of the doctors went into the furnace room and switched off the light so that the room's use would not be apparent. Then he joined the others. The adjutant ran through the procedure to come. Two men were ordered to bring the women across from the cell block one at a time and sit them on a bench in the corridor that led to the furnace. The room emptied, leaving the doctors to prepare the syringe. They did this with great care, Phenol could kill just by contact with the skin. They filled the syringe, wafting away the sweet tar-like smell that came from the bottle.

Through a crack a prisoner was able to make out the first of the women being led from the cement building towards the crematorium. It took nearly an hour before they were all sitting on the bench. Then the adjutant told them to remove their clothes for a medical examination. The four prisoners refused, demanding that a female doctor be present.

In the room with beds the two doctors discussed which of them was to administer the injection. The one who was due to leave in the morning said that it would be his last duty as camp medical officer. Their debate was interrupted by the arrival of the executioner with the first patient. Her upper arm was bared and the thick needle pushed into her skin, making her gasp. Just as he had been taught at medical school the administrating doctor gently pushed the plunger home, emptying the corrosive fluid into the woman's body. Almost at once the poison began to take hold. She slumped and had to be helped to her feet back out to the bench in the corridor where she sat sagging and softly moaning.

The doctors found the experience upsetting and decided to share the work between them. The process was repeated twice. When the fourth woman was brought in she asked in a loud voice what the injection was for and was told it was to protect her against typhoid. The stoker in his cell heard the commotion, then the noise of a struggle followed by muffled shouting as though somebody was holding a hand over the woman's mouth.

The four women sat on the bench, stiff, stupefied, and occasionally groaning. One by one they were taken into the dissecting room, laid on the brilliant white ceramic table and stripped of their clothes. The fourth woman had become very stiff and the man undressing her began to tear open her cardigan. One of the doctors shouted at him, telling him not to be so disrespectful and ordering him to take the clothes off in a 'decent manner'.

Once undressed the first woman was dragged to the furnace room where she was laid on an iron stretcher. The door to the firebox was opened and the woman pushed in. The first body went in head first, the second feet first and the third head first. In his cell the stoker could hear the familiar noise of the furnace door opening and closing and the groans of the women as they were slid in. In the huts the prisoners saw a burst of white flame and sparks erupting from the crematorium chimney each time the furnace door was opened and closed.

When the fourth woman was laid on the iron stretcher and lifted towards the flames she woke up, flayed about, struggling and clawing at the executioner's face, tearing open the skin with her nails, shouting '*Vive la France.*' The men in the room struggled to stop her falling off the stretcher. They slid her feet first into the oven and slammed the door.

The execution party dispersed and headed back up to the camp gates. As they walked through the darkness the two doctors talked about what they had just done, repeating the details over and over. They said that they would rather have used Evipan for the injections. Then they agreed that the women had been spies and it was only just that they had been executed. Poisoning they thought was more humane than shooting or hanging. At the top of the slope the gates swung open and the party went through, heading for the officers' mess, looking forward to the party they were throwing to say goodbye to their comrade, the doctor who was leaving.

The next day the executioner was still drunk, the skin on his face torn from the nails of the woman from the night before. He complained to a medical orderly that he had spent a long time in the camp at Auschwitz and in his time 4 million people had gone 'up the chimney'. But he had never, he said, experienced anything like the death of the four women. He was, he moaned, finished.

A letter marked 'Secret' was written outlining the details of what had happened in the crematorium on the night of 6 July. The now cold oven was emptied of the four charred bodies. A woman's blue shoe remained unburnt. A few days later Brian Stonehouse was working on a trench when he saw one of the guards walking up the long flight of steps from the crematorium block; in his hand he trailed a fur coat.

'SHE LED US LIKE A MAN.'

On the night of 6/7 July, a bomber appeared over the Vercors. Sitting in it, with her legs dangling over the Joe Hole, was Christine Granville with orders to join Francis Cammaerts as part of a mission called *Paquebot*, led by a French Air Force captain. They were to build a landing strip for heavy equipment that could not be brought in by parachute: field guns, anti-tank guns, and mortars. Christine was equipped with a loaded revolver (which she hated), a knife, a torch and suicide pills. In the money belt round her waist she carried gold sovereigns, ration coupons and identity cards with the name 'Pauline Armand'. In the last two months she had been taught to use the Mark B wireless set, had learned to parachute, become proficient in simple explosive demolition, knew about the preparation of a night-time agent's reception committee and been instructed in the use of personal disguises.

The green light flicked on and Christine dropped straight into a blasting gale, her low-level static line pulled her parachute open 'like a great flower', the wind got under it dragging her away from the landing zone. She hit the ground four miles off target, hurting her ankle, her lower back and smashing her revolver. Limping, she buried her parachute, her jumpsuit and her now useless weapon. She was found by the Maquis the next morning, walking in the summer sun looking like a young French country girl. They asked her if she was aware that there were parachutists in the area. At first she said she did not know what they were talking about, but once she was certain that they were members of the Resistance she told them who she really was. They told her that one of her team had landed so badly he had broken his thighbone and been taken to hospital.

Later that day she sat with her comrades outside the Mairie at Vassieux-en-Vercors, where the French tricolour with its Cross of Lorraine, emblazoned with a V, had been flying for a month over the 'Land of the Free'. The town was alive with housewives, anxious to get their share of the sixty tons of sugar and tobacco and 60,000 litres of wine, which had been captured from an ambushed train. The townspeople were overjoyed at the arrival from the air of the agents and were certain that the Allies were soon going to arrive in force. The agents were issued with local French forces permit cards, making them members of the Forces Françaises de Vercors and giving them *Autorisation de Circuler sur le Plateau de Vercors*. Christine's was number 504, and as the only woman in the group, she was the centre of attraction and excitement. There was a rumour that she was Irish.

Four days later Francis Cammaerts came back from a tour of all the sub-circuits in the main *Jockey* circuit in the south-east of France and met Christine. Cammaerts was a very big man, youthful-looking, modest, unassertive and charismatic. The Maquisards called him 'le diable Anglais' and more affectionately 'Grands pieds' because he had huge feet that no French shoe fitted. He described his new recruit as a 'beautiful, slender, dark haired woman'. He loved her 'features and her bearing' and found her face to be 'sensitive and alert' and thought she had the appearance of an 'athletic art student'. He signalled to Brooks Richards, head of SOE in Algiers, 'Christine is magnificent'. Christine's message to the same man read: 'I am very happy with my work. Roger [Cammaerts's code name] is a magnificent person. The unity of the whole of the south of France depends upon him.'

Christine was billeted in Saint-Julien-en-Vercors, in a hovel which

Cammaerts called 'a bungalow' but which was not much more than a ruin with a roof. The Maquisards christened it 'La Maison de Miss Pauline'. It stood on a small plateau surrounded by rugged mountainous country, deep gorges, towering chalk cliffs and the epic Col de Chalimont.

Cammaerts was now acting as liaison officer to Colonel Henri Zeller, a career French officer in his forties who had been made military commander for the south-east of France. In the days before Christine's arrival the two men had sent message after message to London and Algiers asking for supplies and support: DELIVERANCE ONLY POSSIBLE IF LARGE SUPPLIES OF MATERIAL SENT IN. FAILING WHICH RESISTANCE ORGANIZATION IN SOUTH EAST WILL COLLAPSE.

Another read: ... NEEDED HEAVY AND LIGHT MACHINE GUNS RIFLES AND GAMMON GRENADES NOT STEN GUNS STOP ... NEEDED TEN MILLION ROUNDS OF AMMUNITION IMMEDI-ATELY STOP.

On 14 July, Bastille Day, the new Republic held a parade in Die on the southern edge of the Vercors. Christine went along, accompanying Cammaerts and a crowd of senior Maquis officers. At 9.30 a.m. the sound of the march-past was drowned out by the roar of aircraft engines; high above them in the bright blue sky was a formation of 100 American heavy bombers, protected by a fighter escort. The formation circled and flew in low over the unfinished landing strip, bomb doors open. Black objects tumbled out of the aircraft and hundreds of coloured parachutes blossomed in the air, like a firework display. The pilots also dropped personal gifts including packets of Camel cigarettes tied round with a tricolour sleeve of paper inscribed with the words 'Bravo lads. Vive la France!'

On the plateau men had been working since the small hours of the morning preparing to receive the equipment they had been begging for. The last of the 1200 canisters thudded onto the plateau, its parachute collapsing, billowing in the breeze. The pilots waggled their wings from side to side in salute before climbing and setting course for home. The formation dwindled in the sky, the sun glinting off the silver fuselages, the engines fading. The operation had taken half an hour.

At Chabeuil, two German dive-bombers lifted into the air and banked east, heading for the plateau, ten minutes' flying time away. At the airstrip the air was filled with the noise of people shouting to each other, the horses whinnying as they took the strain from the loaded carts. When they heard the sound of the aircraft everyone fell silent. Maquisards shaded their eyes, peering west into the sun thinking that more Allied planes were arriving. The pitch of the engines changed as the planes began their dive towards the landing strip, the swastikas on their tailplanes clearly visible. People threw themselves to the ground as the noise of the howling dive-bombers grew louder and louder. Bullets sprayed from the 7.92mm wing-mounted machine guns at 1200 rounds a minute. The earth erupted in six huge explosions. Canisters were hurled into the air, their contents buckled and ruined. Thirty feet above the ground the planes pulled out, banked round and then flew fast and low over the plateau firing their guns at the helpless Maquisards. Their ammunition spent, they turned west into the sun, heading for the airfields where reinforcements were already landing and ground crews were standing by to rearm them.

For the rest of the day, German planes of all sorts arrived in waves dropping high explosives, incendiaries and hand grenades. Terrified animals bolted, overturning their carts, lorries bogged down in ground churned up by the bombs. People fell in the road, machine-gunned by marauding fighters. Soon contact with the plateau was lost. Between attacks the Maquisards struggled to haul the containers onto whatever transport could get to them. By late afternoon, Vassieux-en-Vercors was in flames, its old church a pile of burning rubble while the temporary hospital at Saint-Martin-en-Vercors was being machine-gunned from the air.

The attacks continued until the sun had set and the pilots could not see their targets. Every space in the hospital, the corridors and even the grounds around it was packed with the wounded – men, women, children, even a baby being breastfed by its mother. Francis Cammaerts was furious. He had been given no warning of the drop and raged to Christine that it was 'wicked lunacy' to stage it in full daylight. Cammaerts was an SOE agent, not a trained military man and did not realise that it was impossible to mount such a huge operation in the dark.

Christine and Cammaerts retreated a mile south to the village of Saint-Agnan-en-Vercors and went into a hotel, part of which was on fire. They did not care, they were certain that this was the end and that even if they survived the night they would be killed the next day.

At dawn Christine and Francis woke together and stumbled to a window. In the distance was a fighter-bomber heading straight for the hotel. They could see the pilot's face staring through the blur of the yellow propeller, concentrating on his bomb-run. Francis grabbed Christine, shouting something, at the same time the bomb detached from the fuselage, wobbling in slow motion towards the burning hotel. As they hit the floor his last words were: 'We've had it ...' The plane roared over the hotel, obliterating the sun, drowning all sound. This was followed by a skidding noise and the sound of breaking tiles, a moment's silence and then a strange thump as a bomb buried itself deep in the earth behind the hotel. Then there was quiet and no explosion. The pair scrambled to their feet, Christine laughing, grabbing Francis's hand, hugging and kissing him, shouting: 'They don't want us to die.'

By mid-morning, 10,000 troops, including two light infantry battalions, two artillery battalions, a police battalion and 400 glider-born paratroops were massing with orders to eliminate the Maquis and all resistance in the Vercors.

In her prison at Pforzheim, Noor's days passed very slowly. People who caught a glimpse of her thought she looked sad, weak and lonely. At night they could hear her crying. On American Independence Day she scratched *Vive le 4 Juillet* on her bowl and on Bastille Day she wrote *Vive la France Libre*. Her neighbours often heard her cell door being kicked open, and her cries as she was dragged to the basement to be thrashed.

*

Violette was moved down to the third floor of Fresnes Prison. Her new cellmate was an elderly woman, a portrait artist. At eleven o'clock one night the cell door was flung open to reveal a woman of about forty whose face was covered in cuts, badly bruised and swollen. She said her name was Marie Lecomte, that she was a member of the Resistance in Brest and that she had been condemned to death. Her injuries were the result of her interrogation. Over the next days she and Violette came to regard each other as mother and daughter; Violette called her 'Maman Marie'.

After D-Day, Allied troops had fought a slow and bloody battle across the tiny fields, sunken lanes and ancient banks that made up the Normandy countryside, known as the 'bocage'. Caen had been a D-Day objective but it took six weeks before the first Allied troops entered the battered ruins of a town which had been almost destroyed. The area held by the Allies was less than a quarter of what they had hoped to gain and the German front line was holding.

Operation *Goodwood*, an attempt to break out, was mounted on 18 July. The Allies dropped thousands of tons of bombs on the German front line. Fifty-ton armoured vehicles were tossed onto their backs and German troops were left stupefied with shock but they quickly recovered and fought back killing or wounding thousands of Allied troops.

On 20 July, a dazed and bewildered Adolf Hitler staggered out of the ruins of his conference room near Rastenburg in East Prussia, the Wolf's Lair. His trousers had been blown off at the belt revealing a badly burned left leg, his hair was burnt, his face was bleeding and blackened and his eardrums had burst. Sheets of conference paper drifted down through the smoke landing softly around him. In his thighs were 100 wooden splinters, torn from the map table against which he had been leaning. He was calm as Field Marshal Keitel led him to safety, his face bearing a livid scarlet burn and his right arm dangling slack at his side. He had survived the twenty-seventh attack on his life. That afternoon he had a meeting with Mussolini and showed him the ruined uniform as if it was a holy relic. He then took him to the site of the explosion and told him, 'Having now escaped death so miraculously, I am more than ever sure that the great destiny which I serve will transcend its present perils and that all will be brought to a triumphant conclusion.' Later they had tea and at first Hitler sat silent, sucking brightly coloured lozenges while around him some of the most senior men in the Third Reich, Göring, Ribbentrop and Dönitz reflected on the miracle of their Führer's escape. Suddenly Hitler jumped to his feet and screamed in fury, spittle foaming on his lips. He declared that everyone who had betrayed him would be found and destroyed along with their wives and children and their children's children. His revenge would never end. When he eventually collapsed he said, 'The German people are unworthy of my greatness. No one appreciates what I have done for them.'

The next day, Field Marshal von Kluge wrote to Hitler giving him a situation report on the battle in Normandy: '... The moment is fast approaching when this overtaxed front line is bound to break. And when the enemy reaches open country a properly coordinated command will be almost impossible. I consider it my duty as the responsible commander on this front to bring these developments to your notice ...'

On the same day a signal arrived in London from Colonel Zeller on the Vercors plateau: FIERCE BATTLE FOR CAPTURE VERCORS IMMINENT. STOP ... URGENTLY REQUEST REINFORCEMENTS FOR ONE PARACHUTE BATTALION AND MORTARS STOP ... COME TO OUR AID BY EVERY MEANS.

Stukas arrived over the airstrip where canisters still littered the landscape. The ground heaved, red-hot shrapnel sliced through the air, wounded men bellowed in pain. The planes passed and for a minute or two there was a kind of silence.

Then once more there was the drone of engines and low in the sky came nearly twenty aircraft towing small gliders which detached and headed down in steep dives. At the last minute each one levelled out and white parachutes billowed from the tailplanes dragging each to a halt. Armed men emerged, dressed in camouflage jackets, fifteen or twenty from each fuselage, advancing in well-organised, coordinated moves.

Christine and Francis were with Colonel Zeller at his headquarters on the eastern edge of the plateau, between Saint-Agnan and Saint-Julien. Intelligence poured in – heavy tanks were coming down the route nationale, heading for Grenoble ready to fan out and block escape to the east. The south was cut off and to the north-west the Isère valley was guarded by troops who could deploy one man for every fifty metres of ground. The Maquisards had Bren guns, Sten guns, rifles and grenades. Against them were aircraft, tanks, half-track troop carriers, artillery, mortars, heavy machine guns and field artillery.

At Zeller's headquarters it was decided that a mass breakout of the 4000 Maquisards was impossible. So they were ordered to disperse, small groups to get away as best they could. Christine encoded Suttill's last signal, sent on behalf of Zeller: WE PROMISED TO HOLD OUT FOR THREE WEEKS STOP TIME PASSED SINCE TAKING UP ACTION SIX WEEKS STOP . . . MORALE OF PEOPLE EXCELLENT IF YOU DO NOT TAKE ACTION IMMEDIATELY STOP THOSE IN LONDON AND ALGIERS . . . ARE CONSIDERED CRIMINALS AND COWARDS STOP YES REPEAT CRIMINALS AND COWARDS.

He signed off: WE HOPE TO BE ABLE TO MAINTAIN RADIO LINK. ADIEU.

There was nothing more that Christine and Francis could do. They had huge responsibilities towards their *Jockey* circuit and there was no point in dying in a battle already lost. On 22 July they pulled out. With them went Auguste Floiras their radio operator, Zeller and a few key men. They escaped by car, driving through a tunnel that led off the plateau. They abandoned the vehicle and travelled for the next twenty-four hours on foot to Seyne-les-Alpes, about 110 miles away. Later the tunnel was dynamited by the Germans, cutting off further retreat from the plateau. Christine was unhappy at having left the Maquisards to be 'slaughtered like sheep'.

The Germans rampaged through the Vercors. They found a cave

where the badly wounded from the hospital at Saint-Martin were lying, protected by three doctors, nine nursing nuns, a priest and an almoner. One of the nurses was a friend of Christine's, among the patients was an agent who had parachuted in with her and broken his leg. The patients, priest and doctors were shot, their bodies rolled down a slope and left. The nuns were sent to Ravensbrück concentration camp. In another place a nineteen-year-old nurse was bayoneted to death and left tied with her entrails wrapped round her neck. When the fighting ended 639 Maquisards and more than 200 civilians were dead.

In Normandy at 6 a.m. on 25 July, the Allies launched Operation *Cobra*. After a bombardment by 3000 aircraft the German front line collapsed and the Allies began to break out of the bocage, chasing the retreating Germans towards Falaise. At the same time plans were finalised for a second landing on the beaches in the south of France. Part of the SOE's role in this was to prevent German reinforcements coming across the Alps from Italy.

Near the Italian border, a lorry rolled into a group of chalets above the village of Bramousse and was waived down by armed men. Christine Granville leapt out; it was only days since she had taken part in the withdrawal from the Vercors plateau. She was heading for a rendezvous with two leaders, Gilbert Galletti and Paul Héraud. Galletti was one of the most important Resistance leaders in the south of France, and Cammaerts described Héraud as 'the greatest man he had ever met'.

When Christine met Galletti she found a 34-year-old of great charm and humour, suntanned and always clowning. With Paul Héraud she had an instant and profound rapport. He was thirty-eight, a wiry cabinet maker who had blown up locomotive sheds, roads and communication centres, had organised reception committees for parachute drops and incoming agents. He was already a friend of Cammaerts and had shared a flat with him. Before going to bed at night they set booby traps to blow up any intruder, and probably themselves at the same time. He was a born leader of whom one friend said he was: 'A complete man. I never met anyone like him.' Francis Cammaerts realised he had become Christine's 'very special friend' and that she 'recognised the purity and perfection of his personality' and needed 'his level of grace'.

Galletti knew that across the border in Italy was the mountain headquarters of a leader with 2000 partisans under his command and that they guarded the heights over two of the main roads into France. The leader's name was Marcellini. Héraud knew that part of the German force guarding the border passes were Poles, conscripted into the Wehrmacht and wondered if Christine could persuade them to defect.

By now Pearl Witherington had 4000 men under her command. Worried that they would become a disorganised shambles, she split them into four groups and appointed four senior men to command them. The men were paid twenty francs a day and the groups were sent 121 tons of supplies, all organised by Pearl. The whole army thought of her as their invisible leader. One man wrote a poem and called her L'Arlésienne, a famous character in a French play who never appears. They called her 'our mother'; she was thirty. What she badly wanted was a French military commander, a Jedburgh team or an inter-Allied mission to help her.

On 25 July, Captain Francis Perdriset arrived to help Pearl. Henri, her second in command, did not trust him. He knew that there had been odd stories floating around about Perdriset and that at one time he had been seen in a Gestapo car outside the house of a family who were about to be arrested and sent to Auschwitz.

Perdriset wanted to organise things along military lines, giving everybody ranks but Pearl disagreed, telling him, 'Look, they're all volunteers. I am not sure it's a good idea giving them all ranks as if they were in the army. ... It's up to each leader to decide how to organise his Maquis.' She got her way. She knew that the important thing was to harass the Germans, to prevent them sending reinforcements to Normandy, lower their morale and make them frightened to move about. Now the invasion had happened she no longer had to work undercover and could wear a uniform, although she complained to London that her trousers were 'flying at half mast', her shoes were skiing boots she had inherited from a dead man and she had been forced to borrow a beret from 'one of the chaps'.

In the foothills of the Italian Alps a motorcycle roared out of Galletti's headquarters in Bramousse. The driver was Gilbert Tavernier, a superb winter sportsman, on the pillion sat Christine Granville, her plain skirt hitched to her knees, her suntanned arms hugging Tavernier's waist and her head pressed between his shoulder blades. A headscarf fluttered round her neck; she had a jersey tied round her waist and on her back was a rucksack full of hand grenades. Her mission was to make contact with Marcellini and, if she could, contact the Polish troops.

On the way the bike ran into a German roadblock. Christine dismounted and stood slightly away while Tavernier was interrogated and his papers examined. Once they were satisfied that all was in order the patrol leader gestured to Christine that she could remount. They were not interested in searching or talking to her thinking she was harmless. Tavernier dropped her at l'Echalp from where she walked on foot over the Col de la Croix de Fer into Italy. The route took her from the shady wooded lowlands up nearly 7000 feet above sea level to above the snow line. She reported that the going was hard, that there was no transport and everything had to be done on foot.

Christine spent the next fortnight on a reconnaissance tour sending reports to Cammaerts and to Brooks Richards in Algiers. She asked for more Jedburgh teams and missions telling Richards that they had to listen to Cammaerts. As she crossed and recrossed the border she saw that the morale of the German soldiers was low and reported that they seemed to know the war was lost.

She was never far away from danger. In the mountains she was stopped by two inexperienced Italian soldiers. She lifted her arms above her head to reveal that in one hand she held a grenade and in the other the pin. If she dropped the grenade it would explode. The soldiers watched her as she walked backwards away from them, staring them in the eyes, mesmerising them before vanishing into the trees. Christine claimed that the grenade was her favourite weapon, much more useful than a handgun or a rifle: 'With a pistol you can defend yourself against one person, with a hand-grenade against five, perhaps ten.'

On another occasion she and a group of French partisans were spotted on the border by a patrol with dogs. The group flung themselves into the undergrowth. The dogs cast about, sniffing the ground. One came upon Christine, a deep growl developing in the back of its throat, its teeth bared as it snarled. Christine slowly raised her arm, letting it sniff the back of her hand, then she stroked its head, murmuring in Polish. She let the dog know that she was stronger and more important. In the distance she could hear the handler calling and whistling. The dog pricked its ears, cocking its head as it heard the commands to return. Christine continued to mesmerise the animal, which slowly relaxed at her side. The patrol moved on, the shouts of the handlers becoming fainter and fainter. The dog licked Christine's face; she ruffled the coarse hair round its neck and scratched its ears. Then she stood up and walked on with the animal following.

When she finally found Marcellini he and his men were in a firefight with German units trying to clear the passes of 'terrorists'. She hid and watched the Italians beat off the attackers. She was the first British agent to make contact with Marcellini. He told her what he needed, which included ammunition, shoes, uniforms and 'packed meat'. He briefed her on the disposition of German forces and showed her his own. She left under fire, heading back, with the dog, to Galletti's base at Bramousse. She gave him the dog, which became a devoted follower of the partisans.

By 26 July, the Maquis had succeeded in their task of lowering morale in German troops in south-east France. Motorcycle couriers were frightened to travel alone on the roads. Columns leaving the town to collect supplies or inflict reprisals were invariably attacked and in some areas could only move with a heavily armed escort. General Blaskowitz, leader of the German Army Group G, admitted in his diary: 'The activity of bands in the rear of the Army Task Force has been allowed to reach the point that the control over a greater part of the area can no longer be assumed.'

At the beginning of August the Allied plan to invade the south of France, which since 1942 had been called *Anvil*, was renamed *Dragoon*. Eisenhower had wanted this to coincide with *Overlord* and the invasion of Normandy but there were not enough landing craft for both operations so he postponed it. On 15 August he planned to put 60,000 troops ashore along a thirty-five-mile stretch of coast that included the towns of Saint-Tropez and Saint-Raphaël. The primary objective was to capture the ports of Marseille and Toulon and then head up the Loire Valley where Nancy Wake, Virginia Hall, Pearl Witherington and Christine Granville were operating.

Bored with the discomforts of camp life, Nancy asked another Maquis leader, Henri Tardivat, to find her a bus to live in. The next day a roadblock appeared, manned by heavily armed young men. Each bus that passed was waved down and the terrified passengers made to clamber out and wait under the suspicious eyes of the Maquis with their guns. The civilians were used to the Germans stopping their vehicles and knew that searches could end up with arrests and disappearances. While the passengers waited, Tardivat climbed aboard and moved down the bus, looking for something. When he didn't find it the passengers got back on board and the bus went on its way. After several goes he found a bus that suited him and requisitioned it. The driver and passengers had to make their way back as best as they could.

That evening the bus stood parked in the Maquis camp, its curtains drawn. Inside was Nancy who had converted the seats at the back into a bedroom, using a stolen mattress and nylon parachutes as sheets. Draped over a seat were two frilly red nighties that she changed into when the day's work was done. The front of the bus became her sitting room, where she planned, drank and entertained.

The Maquis were careful not to stay in one place for too long, a week at most, and usually only for a few days. The first decision on arrival at any new camp was where the next one would be. If they were attacked, the bus was loaded up with equipment, the radios, Nancy's bike, the operators and driven at speed to the next rendezvous. A special two-man team was detailed to make sure the bus got away, slithering along the wooded tracks. The first time this happened, German soldiers arrived, blazing away with their weapons to find nothing but a deserted farmhouse. The whole camp had gone.

On 8 August, Paul Héraud addressed a meeting to outline his plans for the liberation of the area once the long-awaited Allied invasion of the south of France had taken place. Christine and Francis were at the meeting and when it was over Francis said that in Héraud the Maquis 'have a leader ideally qualified to carry through these operations' and that they must have 'total confidence in him'. The next day Héraud left on the pillion of a gendarme's motorbike to meet another Resistance leader. They were travelling on small side roads to avoid roadblocks and ran into a German convoy, which stopped them and asked to see their papers. Héraud made a dash for it and in the panic to stop him the gendarme was shot dead. Héraud hid, tearing up incriminating papers that he was carrying. Then he stood up and ran for the cover of some buildings. There was a brief burst of automatic fire and he fell. A few days earlier Héraud had said to a comrade, 'The end is coming but not every-body will see it.' The Germans did not find the papers which he had scrunched into a ball; the identities of the two men were checked and their bodies buried without ceremony.

Violette Szabo heard footsteps on the iron staircase that led to her cell. The door opened and she was hauled out. Her hands were cuffed together and joined by a short chain to a manacle round her ankles. The chain made it impossible for her to stand upright and the manacles meant she had to shuffle. Before leaving Fresnes she was chained to another woman, herded into a group and put on a lorry, which took them through the suburbs of Paris to the Gare de l'Est where, with thirty-seven other prisoners, they waited to see what would happen next. Some of the prisoners thought they recognised fellow students from the SOE training schools.

A train appeared, smoke coming out of its funnel as it came to a halt. The men were locked into a cage and the women bundled into third-class carriages, their chains clanking, the cuffs cutting into their wrists and ankles.

On the night of 7/8 August, two Americans, John Alsop and Reeve Schley, were parachuted in to join the *Freelance* network. Both the men were graduates of Yale University and from well-to-do families. Schley was thirty-six and Alsop twenty-nine. They were part of a seven-man team tasked with identifying enemy airfields and training the guerrillas. Suspended from his parachute, Schley could see crowds of people, lights and automobiles. Noise from the crowd drifted up to him reminding him more of a political rally than a group of insurgents. A container with Schley's suitcase was lost in the melée. The two were taken to Nancy's boudoir on the bus. They talked and drank champagne until four in the morning. Schley and Alsop wore smart American uniforms and Schley had on a pair of shiny leather cavalry boots. Nancy's men were making do with basic-issue British battledress, socks and heavy ammunition boots. Neither Schley nor Alsop could speak French but Nancy thought this was only a minor drawback; so long as they could teach her recruits how to use small arms and how to apply and detonate plastic explosives, they would do. Later she took them to their quarters, which she had tried to make homely with flowers in a jam jar by their cot beds. She left them saying that because the camp had been under attack the day before they were probably safe for a few days. They were woken by rifle and machine-gun fire and shouts of 'Les Boches'.

Schley pulled on his cavalry boots then found he could not get his breeches on over them. He took his knife and slashed off the tight lower leggings, pulled them on and ran out, to find Nancy and Denis Rake loading up the bus. Schley looked as though he was wearing an eccentric pair of shorts while Nancy's silk nightgown billowed under her khaki shirt. Farmer had disappeared, looking for the missing container. The 200 trained men were already moving forward against the enemy. The muffled sound of automatic fire and exploding hand grenades came from outside the wood.

Several Maquis ran into the clearing with the news that the Germans had dug in. They wanted to use the bazookas that had been dropped the previous night, but which only the Americans knew how to use. By now wounded men were being brought in. The men who wanted the bazookas began to gabble at Nancy that if someone would show them how to use them they could push the Germans out of their positions. She ordered them to get the weapons and carry them into the wood. At the same time she ordered Rake to look after the wounded. He began to complain that he could not stand the sight of blood. She threw bandages at him, gave him a gallon flask of pure medical alcohol and told him to get on with it. Some of the young fighters were moving down the middle of the road, oblivious of the incoming fire. Nancy ordered them into the cover of the woods. Four boys ignored her, a machine gun opened up, blood spurted from them as they took the force of the rounds sending them sprawling to the ground, alive but badly wounded. Men stumbled along, some carrying the long tubes of the bazookas in their arms, others with haversacks full of ammunition slung over their shoulders.

In the cover of the trees Schley and Alsop showed the young Resistance men how to operate the bazookas. Then the fighters took the tubes, ran forward and, flinging themselves on the ground, began firing. Nancy ran between each group yelling instructions passed on from the two instructors. She kept them moving and stopped them from standing in the path of the lethal back-blast. Ahead they could see fires burning in the brush where the rounds had hit and hear the screaming of men in pain. Nearby a farm building was on fire. Soon they ran out of ammunition and began to pull back while Nancy sent an SOS to Henri Tardivat, asking him to come and help.

She found Rake draped in grenades and weapons, tending the sick. He had organised the withdrawal of all the vehicles including Nancy's bus; only a car that would not start remained. Schley handed round cigars saying his father had given them to him in New York and he did not want the Germans to get them. He had lost his glasses in the fight and blinked in the sun. The familiar noise of a Bren came from behind the German positions, followed by the crump of mortar rounds falling. Nancy shouted, 'It's Tardivat, let's go!' The guerrilla leader was drawing German fire, allowing Nancy and her boys to retreat. Then he too vanished with his men. The Germans were left with casualties and a deserted camp.

Later Nancy was found washing the bodies of the boys who had been severely wounded in the road. Their faces were unrecognisable; they had been shot at close range in the face by the enemy. As she bathed them Nancy thought that what she was doing is what their mothers would have wanted. When she had finished, men shrouded the bodies in cut-up parachutes. By nightfall the camp was deserted and empty; even the car had somehow been fixed and driven off.

The following day Nancy and the Americans attended a burial service for their comrades who had died in the battle. They guessed that they had been attacked by a force of about 300 and they had killed about 40. It was impossible to be sure. Schley and Alsop were deeply impressed by Nancy's bravery. Schley reported: 'She led us like a man.'

The first part of Violette Szabo's journey lasted for thirty-six hours, the train rumbling very slowly through the French countryside until it arrived in the early afternoon at Châlons-sur-Marne, and stopped.

The noise of aircraft filled the air. The German guards panicked and jumped off the train, shouting that they would shoot anyone who tried to follow them. Bombs began to fall, rocking the carriages. The chained prisoners became agitated, the men were trapped in their cage, dying of thirst. Some panicked. Edward Yeo Thomas, code-named *The White Rabbit*, prayed that no incendiaries would hit the train. They were calmed by the sight of Violette and her chained companion crawling along the corridor bringing water that they had scavenged from the lavatories. Outside German soldiers were being killed in the attack.

The planes disappeared into the sky and the prisoners ordered off the train. Guards shouted at them that if they tried to escape they would be shot. The prisoners spent the night in stables. In the morning the men and women were separated and bundled, still chained, onto heavy lorries and driven to Saarbrücken were they disembarked at a concentration camp called Neue Bremm, a small transit camp designed to break the spirit of anyone passing through it. Prisoners stayed until there were enough of them to fill a train of cattle trucks taking them on to the bigger camps. Punishment was part of their short stay. Some inmates were made to crouch and hop for up to eight hours at a time. Others were flogged for just being there. Nothing was provided for the inmates; they were lucky if they were issued with a few slices of bread. The fortunate stayed for a few days, the unlucky for as long as a month.

Violette stayed at Neue Bremm for ten days during which she met Yvonne Baseden, a fellow SOE officer. They had last met in Baker Street when Violette introduced her baby daughter, Tania, to some of the men and women she was working with. They saw each other for a few days before Violette was wedged into a cattle truck heading towards Berlin.

In Normandy the quiet Calvados countryside lay in ruins. The roads leading to Paris were lined with the burning ruins of towns and villages. Smoke and flames rose from burning farms and the fields were littered with the burnt-out remains of vehicles and the bloated corpses of men and animals. By 12 August the German Army was trapped with its back to the town of Falaise. General Omar Bradley, in command of the US 1st Army said: 'This is an opportunity that comes to a commander not more than once in a century. We're about to destroy an entire hostile army and go all the way from here to the German border.'

A disgruntled Maquis leader who thought that Nancy was withholding arms and money waited for her to arrive for a meeting in a bar. He was drunk. As he heard her car approach he pulled the pin from a grenade, let go of the clip and waited to throw it, forgetting that with the clip gone the fuse was burning. The explosion four seconds later showered Nancy's car with the remains of the man.

After the incident it was decided to give Nancy a bodyguard. Six tough Spaniards were chosen, men who had fought in the Spanish Civil War. From then on she travelled round in a convoy of three cars, the front and rear windows removed to allow a Bren gun to be deployed.

Nancy heard that three women had been captured by a band of Maquis and were being raped and abused. She asked what was going on and was told the women were spies and this was their punishment. Nancy demanded that they were brought to her. The next day the women arrived, dressed in rags and in a bad physical state. One by one Nancy interrogated them.

The first was a pretty seventeen-year-old girl, her face bruised and swollen, her eyes puffy with tears. She denied being a spy and to Nancy it was obvious why she had been 'arrested' by the guerrilla fighters. She released the girl at once and caused the men who had raped her to be heavily disciplined, showing that she was not prepared to tolerate such behaviour. The second woman was in her late thirties and had been caught having an affair with one of the dreaded Milice. She too had been beaten and raped. Nancy thought she had suffered enough and told her to go.

The third woman, dressed in rags, battered and bruised like the others, was German and admitted to being a spy. She was arrogant and clearly hated the Maquis. Nancy told her that she could not release her and had no facilities to keep her a prisoner. Her fate was to be the same as many other spies captured in wartime, she was going to be shot. She, Nancy, would find her a dress to replace the rags she was wearing. The woman did not show fear or remorse. At first the men of the Maquis said they could not shoot a woman in cold blood, even if she was guilty. These were the same men who had lined up to abuse her. Nancy called them cowards and said that if they couldn't do it, she could.

The next day at dawn as she was led past Nancy the woman spat at her. She was made to stand against a tree; she refused a blindfold. As the men raised their rifles she shouted, *'Heil Hitler!'* Nancy watched without emotion. The spy's body was buried without ceremony in the wood. The young girl who Nancy had released said that she had no family and asked if she could stay and work for her.

By 11 August, Christine and Cammaerts were back at their HQ in Seyne-les-Alpes where they were contacted by Xan Fielding, who had been operational on Crete. He was now a member of a recently arrived two-man Inter-Allied mission. His partner had been injured on landing and was being treated in a Maquis hospital. Cammaerts explained that there was not really anything for the new arrival to do and suggested that he come on a trip round the area to see what was going on. Christine could not go with them as she was going back into the mountains to a garrison located in a pass called Col de Larche. It was manned by about 150 troops, over 50 of whom were Poles.

The garrison was nearly 6500 feet above sea level. In order to reach it Christine had to climb through a dense forest of larch. She was driven part of the way in a car and then started up the mountainside, following a steep track ankle-deep in a slippery carpet of tiny, stinging larch needles and hard round pine cones. She was escorted by a guide code-named *Tartar*.

The pair climbed for a day and a half. Christine often slipped and her legs were covered in tiny, bloody scratches and swollen from the resin in the needles. Eventually they reached the fort, a huge, stubby concrete structure protecting heavy guns sighted to shell the pass. The site was surrounded by barbed wire and machine-gun platforms.

Carefully Christine recced the fortification and eventually made contact with a Polish guard. He told her that there were sixty-five of his countrymen in the 500-strong garrison. She asked him where and when they held their roll calls. Armed with this information, she turned back down the mountain, taking an easier and quicker route. Her guide *Tartar* described Christine's assault on the terrifying heights of the Col de Larche as a triumph of mind over matter.

She returned on the 13th. Round her neck she wore a red and white scarf, the colours of the Polish flag. She now managed to address almost the entire Polish contingent and persuaded them that they should desert. When the time came, she said, they would be contacted and this was the signal for them to sabotage as much of the installation as possible. One of their tasks would be to dismantle the breechblocks and delicate optical-dial sights of the heavy guns and throw them over the wall onto the mountain slopes. When they had done this they were to move down the mountain in groups of ten, carrying white flags. Once they were in contact with the Maquis they could choose to either join the Free French Forces or become honourable prisoners of war. She then distributed typed sheets, which summarised what she had just said. For the second time she left the redoubt, taking a now familiar path down the steep slopes.

When she got back to the HQ at Seyne she was told that Francis Cammaerts, Xan Fielding and a French officer named Christian Sorensen had been arrested by the Gestapo.

On 14 August, Henri Tardivat and Nancy Wake and a large group of heavily armed men assembled outside the 'Restaurant Tailhardat' outside Montluçon. The men came by bicycle, on foot, in Citroën cars, some fuelled by charcoal and others with the luxury of forbidden petrol. A large contingent was delivered in an open-sided lorry. At a signal they moved off, silently working their way through the town; it was a little after midday. They were heading for the Gestapo headquarters at Montluçon, where it was hoped that the German officers would be having drinks before lunch. Their first stop was a house near the headquarters where they were issued with weapons and ammunition stored there the night before. Nancy was armed with hand grenades. When they arrived she ran to the back of the building, through the kitchen door, and up the stairs onto the first floor where she kicked open a door. For an instant she glimpsed the startled faces of the enemy as her grenades bounced onto the floor in front of them. She pulled the door closed and ran back. Behind her the noise of her grenades exploding was joined by the sound of Sten guns, more grenades and the harsh crashing of Bren guns cutting down any German who managed to escape the inferno in the house. Along the road the transports were waiting. Nancy dived into her car and was driven off. In under fifteen minutes the raid was over. Excited villagers rushed out to cheer them. They had to clear a path through, telling them to get back inside their homes, and that this was not the start of the invasion. Eventually the Maquis band vanished back into the forest, leaving dead and dying Germans everywhere, their head-quarters wrecked and burning. In retribution for the raid the Gestapo arrested forty-two hostages and took them to a quarry outside the town. There they were tortured and mutilated before being made to dig a pit in which they stood while the soldiers shot them.

At 6.00 a.m. on 15 August, 1300 Allied bombers flew in from the sea towards the south of France heading for a fifty-mile stretch of coast south-west of Cannes and some of the most glamorous beaches in the world. Their targets included Saint-Raphaël, Sainte-Maxime and Saint-Tropez. For the next ninety minutes they dropped their bombs. At 7.30 a.m. the guns of large Allied battleships joined the bombardment while landing craft of all types ploughed towards the shore. Operation *Dragoon* had begun.

Facing the invaders was Army Group G, which was under strength and had been stripped of many of its best units and equipment. A significant proportion of the troops were wounded veterans and vol-unteer Russian prisoners of war armed with weapons captured on the battlefields of Europe and Russia. The commander of Army Group G had recently reported that his force had been so weakened 'from the reassignment of men and weapons that the successful defence of the [south] coast can no longer be guaranteed'. It did though have one real asset, the 11th Panzer Division, which, even though it had lost two battalions was still considered one of the strongest units on the Western Front. The land forces were augmented by 200 aircraft and a handful of coastal batteries.

Before the landing the Resistance had concentrated on cutting telephone cables, disrupting communications with catastrophic consequences for the Germans. By the end of the day the Allies held a bridgehead that extended up to ten miles inland, held by 60,000 troops.

In Paris on 15 August, convoys of vehicles poured through the city retreating from the Normandy front, heading east for the Fatherland and home. Resistance prisoners from Fresnes and other jails were packed into cattle trucks, 120 people per wagon with little sanitation and no heat and sent to concentration camps, including Natzweiler, Buchenwald and Dachau. Among those crammed together in the stifling heat were several SOE agents, including the radio operator Eileen Nearne and French agent Alix d'Unienville, a woman who had been arrested on D-Day outside the Bon Marché store in Paris.

On the same day 300 SS troops from Das Reich, with tanks and half-tracks, rampaged through the town of Valençay in Pearl's area, setting fire to houses, shouting 'Raus Raus' looking for a Resistance leader wounded in an attack a few days before. He and other FFI comrades were hiding in a local hospital run by nuns. The Germans found nothing and moved on leaving forty-eight buildings in ruins. Pearl, whose Maquis had withdrawn to the safety of the Gâtine Forest just north of the town, thought that the attack was senseless and vindictive. She said that while it was not on the scale of Oradour, it 'wasn't pretty'.

News reached Christine and her comrades that Cammaerts and the other two had been sentenced to death. They were to be executed within the next few days but no one knew precisely when. Christine began to plan how to rescue them. At first she wanted to lead a raiding party to attack the prison to snatch the condemned men. The Maquis leader quashed the idea. He thought it was too dangerous and in any case they did not have the time, the transport or the equipment to carry out a raid. Meanwhile Jedburgh teams had arrived with heavy equipment; and there were ten new agents with orders to penetrate German units and destabilise any foreign troops in their ranks. It had been Cammaerts's job to organise everything and liaise with London. Christine took over and sent the Jedburghs off with a driver and a guide and a list of her contacts. She was stressed and curt with everybody, but everyone did as she instructed.

The streets of Paris were still clogged with German vehicles trying to move east to safety. Tanks, half-tracks and trucks pulling trailers streamed down the Champs-Elysées carrying troops and their possessions. Soldiers billeted in hotels all over the city were ordered to proceed to the Hôtel Majestic where the military had its headquarters. By the afternoon the administration of the Wehrmacht had almost all gone, leaving the fighting men. Robert Alesch wobbled along on a bicycle behind the retreating columns, hurt that he had not been invited to join them.

In the Hôtel Le Meurice, General Dietrich von Choltitz, the commander of Paris, met the chairman of the Paris council, the prefect of police and the prefect of the Seine. He warned them that he would do anything necessary to 'maintain order and pitilessly repress disorder'. Later he stood with them on a balcony with Paris spread below. In a low voice he said, 'It would be a real pity if such a city were to be destroyed.'

Pearl moved into the chateau at Valençay where some of the treasures from the Louvre were stored including the *Venus de Milo*. The bed she shared with Henri was huge and situated in the middle of a ballroom.

Her job now was to help 'mess up' the Germans as they withdrew. After one firefight two prisoners were taken, an officer who had been wounded in both legs by shrapnel from a bazooka fired at the truck he was travelling in, the other a young soldier who was taken to be treated at a hospital run by nuns. The officer was a fanatical Nazi who told his captors that he wanted to be shot. The Maquis had no facilities for keeping him a prisoner and it was decided to grant his request. He was allowed to write a letter to his family and a short while later the execution order was read to him. The man sat at the foot of a tree, unable to move because of his wounded legs.

With the Maquis was a man in German uniform, who was from Alsace and had deserted. A group of about twelve prisoners were led past. The condemned officer called them over, ordered them to stand to attention and began to harangue them about their duty to the Führer. The Alsatian took out a Walther P38 pistol and shot him twice in the head.

News reached Seyne-les-Alpes that Cammaerts, Fielding and Sorensen were going to be executed on the evening of 17 August. Christine decided to risk everything in an attempt to rescue them. Other Maquis commanders agreed and thought 'his [Cammaerts] presence was essential'. She set off for the prison at Digne twenty-five miles away, travelling by bicycle, a form of transport which she hated and which frightened her. She had been given the name of one contact, a captain in the Gendarmerie, Albert Schenck, who it was thought was a double agent. The ride took her over rugged, mountainous terrain that exhausted her. At the last hill she saw the town spread out before her with its huge bridge across the River Bléone. The town itself was in chaos. The day before a flight of American P47 Thunderbolts had screamed out of the sky, heading for the bridge. These stubby, bulldog-like planes had been wreaking havoc in Normandy, machine-gunning convoys of lorries, blasting troop trains and reducing Panzer tanks to heaps of red-hot scrap metal.

When the Thunderbolts let fly, one bomb had hit the bridge, destroying several houses and killing twenty-four civilians and two Germans. Now German military police struggled in the heat to keep vehicles moving across the Bléone.

A large crowd surrounded the prison, desperate for news of

relatives and friends. Wearing a dark scarf tied round her face and looking like a peasant, Christine pushed through the forbidding outer gates into the inner courtyard milling with people, some shouting names in the hope of hearing an answering cry. She moved slowly along the wall under the barred windows humming 'Frankie and Johnny' as loudly as she could. The song was one that Cammaerts and she used to sing together on their long drives. Then she heard Cammaerts's voice singing in unison.

Next Christine tried to see if she could visit the prisoners. No official was interested in helping her, visitors were not allowed. Eventually she tracked down the contact she had been given, Schenck, and bamboozled her way into his office. He spoke French and German and as the liaison officer between the Préfecture and the Gestapo was very well connected.

Christine began by telling Schenck that she was an SOE agent, that the three prisoners were also agents and one of them was her husband. The Allies, she said, were going to arrive at any minute, the bombing of the bridge was just the start. Then, getting into her stride, she said she was the niece of Field Marshal Montgomery and a relation of Lord Vansittart who had said the year before that the only hope of peace in Europe was a crushing and violent military defeat for Germany. Once this had sunk in she told Schenck that if anything happened to the prisoners the Maquis and the Allies would arrest him and he would be 'handed to the mob'. She sat staring at the man, waiting to see if he was going to arrest her. He said he had no authority to do anything but there was someone in the prison who might be prepared to help. That man was Max Waem, the officer in the Milice who had arrested the three agents. He was prepared to ask for Waem's help if she gave him 2 million francs, more money than he could earn in his whole career as a policeman. Christine told him she would be back in two days with the money, adding that if anything went wrong she was going to shoot him herself. She cycled back over the mountains to Seyne, arriving long after the sun had set.

From Seyne a message went to SOE headquarters in Algiers, where immediate arrangements were made for the money to be delivered within forty-eight hours. Buckmaster was in the signals room with Vera Atkins when the news came through. A young assistant, Noreen Riols, who was also in the room, said there was a silence in which 'You could have heard a pin drop.'

The next day, 16 August, Hitler finally allowed Army Group G to withdraw from the south of France to move north along the Rhône Valley to link up with the remains of Army Group B in the north. They were heading for the areas where Pearl Witherington and Nancy Wake were fighting alongside their FFI comrades.

Twenty-four hours later Christine once more laboured up and down the steep mountain roads, heading for Digne. In her panniers were gifts for the guards, alcohol and 2 million francs. The money was in small rubber bags, which had protected it during the parachute drop. She met Schenck in his office, and handed over the cash. The meeting with Waem was arranged for 4 p.m. that afternoon in Schenck's flat. The execution was set for 9 p.m. that evening.

When Waem appeared he was holding a gun, which he trained on Christine. He was small and aquiline with blond hair and had dressed himself in an SS uniform. In the distance could be heard the unfamiliar sound of Allied fighter planes scouring the hills for German convoys to shoot up. Frau Schenck brought in a tray with real coffee and milk. She left it on the table between them and Waem put his gun down next to it. Christine began to talk, running through the same routine she had used with Schenck two days before. She told him the war was almost over and the Germans had lost. The Allies were on the doorstep. If anything happened to her husband and the other agents Waem was certain to be captured and executed, if not by the Allies, then by the Maquis. Schenck's hands began to shake. From her pocket Christine pulled wireless crystals and threw them down in front of him. He tried to pour her another cup of coffee. His hands were now shaking so violently that he spilled it, apologised and said that perhaps she would like to pour the contents of her saucer into her cup. Christine went on for three hours painting a darker and darker picture. There was no escape for him, the town was surrounded by Maquis, only she could arrange his safe conduct to the Americans. She was not prepared to do this until she was certain that the SOE prisoners were going to be released.

By seven in the evening Waem was a nervous wreck. He promised that he would do what she wanted provided that she guaranteed him a safe passage to the American lines and that he would be treated as a free man, not a prisoner of war. He gabbled that he wanted to volunteer for an undercover mission.

In their cell the three men were brought what they thought was going to be their last supper – vegetable soup and brown bread; for prison food the captives thought it was surprisingly good. A key sounded in the lock and the door opened to reveal the slight, blond-haired figure of Max Waem, a gun in his hand. Instead of his immaculate SS uniform he had on civilian trousers and the jacket of an officer in the Wehrmacht. Fielding thought he looked like a judge who had put on the black cap to pronounce sentence of death. The officer ordered them out of the cell. He spoke directly to Cammaerts, congratulating him on his wife, 'What a wonderful woman you have.'

They left the building, passing into the now deserted outer court-yard. The sun had set, a drizzle fell from the grey sky, silver from the last rays of light. Arc lamps round the walls reflected yellow on the cobblestones. The guards stiffened and came to attention, their anonymous faces shadowed by their helmets. The party walked towards the outer prison gates, Waem in front with Cammaerts by his side. Once through the gates they would turn left towards the football field where they expected to see a firing squad drawn up and waiting. Fielding wondered whether this was going to be their last chance to escape, to run into the darkness, waiting for a bullet in the back.

Instead, they turned right. They walked on until they came level with a big black Citroën, its engine running. Waem said, 'Get in quick, all three of you.' The three men squeezed into the back. The doors were slammed. Waem climbed into the front and the car pulled away;

behind them the prison disappeared into darkness. The driver sped through the streets. At the edge of the town was a roadblock – armed men stood in the road, one holding up his hand for the car to stop. Waem wound down his window and leant out, waving a uniformed arm and shouting, the headlights blazed, dazzling the guards who, seeing an officer in an official car, stood aside to let it through. It was now totally dark, the windscreen wipers struggled with the rain pouring down the windscreen. The car rounded a bend and slowed; ahead in the darkness a figure stood black against a white wall. Through the rain Fielding could see it was Christine, her shoulders wet.

Waem got out, Christine approached the car and climbed into the front, then Waem squeezed in beside her. Once more the car sped off, Christine staring silently ahead. Fielding was bewildered, his life had become a dream that he could not make head or tail of. He assumed that Christine's silence meant she too had been captured and did not want to betray them by the slightest sign of recognition.

The car stopped on the edge of a steep embankment. Waem leapt out and pulled open the back door, ordered Fielding out and told him to follow him down the bank at the bottom of which was a stream. The two men slithered towards the water where Waem took off his uniform jacket and told Fielding to help him bury it in the mud, pebbles and rocks at the edge of the stream. They scrabbled about, unable to see what they were doing and finally hauled themselves up the slippery slope back to the car. Once they were back in, the driver let out the clutch and accelerated off into the rain. In front Christine turned round and grinned. They were free.

By midday on 18 August the BBC broadcast the news that the Allies had taken Chartres sixty miles to the south-west of Paris. It was a very hot day, the Metro was closed and most of the police were on strike. In the police station in Saint-Germain the divisional commander, a collaborator, faced one of his men who told him, 'You are the *ex* Divisional Commander, you are no longer in command here. We obey only the orders of our Resistance leaders ... until the Germans have gone.'

As night fell a thunderstorm broke. A woman wrote in her diary:

'Night falls. Another day has passed, a day that brings us closer to that marvellous liberty, which is already sweeping towards us along our French roads.'

During the night of 18 August the Vichy government representatives left the French capital. Loud explosions could be heard. Jumpy German soldiers fired indiscriminately at civilians and got ready for the battle of Paris. A curfew was called for 9 p.m. with the death penalty for anyone caught breaking it. In his office Dietrich von Choltitz began to prepare for the destruction of the city, obeying Hitler's orders that the city 'must not fall into the enemy's hands, except lying in complete debris'. German engineers clambered in the ironwork of the Eiffel Tower or swung from the bridges across the Seine, connecting bundles of explosives to electric wires.

By mid-August in the Haute-Loire, where Virginia Hall was operating, the German forces began to collapse. At Le Puy-en-Velay 500 soldiers were taken prisoner and the next day the garrison itself surrendered. That evening the commander of the garrison at the Col de Larche sat down to dinner with a delegation that included a French local government official and Captain John Halsey, who had arrived a few days before with a Jedburgh team. They were there to discuss the terms of surrender.

As they talked, the Poles in the fort, obeying Christine's orders, dismantled the breechblocks of the heavy guns and threw the dial sights down the mountain. Then they deserted, carrying with them small arms, mortars and machine guns.

At 2.30 a.m. the commander accepted Halsey's terms, gave up his command and was led away with his dog.

By the morning of 19 August the French flag flew from the top of Notre-Dame and the Hôtel de Ville in Paris. Vehicles began to appear on the street painted military green with the Cross of Lorraine on the doors, or the words *Police* and *FFI* daubed on the bodywork.

By 21 August the remains of the German forces trapped in the Falaise pocket had escaped. For ten days Allied shells had poured down on them, tanks weighing more than fifty tons were flipped on their backs, vehicles and men were blown to pieces, crazed and wounded horses galloped along roads choked with burning vehicles, their hooves slipping on the bloody remains of the dead.

Two days later, General Eisenhower was taken to see what had happened in the fighting round Falaise. He found a scene that he thought could only be described by Dante, describing the stench of rotting bodies and the fact that it was possible to walk for hundreds of yards at a time on the bodies of the dead.

In spite of the devastation the survivors of Army Group B, the 7th Army and the 5th Panzer Army, 60,000 men, were moving east, in good order, but without tanks or heavy artillery. The Allied commanders squabbled about who had done what and whether they could have done it better.

The Allies were now advancing east through Normandy and north from the south of France. Nancy's work became more systematic. Even her clothes changed. She wore her uniform khaki shirt and tie, battledress trousers and military boots on her feet.

Her SOE training came into its own in an attack on a factory near Mont Mouchet. The plan had been to isolate and immobilise two sentries. Nancy overpowered one of them and killed him with a karate chop to a point just below his ear. In the tussle she received a bad bayonet slash on her arm. She said, 'No I did not weep for that sentry. It was him or me and by that time I had the attitude anyway that the only good German was a dead one.'

In Montluçon there was a garrison of 500 German soldiers. Nancy's boss, John Farmer, suggested to his French superior that they send the garrison commander an ultimatum demanding his surrender. In return he and his men would be treated as prisoners of war under the Geneva Convention. The commander was willing, but his lieutenants, both members of the SS, refused. As a result the Maquis surrounded the town, cutting off water, electricity and gas to the garrison. After four days of fighting the commander asked for a temporary armistice so that he could bury his dead and get his wounded into a French hospital.

Nancy swapped her bus for the Château de Fragne, a large empty building with no running water or electricity. She moved in a week before her birthday and for the first time in months slept comfortable and dry in the chateau's huge rooms. Nancy decided to abandon the places she had organised to receive parachute drops and concentrated her efforts on the fields around the chateau, even managing to set up a permanent system of signal lights run from car batteries.

The next day a German relief column arrived from the south heading for Montluçon. The route led them alongside the grounds of the Château de Fragne. More than 200 vehicles passed by the gates not realising that Lieutenant Schley and others were lying in the undergrowth watching and photographing them. With the help of the relief column the Germans trapped in Montluçon broke out and escaped. Later the corpse of the garrison commander was found; he had been beheaded.

On 24 August the Germans pulled out of Montluçon in a bedraggled convoy of lorries, cars and motorbikes, loaded with their possessions and the property they had stolen from their French billets. For hours the column passed the main gates of Nancy's chateau still, watched and photographed by the Maquis. Then the garrison in Vichy cleared out and the Maquis raced to the town. Virginia Hall told London that her area was clear of Germans.

Several days later a team of five arrived by parachute to join Nancy and John Farmer, keyed up to play their part in the war. They arrived at the chateau and were shocked to find it in a party mood. As far as Nancy was concerned the job she had come to do was done, it was time to relax, eat good food and drink fine wine liberated from the chateau cellars. The new arrivals quickly realised they were not welcome and decided to look for the war somewhere else.

On the eastern flank of the Allied invasion of south-east France, things moved quickly. The main roads north, the routes nationale

7 and 51 were lined with the wreckage of the retreating German Army – burnt-out vehicles, shattered armour, spiked guns and abandoned equipment. Soldiers of the Wehrmacht and the SS surrendered in their thousands, tramping south under the hot sun, covered in white dust, forced to keep to the verges, making room for the endless stream of Allied units heading north.

The town of Montelimar lay across the German escape route and it was there that the Allies tried to stop them; after several days of heavy fighting the Germans broke contact and escaped north leaving smoke and flames from burning buildings. Some 130,000 men in good fighting order lived to fight another day. The retreating column of Army Group Blaskowitz, named after its commander, stretched for more than 100 miles. They left behind over 2000 wrecked vehicles, 300 pieces of artillery, 1500 dead horses and 10,000 men, dead, wounded or prisoners of war.

In his mistress Marie-Thérèse's apartment Pablo Picasso was painting, bellowing at the top of his voice, drowning out the noises echoing round the streets outside, the crash of grenades, the shouts and the stutter of machine guns. He was reworking a painting by Poussin, *The Triumph of Pan*, a wild Bacchanalian scene.

At 9.15 p.m. the twenty-two armoured vehicles in the vanguard of the liberating army roared into the square in front of the Hôtel de Ville, the heart of the capital and the symbol of liberty. They swung round and parked line abreast in front of the building. Crowds flooded in from all over the city. Flares were lit, bathing the armour in a yellow glow; the lights in the Hôtel de Ville shone over the scene but were rapidly extinguished when a machine gun opened up.

By dawn several of the roads out of the city were littered with dead soldiers and burning German and Allied vehicles. General von Choltitz and his staff ate their lunch in the Hôtel Meurice with the tables pushed away from the windows as a precaution against bullets and masonry ricocheting into the dining room.

A Grenadier Guards officer escorting a party of BBC corre-
spondents reported that they were fired on as they drove into the
city. They retreated through streets littered with burnt-out German
vehicles, lamp posts torn down and streets torn up to make barricades. Later the party was led to the Hôtel de Ville by a van playing
the Marseillaise over loudspeakers strapped to the roof. Inside the
building they were taken on a tour of some of the rooms. In one
they found German soldiers, 'sour and embittered with evil faces';
in another were officers 'sitting on the floor in their smart uniforms,
disconsolate and miserable'; another held women with shaved heads,
their cheeks daubed with the swastika, sobbing; in a fourth were men
who had collaborated with the Gestapo, 'badly beaten with bruised
and swollen faces, pondering miserably the future that awaited
them ... mad terror written on their faces.'

By nightfall General Dietrich von Choltitz had surrendered to
General Leclerc. Later de Gaulle arrived and broadcast to the nation
from the Hôtel de Ville and declared Paris liberated after 1442 days
of occupation. Hundreds of thousands of cheering people lined the
Champs-Elysées as de Gaulle drove towards the Arc de Triomphe
where chaos reigned, cars and tanks 'inextricably entangled'.
Photographers jostled, people screamed with joy, as their liberator
approached the tomb of the unknown warrior.

Picasso finished his picture, signed and dated it 'Paris 25 August
1944', 'because it is not sufficient to know an artist's work – it is
necessary to know when he did them, why, how, under what circumstances'. The colours that dominate Picasso's picture are those
of France, red, white and blue. In the background, behind the hills
framing the scene, a golden sun is rising.

To the west Pearl Witherington's group was still fighting hard. The
last German troops left in southern France, a rearguard column,
led by 50-year-old General Botho Elster, was heading north hoping
to fight its way through to link up with the armies retreating out of
Paris towards Germany. The column stretched for miles, 20,000

men transported by 300 lorries, 1000 horses, 700 bicycles and their own feet. Since being ordered north it had been bombed and strafed by Allied planes, many of them brought on target by the Jedburgh teams. The column was also under continual attack from the Maquis.

Elster was heading for the Loire where his way was blocked by General Patton's 3rd Army. Coming up behind him were the Allies and directly in front of him was Pearl Witherington with orders to stop him. Her four Maquis units positioned themselves astride routes nationale 76, 17 and 156. They had mined the roads, blown up bridges, set up roadblocks and were ready to do anything to bring the column to a halt.

From the first contact they attacked the enemy without ceasing. Small quantities of plastic explosive overturned vehicles or tore tyres to shreds. Larger quantities buried in the road blew lorries into the air, lacerating them so that all that remained was the chassis and the mutilated bodies of the occupants. One battle went on for five hours with only minor Maquis losses; in another the partisans took more than a hundred casualties. Pearl radioed urgently to Allied high command asking for the immediate bombardment of the convoy as it travelled up the Châteauroux to Issoudun road.

The fighting forced the column to do a U-turn, trying to pull back. In their anger the soldiers tortured, mutilated and shot captured Maquisards; civilian hostages were rounded up and shot. The damage to the area was immense. In the end the German forces were trapped in the flat fields hedged by the towns of Châteauroux, Vierzon and Bourges. The same places that Nancy Wake had travelled round on her epic cycle ride. General Elster was contacted by French negotiators. He told them he was prepared to surrender but only to regular military forces and to a commander of equivalent rank to his own. He was not prepared to deal with the Maquis or irregular forces like the SOE.

As August turned into September, Violette Szabo arrived at Ravensbrück concentration camp, a place where 80,000 women prisoners lived in quarters that had been designed for 6000. In the same transport arrived other SOE agents: Denise Bloch, who in peacetime had been a secretary, and Lilian Rolfe, a thirty-year-old wireless operator, highly intelligent, painstaking and an idealist. Another agent, Eileen Nearne, was already there. Ravensbrück stood in the middle of a huge sandy plain covered in pine trees where the smell of resin floated on the air. Winter was approaching and Violette wore only the blue, silk, short-sleeved dress she had been arrested in. She was worn out, depressed, exhausted. 'Devoid of hope' she only wanted to sleep. At one point she began to scream and shout over and over again, 'I am so cold, so cold.'

In early September Noor Khan was seen walking in the prison yard wearing sackcloth. Later she scratched a message on her bowl saying that her own clothes had been removed. The last message she sent read 'I am leaving', after which she disappeared. Her fellow prisoners did not know that orders had arrived from Berlin on the teleprinter saying that she was to be transferred to the concentration camp at Dachau. On the way she was joined by three other SOE agents, Madeleine Damerment, Eliane Plewman, and Yolande Beekman, who she had trained with in England. When they arrived at Dachau the SS man escorting the four women was informed he would be given a receipt for them in the morning. He told the reception committee that one of the women – 'the Creole', by which he meant Noor – was especially dangerous and was to be kept separate from the others and given the 'full treatment'. They were locked in separate cells. Noor was chained, slapped and, almost naked, ridiculed. A few hours later the other three were dragged from their cells, punched and kicked and taken to a place near the crematorium. They were violently stripped of their clothing and shot.

An officer called Ruppert then visited Noor. He spent the next few hours tormenting and beating her. By the time he had buttoned himself back into his jacket and breeches she was 'a bloody mess'. Then he made her kneel in front of him and pulled out his pistol. Before he pulled the trigger she uttered one last word – '*Liberté*'.

*

On 17 September General Elster surrendered to an American general at Issoudun. To the outrage of Pearl and her Maquis comrades the German troops were allowed to march out of the area armed, flying flags and singing marching songs. The Resistance felt cheated as the swaggering troops went on their arrogant way; the surrender should have been theirs. Pearl's fury deepened when she heard that the US Army welcomed the troops into captivity with speeches, a march-past that included the Nazi salute and gifts of chocolate, oranges and cigarettes.

Four days later, on 21 September, Pearl Witherington received a signal from London. It read: '... Personal for Mairie [Pearl] from Colonel Buckmaster. Want you to return soonest as no further work for you in France ... bring with you all British commissioned personnel ... bring with you all crystals and store in safe place ...' The survivors of F Section SOE were going home, mission accomplished.

EPILOGUE

At a memorial service by the Cenotaph in the newly liberated town of Vichy, Nancy Wake met an old acquaintance who told her that her husband, Henri, had died in a Gestapo prison. She burst into tears, unable to believe the news. Denis Rake led her away; he had never seen her so distressed. Rake and her other close friends drove her at once to Marseille to find out what had happened. The trip took a long time, Nancy sat in the car barely speaking. Eventually they discovered that the Gestapo had arrested Henri and realised that his wife was the woman they were after – *The White Mouse*. Henri had endured torture and been beaten almost to death with clubs, but revealed nothing. He was executed at dawn on 16 October 1943. Nancy said, 'I just had to turn and walk away. Get into the car and go. It had to end sometime, and that is when it ended.'

Violette Szabo's war ended in Ravensbrück concentration camp with fellow SOE agents Denise Bloch and Lilian Rolfe, both of whom were too ill to walk. The three emaciated women, blackened and dressed in rags, were taken to a spot near the camp crematorium and murdered. None of the prisoners in the camp were certain whether they had been shot or hanged from butchers' hooks by rope or piano wire.

*

After reporting that her area was clear of Germans, Virginia Hall received two new agents, both American, Henry Riley from Connecticut and Paul Goillot from New York. They arrived with equipment and 2 million francs. Virginia told them they were too late, the Yssingeaux plateau had been liberated, the Germans had all gone. Virginia and Goillot tried to form a freelance mobile unit and take it to wherever the war was being fought. When London heard what they were trying to do they told her to stop, forbidding the mission to go on.

Christine Granville and Francis Cammaerts had a similar problem and were looking for something to do. Even before south-east France was cleared of the enemy they were driving round in a jeep, wearing makeshift uniforms, trying to sell their services to whatever American commander would take them. General Butler, who was at the time at Sisteron on a salient deep inside enemy territory, had other things on his mind and told Cammaerts to 'bugger off', he was not interested in private armies.

Later Christine persuaded 300 Poles to desert from the Wehrmacht. When she pointed out that under the Geneva Convention they could not fight in enemy tunics hundreds of men began to strip to the waist. Butler intervened, saying he would court-martial Christine and Francis if they did not clear off.

Eventually she reached London where she asked to be sent to Poland to help the resistance. She spent Christmas and the New Year in southern Italy waiting for the go-ahead to start a new mission in her homeland.

On 17 January 1945, the Soviet Army entered Warsaw. The Germans had left almost nothing but rubble. One local radio transmission described it as 'Absolutely everyone has lost absolutely everything'. Poland was occupied by Soviet troops. The US ambassador in Moscow wrote to his president warning him that Soviet intentions in Poland were to establish a totalitarian state that would end all notions of personal liberty. The free Poland that Christine had fought for and hoped to return to no longer existed. Her mission was cancelled and she returned to Cairo. She burnt the clothes that had been issued to her for disguise, saying, 'That's the end.'

In September 1944, Virginia Hall returned to London having spent a lot of time with Goillot. She transferred to OSS Western Europe in the hope of being sent into Vienna to help organise the resistance in advance of the Allied armies entering Austria. Events moved too fast and the operation was cancelled. She then became part of Western Europe Special Operations but the war ended before she could be deployed.

Before Pearl and Henri left France they attended a formal lunch given by a visiting French delegation. Henri was wearing British battledress and one of the delegation began to talk to him in English. Henri told him to relax as he was French. At this point the man asked Henri what he, a Frenchman, was doing in a British uniform and said he considered him to be a deserter. When Pearl heard this she cornered the man and told him that they had just fought a war, English and French side by side, and nobody had cared so long as they were killing Germans and throwing them out of France.

In January 1945, Pearl was recommended for a Military Cross but she was ineligible because she was a civilian. She was then nominated for an MBE (Civil Division). Because she had fought as a civilian she was not entitled to the military form of the decoration. She turned it down saying that there was nothing remotely civil about the battles she had been fighting in France.

Hitler spent the last four months of the war in Berlin, living underground in a bunker constructed below the Reich Chancellery where his reign had started with such swagger in 1933. Above his head the Russians were swarming into the capital and Germany lay in ruins. In the early hours of 29 April he married his mistress, dictated his will and shot himself. A week later, at 2.41 a.m. on 7 May, the Germans surrendered unconditionally to the Allies. The Thousand Year Reich was over.

AFTER THE WAR

Andrée Borrel

Andrée Borrel was awarded a posthumous Croix de Guerre.

Christine Granville

Christine Granville was eventually awarded the George Medal. Part of the very long citation describes her negotiations to get the release of Cammaerts, Fielding and Sorensen:

> The nerve, coolness and devotion to duty and high courage of this lady which inspired and brought to a successful conclusion this astonishing coup de main must certainly be considered as one of the most remarkable personal exploits of the war and in the circumstances I have the honour to recommend that her courage be recognised with the immediate award of the George Cross.

The recommendation was downgraded to an OBE and then later upgraded again to the George Medal.

Christine badly wanted to be made a British citizen. Xan Fielding wrote about her:

After the physical suffering and mental strain she had suffered for more than six years in our service ... she needed, probably more than any other agent we employed, security for life. After her outstanding personal contribution to our victory, she deserved it. Yet a few months after the armistice she was dismissed with a month's salary and left in Cairo to fend for herself.

An official reported: 'She is no longer wanted ... Unless we have any likely job in the offing I suggest it would be a simpler matter to arrange for her to resign her commission and go back to that civilian life from whence she came. No employment here.'

In 1946, after a long battle, Christine was finally recognised as a British citizen. For the next four years she lived a peripatetic and unsettled life of great emotional complexity. In 1950 she enrolled as a stewardess with the Union-Castle Line. A fellow steward became obsessed with her and on Sunday 15 June 1952 he stabbed her to death in the Shelbourne Hotel in South Kensington where she had a room. She was buried in the Roman Catholic Cemetery in Kensal Green. Her portrait and some of her effects including her Fairbairn–Sykes SOE-issue dagger and her medals are held by the Polish Institute and Sikorski Museum in London.

Several biographies have been written about her, of which by far the best is Clare Mulley's authoritative and informed *The Spy Who Loved: The Secrets and Lives of Christine Granville, Britain's First Female Special Agent of World War II*.

Virginia Hall

Virginia was awarded the US Distinguished Service Cross, the highest award that can be given to a member of the United States Army. It is given for extreme gallantry and risk of life in actual combat with an armed enemy. Virginia Hall was the only civilian woman to receive the award in the Second World War. On 12 May 1945 a memorandum was sent by the director of OSS, William J. Donovan, to the president, briefing him about Virginia's award:

Miss Virginia Hall, an American civilian working for this agency [OSS] in the European Theatre of Operation has been awarded the Distinguished Service Cross for extraordinary heroism in connection with military operations against the enemy. We understand that Miss Hall is the first civilian in this war to receive the Distinguished Service Cross.

Despite the fact that she was well known to the Gestapo, Miss Hall voluntarily returned to France in March 1944 to assist in sabotage operations against the Germans. Through her courage and physical endurance, even though she had previously lost a leg in an accident, Miss Hall, with two American officers, succeeded in organising, arming and training three FFI Battalions which took part in many engagements with the enemy and a number of acts of sabotage including the demolition of many bridges, the destruction of a number of supply trains, and the disruption of enemy communications. As a result of the demolition of one bridge, a German convoy was ambushed and during a bitter struggle 150 Germans were killed and 500 were captured. In addition Miss Hall provided radio communication between London Headquarters and the Resistance forces in the Haute Loire Department, transmitting and receiving operational and intelligence information. This was the most dangerous type of work as the enemy, whenever two or more direction finders could be tuned in on a transmitter, were able to locate the transmitting point to within a couple of hundred yards. It was frequently necessary for Miss Hall to change her headquarters in order to avoid detection.

Inasmuch as an award of this kind has not been made in the present war you may wish to make the presentation personally. Miss Hall is currently in the European Theatre of Operations.

Virginia declined to accept the president's offer, saying she was 'still operational and most anxious to get busy'.

In June 1945 Virginia wrote a detailed report about the double agent Alesch in the hope that she might mobilise American counter-intelligence to find him. She then went to Lyon to find out what had happened to the comrades she left behind. Many had been arrested and died in captivity. Some like Mme Guérin and Dr Rousset had survived torture and starvation and had returned.

In 1950, Virginia married Paul Goillot and a year later joined the CIA. She died on 12 July 1982; Goillot died five years later.

Noor Inayat Khan

Noor Inayat Khan was awarded the Croix de Guerre and the George Cross. Her citation for the George Cross contains several major inaccuracies but nevertheless sums up her courage:

> Assistant Section Officer Nora INAYAT-KHAN was the first woman operator to be infiltrated into enemy occupied France, and was landed by Lysander aircraft on 16th June, 1943. During the weeks immediately following her arrival, the Gestapo made mass arrests in the Paris Resistance groups to which she had been detailed. She refused however to abandon what had become the principal and most dangerous post in France, although given the opportunity to return to England, because she did not wish to leave her French comrades without communications and she hoped also to rebuild her group. She remained at her post therefore and did the excellent work which earned her a posthumous Mention in Despatches.
>
> The Gestapo had a full description of her, but knew only her code name 'Madeleine'. They deployed considerable forces in their effort to catch her and so break the last remaining link with London. After 3 months, she was betrayed to the Gestapo and taken to their H.Q. in the Avenue Foch. The Gestapo had found her codes and messages and were now in a position to work back to London. They asked her to co-operate, but she refused and gave them no information of any kind. She was imprisoned in one of the cells on the 5th floor of the Gestapo H.Q. and remained there for several weeks during which time she made two unsuccessful attempts at escape. She was asked to sign a declaration that she

would make no further attempts, but she refused and the Chief of the Gestapo obtained permission from Berlin to send her to Germany for 'safe custody'. She was the first agent to be sent to Germany.

Assistant Section Officer INAYAT-KHAN was sent to Karlsruhe in November 1943, and then to Pforzheim where her cell was apart from the main prison. She was considered to be a particularly dangerous and unco-operative prisoner. The Director of the prison has also been interrogated and has confirmed that Assistant Section Officer INAYAT-KHAN, when interrogated by the Karlsruhe Gestapo, refused to give any information whatsoever, either as to her work or her colleagues.

She was taken with three others to Dachau Camp on the 12 September 1944. On arrival, she was taken to the crematorium and shot.

Assistant Section Officer INAYAT-KHAN displayed the most conspicuous courage, both moral and physical over a period of more than 12 months.

Noor is commemorated by a statue in Gordon Square, London and her image appeared on a Royal Mail stamp, part of a set to celebrate 'Remarkable Lives'.

Noor's life and work have been movingly described in Shrabani Basu's *Spy Princess: The Life of Noor Inayat Khan*.

Violette Szabo

The French awarded Violette Szabo the Croix de Guerre. The British gave her the George Cross, which is granted for 'acts of the greatest heroism or the most conspicuous courage in circumstances of extreme danger'. Her citation too contains some major inaccuracies but even so is true to her spirit:

Madame Szabo volunteered to undertake a particularly dangerous mission in France. She was parachuted into France in

April, 1944, and undertook the task with enthusiasm. In her execution of the delicate researches entailed she showed great presence of mind and astuteness. She was twice arrested by the German security authorities but each time managed to get away. Eventually, however, with other members of her group, she was surrounded by the Gestapo in a house in the south-west of France. Resistance appeared hopeless but Madame Szabo, seizing a Sten-gun and as much ammunition as she could carry, barricaded herself in part of the house and, exchanging shot for shot with the enemy, killed or wounded several of them. By constant movement, she avoided being cornered and fought until she dropped exhausted. She was arrested and had to undergo solitary confinement. She was then continuously and atrociously tortured but never by word or deed gave away any of her acquaintances or told the enemy anything of any value. She was ultimately executed. Madame Szabo gave a magnificent example of courage and steadfastness.

Several biographies have been written about her including one by her daughter, Tania Szabó, *Young, Brave and Beautiful*. In 1958 a film about Violette's life was released, *Carve Her Name with Pride*, based on the book of the same title. Among the many other commemorations of Violette's life there is a museum to her memory, and a painting of her on the Stockwell War Monument near her family home. The Royal College of Music offers the Violette Szabo GC Memorial Prize for pianists who accompany singers.

NANCY WAKE

Nancy Wake was one of the most decorated women to work for SOE's F Section. Her awards include the George Medal, the Croix de Guerre and the Légion d'Honneur. When she was offered an award by Australia 'I told the government they could stick their medals where the monkey stuck his nuts. The thing is if they gave me a medal now, it wouldn't be love so I don't want anything from them.' In February 2004 she was made a Companion of the Order of Australia. Her citation for the George Medal read:

This officer was parachuted into France on 29th November 1944, as assistant to an organiser who was taking over the direction of an important circuit in Central France. The day after their arrival she and her chief found themselves stranded and without directions through the arrest of their contact, but ultimately reached their rendezvous by their own initiative. She worked for several months helping to train and instruct Maquis groups.

Lieutenant Wake took part in several engagements with the enemy, and showed the utmost bravery under fire. During a German attack, due to the arrival by parachute of two American officers to help in the Maquis, she personally took command of a section of 10 men whose leader was demoralised. She led them to within point-blank range of the enemy, directed their fire, rescued the two American officers and withdrew in good order. She showed exceptional courage and coolness in the face of enemy fire. When the Maquis group with which she was working was broken up by large-scale German attacks and wireless contact was lost, Lieutenant Wake went along to find a wireless operator through whom she could contact London. She covered some 200 kilometres on foot and by remarkable steadfastness and perseverance succeeded in getting a message through to London. It was largely due to these efforts that the circuit was able to start work again. Lieutenant Wake's organising ability, endurance, courage and complete disregard for her own safety earned her the respect and admiration of all. The Maquis troops, most of them rough and difficult to handle, accepted orders from her, and treated her as one of their own male officers.

In 1957 she married an RAF officer, John Forward, and the couple lived in Australia. In 1985 she published her autobiography, *The White Mouse*, which became a bestseller. After John Forward died in 1997 Nancy moved to England and became a resident at the

Stafford Hotel in St James's Place, near Piccadilly, formerly a British and American forces club during the war. She had been introduced to her first 'bloody good drink' there by the general manager Louis Burdet, who had also worked for the Resistance. In 2003, Nancy moved to the Royal Star and Garter Home, in Richmond, London, where she remained until her death on 7 August 2011. She was ninety-eight years old. Her ashes were scattered near Montluçon, on 11 March 2013.

Pearl Witherington

After turning down the MBE (Civil Division) Pearl was later offered and accepted the military version of the honour. It upset her that she was not given her parachute wings. Officially a parachutist has to complete five jumps before winning the coveted badge. Pearl had only done three when she was sent into battle. She said: '... the chaps did four training jumps, and the fifth was operational – and you only got your wings after a total of five jumps. So I was not entitled – and for 63 years I have been moaning to anybody who would listen because I thought it was an injustice.' In April 2006 she at last received her wings and this was the award she treasured the most. She was also a holder of the Légion d'Honneur and before she died she was granted a CBE.

Pearl and Henri Cornioley were married in London in 1944 and stayed together until Henri died in 1991. The couple had one daughter, Claire. On 24 February 2008, Pearl died in the Loire Valley in France. She was ninety-three.

Agnès Humbert

Agnès Humbert spent four years in captivity and was released by the United States 3rd Army. She immediately went to work helping to track down war criminals and at the same time set up a soup kitchen for refugees. She insisted that the food be given to everybody, including German civilians. After the war she went back to the museum and wrote books on art. In 1949 she was awarded the Croix de Guerre with Silver Gilt Palm for bravery. She spent her last years living with her son and died on 19 September 1963 aged sixty-eight.

MAURICE BUCKMASTER

After the war Buckmaster returned to the Ford Motor Company as a public affairs manager. He wrote his memoirs and was awarded an OBE. He died on 17 April 1992 aged ninety.

VERA ATKINS

After the war Vera Atkins spent some time trying to establish what had happened to the women of F Section who did not return. She then worked for UNESCO as first an office manager and then a director, retiring in 1961. She was made a CBE and died on 24 January 2000 aged ninety-two. Many secrets went with her.

THE OPPOSITION

ROBERT ALESCH

The double agent was arrested and tried. In his defence he claimed that he too had been a victim of the Germans. He was found guilty and executed.

HUGO BLEICHER

At the end of the war Bleicher was arrested, interrogated, tried and imprisoned. On his release he ran a tobacco shop and wrote a memoir. He died in 1982.

KARL BÖMELBURG

He assumed a false identity after the war, and in 1946 died of a fractured skull when falling on ice. In 1950 he was tried *in absentia* for war crimes and condemned to death.

MATHILDE CARRÉ

After the war the French tried Carré for treason. Her death sentence was commuted to twenty years in prison, of which she served five. She wrote a memoir and died in 2007, a blind recluse.

HANS JOSEF KIEFFER

He was arrested and tried for war crimes. He was hanged on 27 June 1947.

THE ENIGMA: HENRI DÉRICOURT

In 1946 Déricourt was arrested and tried by the French. Nicolas Bodington testified that he had authorised Déricourt to maintain contact with the Germans and he was acquitted. There are many theories about what Déricourt was really up to, including one that he was a triple agent working for MI6. He died in a plane crash in November 1962, taking his secrets with him.

ACKNOWLEDGEMENTS

Three people helped at the birth of this book. The first was my wife, Alexandra Pringle, who had always encouraged me to write about the women of SOE. When I started the research she had one word of advice: 'timelines', and how right she was. The second was my literary agent Patrick Walsh, who put in a great deal of effort working with me on the idea and the proposal. The third was my editor and publisher at Simon & Schuster, Iain MacGregor, who was unequivocal in his enthusiasm for the project and his determination to publish the book. I would like to thank all three for their support.

Elspeth Forbes-Robertson is one of three SOE experts who have helped me; she very kindly read the manuscript and gave me notes. The second expert is Dr Steven Kippax, a special-forces soldier turned academic, who knows more about SOE than almost anyone in the world. He gave me good advice and read the manuscript. Alan Ogden, the third expert, has written several books about SOE. He too read the manuscript and gave me the most meticulous set of notes, maps, and links to additional material.

Very few of the men and women who served with SOE are still alive, but I was lucky enough to be introduced to Noreen Riols, who as a very young woman served in Baker Street. I spent a morning with Noreen and she was very generous with her memories. I met and interviewed two FANYs, Jean Argles who was a cipher clerk in Baker Street and Geraldine Norris who is a serving officer. I have talked to some family members of SOE agents and give special thanks to Joanna Cammaerts, Francis Cammaerts's daughter. Tony Neville, who was a neighbour and friend of Vera Atkins, talked to me about the sort of woman she was.

I have interviewed several soldiers for this project and would especially like to thank Charles Guthrie, Mike and Mark Carleton-Smith (father and son), Jamie Lowther-Pinkerton, Geoffrey Matthews, Simon Davie and Victor Gregg who worked for M16 during the Cold War and knows the dangers of undercover work. I would also like to thank two officers of the Royal Navy, Chris Stanford and James Fanshawe. Phillip Athill of Abbot and Holder spent a lot of time talking to me about Brian Stonehouse, for which many thanks. Sacha Llewellyn and Paul Liss, of Liss Llewellyn Fine Art, kindly sent me visual references to England during the war.

Of the people who have written about SOE, I would like to thank, in no special order, Sarah Helm, Giles Milton, Nigel Perrin, Ben Macintyre, Shrabani Basu, Ray Jenkins and Clare Mulley.

From writers working in the London Library, Victoria Hislop, Philip Eade, Rebecca Fogg and Adrian Wilsdon have been very helpful, as has my old friend Nigel Williams. Emily Gunning kindly translated German documents for me and Elizabeth Gres was most helpful about the Polish language. Geoffrey Pigeon helped me with the technicalities of the SOE portable wireless transmitter.

I would like to thank my daughters Nell Gifford and Clover Stroud, also my friends Roger and Wendy Lambert, Jeremy and Kirstie Hardie, Giles Havergal, Kerry Crabbe and the poet Scarlett Sabet, who have all taken a lively interest in the book's progress.

I must thank the staff of the London Library, the National Archive at Kew, the Imperial War Museum in London, the British Library and the National Archives and Records Administration in Washington, where William Cunliffe, special assistant, Archive Operations, was a mine of information on Virginia Hall.

I would like to thank everyone at Simon & Schuster, especially Harriet Dobson, and Sian Wilson who designed the jacket. Last but by no means least I must thank my copy-editor, Martin Bryant.

It goes without saying that any errors in this book are entirely my own.

Rick Stroud, London 2016

NOTES

A NOTE ON SOURCES

In the research for this book I have used the SOE files in the National Archive (NA), especially the HS9 and KV2/3/6 range. In America I spent some time at the National Archives and Records Administration in Washington (NARA), researching the OSS Research Group 226 range of physical files. I also used the microfilm archive RG 226/ M1623 rolls 1–10. I was greatly assisted by William Cunliffe, Special Assistant, Archive Operations. Mr Cunliffe has a special interest in Virginia Hall and has established his own file with copies of almost all the Virginia Hall and related reports. He described this file as the 'fruit of nearly 20 years work'; both by himself and other researchers. It proved to be an invaluable resource and made my time in the NARA very productive. For reference purposes I have called the file NARA/RG226/CF (the CF stands for 'Cunliffe File'). I spent some time at the Imperial War Museum in London, especially the sound archive. The book was written in the London Library, which has an excellent Second World War collection. The maps for the many journeys, especially Nancy Wake's epic bike ride, were all in the Institut géographique national, 1:100 000 series. I am very grateful to Alan Ogden for the loan of his Aurillac St-Flour Map 155 in the same series, marked up with all Nancy Wake's peregrinations. Like the true soldier and SOE expert he is, Alan had walked the course.

Prologue

p.xvii 'Do you understand?': M. R. D. Foot, *SOE in France* (HMSO, 1966).

p.xviii 'Yes, good luck to you.': Imperial War Museum (Oral History) Selwyn Jepson, 9331, Reel 1.

p.xix   'Welcome to Tangmere. My name's Verity': The interior of the house, the details and the procedure are all accurate. I have made up the two lines of dialogue from Verity.

p.xxi   'That book will have to be': Hugh Verity, *We Landed By Moonlight*, p.94.

Chapter 1: 'It was in Vienna that I formed my own opinion of the Nazis'

p.1   The ceremony should: Ian Kershaw, *Hitler 1889–1936: Hubris* (The Penguin Press, 1998), p.433.

p.2   His first order: Radio Broadcast Frankfurt 1933. Quoted in Stephen Henry Roberts, *The House that Hitler Built* (Kessinger Publishing, 2003), p.63.

p.2   Sebastian Haffner, a 25-year-old: Sebastian Haffner, *Defying Hitler*, p.89. Haffner's real name was Raimond Pretzel. He changed his name after he left Germany to protect relatives left behind.

p.2   Later he and his father: Haffner, p.89.

p.3   The crowd went berserk: Kershaw, p.434.

p.3   In the library a: Haffner, p.113.

p.4   The next day he crossed Berlin: Haffner, pp.118–123.

p.4   In a speech to the SA: Quoted in Frank McDonough, *The Gestapo, the Myth and Reality of Hitler's Secret Police*, p.29.

p.4   'Some of them are psychopathic cases': Messersmith papers, University of Delaware, quoted in Erik Larson, *In the Garden of the Beasts*, Kindle edition.

p.5   'Most of the men were': Peter Fitzsimons, *Nancy Wake* (HarperCollins, 2012).

p.7   He described Krystyna as: Karbowska, *Getting to know Mankiewicz*; quoted in Clare Mulley, *The Spy Who Loved* (Macmillan, 2012).

p.10 That afternoon a boy: Alfons Heck, *A Child of Hitler: Germany in the Days When God Wore a Swastika* (American Travel Press, 2011).

p.11 throughout the afternoon and evening: Hugh Carlton Greene, *Daily Telegraph*, 11 November 1938.

p.11 In June 1939 a paper: M. R. D. Foot, *SOE in France*, p.8.

p.11 'Undoubtedly, therefore, the most': Foot, *SOE in France*, p.6.

p.13 Everyone was packing: Nancy Wake, *The Autobiography of the Woman the Gestapo Called the White Mouse*, p.28.

p.14 He told his generals: Address by Adolf Hitler, 1 September 1939; retrieved from the archives of the Avalon Project at Yale Law School.

p.14 He had also commanded: William L. Shirer, *The Rise and Fall of the Third Reich*, p.531.

p.15 Overhead silver barrage: Mollie Panter-Downes, letter to *NY* magazine, 9 September 1939, quoted in Eye Witness to History (http://www.eyewitnesstohistory.com).

p.16 Daily reports about: Giżycki, *Winding Trail*, quoted in Clare Mulley, *The Spy Who Loved*, p.389.

p.16 Next she was interviewed: Mulley, p.37.

p.17 Taylor ended his: NA HS9–612.

p.18 Krystyna's float of £250 would be worth about £15,000 in 2017.

Chapter 2: The Phoney War

p.20 Kowerski was a: Clare Mulley, *The Spy Who Loved*, p.45.

p.20 He told her that: Madeleine Masson, *Christine: A Search for Christine Granville*, p.47.

p.21 They spent that night: Masson, p.48.

p.23 Krystyna met representatives: NA/HS9/612.

p.24 One day, while sitting: 'Krystyna Skarbek: Re-viewing Britain's Legendary Polish Agent', *The Polish Review*, vol. XLIX, no. 3 (2004), p.950.

p.25 A month later: William L. Shirer, *The Rise and Fall of the Third Reich*, p.162.

Chapter 3: 1940: Paris and the Fall of France

p.26 'The great stations': Clare Boothe, *European Spring*, pp.270–1.

p.28 'If we let France': Boothe, pp.289–90.

p.29 By 10 June: Alexander Werth, *The Last Days of Paris*, p.146.

p.29 She was grateful: Agnès Humbert, *Résistance: Memoirs of Occupied France*, p.1.

p.29 On the streets: Werth, *The Last Days of Paris*, p.157.

p.29 She could not bring herself: Humbert, *Résistance*, p.3.

p.31 A little-known French General: Edward Speers, *Assignment to Catastrophe*, quoted in Robert Gildea, *Fighters in the Shadows* (Faber & Faber, 2015).

p.31 'Whatever happens the flame': Reprinted in the *Guardian*, 'Great speeches of the 20th century', 27 April 2007; Charles de Gaulle broadcast the speech on 18 June 1940 with Churchill's permission.

p.32 Nancy Wake heard: Nancy Wake, *The Autobiography of the Woman the Gestapo Called the White Mouse*, p.38.

p.32   The deaths of: Wake, *The Autobiography*, p.12.

p.32   'When we heard': Denise Domenach-Lallich, *Demain il fera beau*, p.62.

Chapter 4: '33 Hints for the Occupied'

p.33   She was transferred: Vincent Nouzille, *L'espionne: Virginia Hall, une Américaine dans la guerre* (Fayard, 2007).

p.34   She arrived at the: Agnés Humbert, *Résistance: Memoirs of Occupied France*, p.9.

p.34   'You won't find copies of these tips': Jean Texcier, 'Conseils à l' Occupé' (available on Musée de la Résistance website).

p.34   Humbert went home: Humbert, *Résistance*, p.41.

p.34   The people who: M. R. D. Foot, *SOE in France*, p.9.

p.36   On the train she met: Nouzille, *L'espionne*, Kindle edition.

p.37   They began to talk: Roman Garby-Czerniawski, *The Big Network* (George Ronald, 1961), p.43.

p.37   He nicknamed her *La Chatte*: Garby-Czerniawski, *The Big Network*, p.45.

p.37   On Bastille Day: The description of the Bastille Day parade is based on Pathé News documentary film of the event. Pathé News ID: 1051.01 Canister 40/58.

p.38   When the general: Charles de Gaulle, *Lettres, notes et carnets*, quoted in Robert Gildea, *Fighters in the Shadows*.

p.38   When the crowd surged round: Henri Frenay, *La Nuit Finira: Mémoires de Résistance 1940–1945*, quoted in Robert Gildea, *Fighters in the Shadows*, p.42.

p.38   She found Pétain: Nancy Wake, *The Autobiography of the Woman the Gestapo Called the White Mouse*, p.43.

p.39   Denise Domenach complained: Denise Domenach-Lallich, *Demain il fera beau*, p.63.

p.39   'Me, I whisper': Domenach-Lallich, *Demain il fera beau*, p.65.

p.42   In Budapest, Krystyna Skarbek's: Clare Mulley, *The Spy Who Loved*, p.40.

p.42   One officer said: Mulley, *The Spy Who Loved*, p.74.

p.42   Krystyna made another: Mulley, *The Spy Who Loved*, p.77.

Chapter 5: 1941: F Section v the Abwehr

p.45   One contact Virginia Hall: Virginia Hall personal file NA HS9/647/4.

p.45   The next day Bodington: NA HS9/647/4.

p.46   After spending an: Clare Mulley, *The Spy Who Loved*, p.97.

p.46   In her cell Krystyna: Wladimir Ledóchowski quoted in Clare Mulley,

The Spy Who Loved, p.98.

p.47 In the embassy: Mulley, *The Spy Who Loved*, p.101.

p.48 The interrogators sniggered: Agnés Humbert, *Résistance: Memoirs of Occupied France*, p.51.

p.49 The tommy guns, knives: M. R. D. Foot, *SOE in France*, p.149.

p.49 A document arrived on: Foot, *SOE in France*, p.150.

p.49 May God help us in this battle: Quoted by Prof. Randal Bytwerk, German Propaganda Archive, Calvin College Michigan. Prof. Bytwerk gives the reference as from Philipp Bouhler (ed.), *Der Großdeutsche Freiheitskampf. Reden Adolf Hitlers. Franz Ihrer 1942.* (*Der Führer an das Deutsche volk*, 22 Juni 1941, pp.51–61.)

p.50 The expert teaching: Arthur Christie, Personal File National Archive HS9/313/1.

p.50 As well as explosives: Virginia Hall personal file NA HS9/647/4.

p.51 To substantiate her: NA HS9/647/4.

p.51 Soon after she arrived she: William Simpson, *I Burned My Fingers*, p.36.

p.51 One was Mme: Vincent Nouzille, *L'espionne: Virginia Hall, une Américaine dans la guerre*, Kindle edition.

p.52 Hall and Rousset: NA HS9/647/4.

p.52 One German staff officer wrote in his diary: William Shirer, *The Rise and Fall of the Third Reich*, p.864.

p.52 While the Soviet Union: Foot, *SOE in France*, p.21.

p.52 His new boss, Colin Gubbins: Maurice Buckmaster, *They Fought Alone*, p.11.

p.53 Her accent was clipped: Tony Neville, author interview. Neville was a neighbour of Atkins.

p.53 One of her staff confessed: Noreen Riols, author interview. Riols served in F Section but was too young to be allowed into the field.

p.53 Buckmaster found that: Buckmaster, *They Fought Alone*, p.21.

p.54 They sent a reply: Roman Garby-Czerniawski, *The Big Network* (George Ronald, 1961), p.232.

p.55 Inside Czerniawski shook: Garby-Czerniawski, *The Big Network*, p.238.

p.55 Renée sat up: Gordon Young, *The Cat with Two Faces*, p.63.

p.57 Suddenly she was grabbed: Young, *The Cat with Two Faces*, p.64.

p.57 She wanted to die: Young, *The Cat with Two Faces*, p.66.

p.57 A steward came in: Mathilde Carré, *I Was the Cat*, p.35.

p.58 Bleicher took over: Lauran Paine, *Mathilde Carré: Double Agent*, p.96.

p.59 The reply was short: Young, *The Cat with Two Faces*, p.98.

Chapter 6: Radio Games

p.61 When the two men left: Gordon Young, *The Cat with Two Faces*, p.115.

p.62 With many apologies: Philippe de Vomécourt, *Who Lived to See the Day*, p.90.

p.62 Through her tears: Young, *The Cat with Two Faces*, p.129.

p.63 A tough young: Benjamin Cowburn, *No Cloak, No Dagger*, Kindle edition.

p.64 Cowburn began to flash: Cowburn, *No Cloak, No Dagger*, Kindle edition.

p.65 De Vomécourt, Cowburn and Carré walked: Cowburn, *No Cloak, No Dagger*, Kindle edition.

p.66 He took the unusual: M. R. D. Foot, *SOE in France*, p.172.

p.67 As a traitor: Foot, *SOE in France*, p.172.

p.67 Back in France: Cowburn, *No Cloak, No Dagger*, Kindle edition

p.67 The year 1941 was drawing to a close: Foot, *SOE in France*, pp.156–7.

p.67 The head of the Political Warfare Unit: Foot, *SOE in France*, p.11.

Chapter 7: 'If you could ever send me a piece of soap I should be both very happy and much cleaner'

p.69 Also in Lyon: Virginia Hall personal file NA HS9/647/4.

p.70 Humbert was accused: Agnés Humbert, *Résistance*, p.97.

p.70 In spite of: Eisenhower's quote comes from Martin Gilbert, *D-Day*, p.7.

p.71 When it was suggested: Sarah Helm, *A Life in Secrets: Vera Atkins and the Lost Agents of SOE*, p.24.

p.71 'Somewhat disinclined': Helm, *A Life in Secrets*, p.46

p.72 She was asked to: Nancy Wake, *The Autobiography of the Woman the Gestapo Called the White Mouse*, p.64.

p.73 If you sit in: Foot, *SOE in France*, p.190.

p.74 'If you could ever send me a piece of soap I should be both very happy and much cleaner': Virginia Hall personal file, HS9/647/4.

p.74 The pointy-nosed priest: NARA OSS Research Group 226. William Cunliffe personal file. Alesch interrogation report.

p.74 The reality was: Foot, *SOE in France*, p.183.

p.74 Then, an artist: Foot, *SOE in France*, p.183.

p.75 A new SOE: Foot, *SOE in France*, p.185.

p.76 The MI5 officer: NA HS9/183. Borrel's personal file.

p.76 Her lover, Maurice Dufour: John Vader, *The Prosper Double-Cross*, p.23. After the war legal action was taken against de Gaulle as a result of Dufour's treatment.

p.77 The Free French movement: NA HS9/183.

p.79 Le Chène gave: Rita Kramer, *Flames in the Field*, p.91.

p.79 Before being sent: NA HS9/183.

p.80 Alesch made contact with: Vincent Nouzille, *L'espionne*, Kindle edition.

p.80 When Virginia was told: NARA RG 226 CF (Virginia Hall, Alesch report).

p.80 She opened it to find: Nouzille, *L'espionne*, Kindle edition.

p.81 When he returned: NARA RG 226 CF (Virginia Hall, Alesch report).

p.81 Later Virginia heard: Nouzille, *L'espionne*, Kindle edition.

p.81 He explained that: NA HS9-647-4 V. Virginia Hall personal file, Alesch interrogation report.

p.83 Virginia checked up: Nouzille, *L'espionne*, Kindle edition.

p.83 Later she radioed: NARA RG 226 CF.

p.83 About the same time: Simon Kitson, *Police and Politics in Marseille 1936–1945*, Online Reference.

p.84 Déricourt admitted that: Robert Marshall, *All the King's Men* (HarperCollins, 1988).

p.85 Maurice Buckmaster heard about Déricourt: Foot, *SOE in France*, p.291.

p.85 MI5 said that: Marshall, *All the King's Men*, Kindle edition.

p.85 Even though he found: in *All the King's Men* Marshall quotes a letter from Selwyn Jepson.

p.85 When Vera Atkins saw: Marshall, *All the King's Men*, Kindle edition.

p.85 Buckmaster thought Suttill had: Francis J. Suttill, *Shadows in the Fog*, p.15.

p.86 He aborted the mission: Francis J. Suttill, *Shadows in the Fog*, p.34.

p.87 They had a plan: NA HS9/183.

p.87 Some of these: Francis J. Suttill, *Shadows*, p.42.

p.88 The American Consul: NARA RG 226 CF.

p.88 London replied that: NARA RG 226 CF.

p.88 'Thank you very much': Rita Kramer, *Flames*, p.97.

p.89 Nancy Wake took: Nancy Wake, *The Autobiography of the Woman the Gestapo Called the White Mouse*, p.60.

p.90 'She must be found': Nouzille, *L'espionne*, Kindle edition.

p.90 The next day the doctor was arrested: Marcel Ruby, *F Section SOE*, p.71.

p.92 a pleasant fellow: Hugh Verity, *We Landed by Moonlight*, p.19.

p.92 Her objections were overruled: Marshall, *All the King's Men*, Kindle edition.

pp.92–3 He assessed that: Shrabani Basu, *Spy Princess*, Kindle edition.

Chapter 8: 1943: 'There are hard blows in prospect ...'

p.95 Later Buckmaster recommended her: NA HS7/121.

p.95 When she was arrested: NARA RG 226 CF.

p.95 During the first weeks: Simon Kitson, *Police and Politics in Marseille, 1936–1945*, Online Reference.

p.96 Without her knowing: Nancy Wake, *The Autobiography of the Woman the Gestapo Called the White Mouse*, p.72.

p.96 Far to the east in Russia: William Shirer, *The Rise and Fall of the Third Reich*, p.930.

p.96 Paulus sat on: Shirer, *The Rise and Fall*, p.930.

p.97 On 5 February, the Combined Commanders: James Fanshawe, late Royal Navy, private collection. The document was written by Fanshawe's father and is labelled 'Top Secret'. The cover is stamped with 'Copy no. 4' and 'Notes by Combined Planning Staff'. It is dated 5 February 1943 and has 'c.c. (42) 108 (P.S.Os' Draft)' typed in the top left-hand corner.

p.98 'I am Nancy Fiocca': Wake, *The Autobiography*, p.83.

p.98 From the end of January: NA HS7/121.

p.99 One SOE officer in London: HS7/121.

p.99 Then he gave her some: Robert Marshall, *All the King's Men* (HarperCollins, 1988).

p.99 At the end of: Marshall, *All the King's Men*.

p.102 One of the most important: M. R. D. Foot, *SOE in France*, p.275.

p.103 He was ambitious: Hugo Bleicher, *Colonel Henri's Story: The War Memoirs of Hugo Bleicher, Former German Secret Agent*, p.52.

p.104 'You cannot imagine': Clare Mulley, *The Spy Who Loved*, p.140.

p.104 'His brother has': NA HS4/201.

p.104 She refused and: HS9/588/2, quoted in Mulley, *The Spy Who Loved*, p.141.

p.105 Christine herself offered: Mulley, *The Spy Who Loved*, p.148.

p.105 She never mentioned her again: Mulley, *The Spy Who Loved*, p.157.

p.105 But she worked hard: NA HS9/83/5.

p.106 Colin Gubbins said: Foot, *SOE in France*, p.95.

p.106 Her instructors worried: NA HS9/836/5.

p.107 One instructor at Beaulieu: NA HS9/836/5.

p.108 She has an unstable: NA HS9/836/5.

p.108 Buckmaster went to: Shrabani Basu, *Spy Princess*, Kindle edition.

p.109 At the mention: Leo Marks, *Between Silk and Cyanide* (HarperCollins, 1998).

p.110 Some documents were: Bleicher, *Colonel Henri's Story*, p.61.

p.112 By the evening: Basu, *Spy Princess*, Kindle edition.

p.113 When he discovered: Prosper Report, 19 June 1943. NA/HS9/91/1.

p.114   During the day: Basu, *Spy Princess*, Kindle edition.

p.115   Suddenly a soldier: 1375 W 70, Archives departmental, Blois, de Loire et Cher, quoted in Francis J. Suttill, *Shadows in the Fog*, p.147.

p.115   Culioli tried to drive: Jean Overton Fuller, *The German Penetration of SOE*, p.66.

Chapter 9: *Nacht und Nebel*

p.117   The next night: NA/HS6/440.

p.117   After a pause: Francis J. Suttill, *Shadows in the Fog*, p.151.

p.118   Madame Fèvre glimpsed: Jean Overton Fuller, *The German Penetration of SOE*, p.74.

p.119   After forty-eight hours: Letter from Jean Overton Fuller to Suttill; Suttill, *Shadows in the Fog*, p.155.

p.119   At first Suttill did: Suttill, *Shadows in the Fog*, p.155.

p.119   On 27 June, Noor: Shrabani Basu, *Spy Princess*, Kindle edition.

p.120   On 7 July, in the: Sarah Helm, *A Life in Secrets*, p.285.

p.120   The Records Officer: Helm, *A Life in Secrets*, p.35.

p.121   Then a signal came in: Helm, *A Life in Secrets*, p.285.

p.121   Penelope Torr went: Helm, *A Life in Secrets*, p.36.

p.122   In London Nicolas Bodington: NA HS9/171, Bodington personal file.

p.122   Noor was now: Basu, *Spy Princess*, Kindle edition.

p.122   The number of arrested: Basu, *Spy Princess*.

p.123   He also reported: NA HS9/171. Bodington personal file.

p.124   From Madeleine – Ops: NA HS9/836. Khan personal file.

p.125   She returned to the bookshop: NA HS9/836/5.

p.125   The doctor had: Basu, *Spy Princess*, Kindle edition.

p.126   Noor's endless dance: NA HS9/836/5.

p.127   Buckmaster sent Noor: Quoted in Helm, *A Life in Secrets*, p.43

p.128   Field Marshal Gerd von Rundstedt had already: M. R. D. Foot, *SOE in France*, p.314. This is what von Rundstedt said at his war-crimes trial.

p.129   Witherington's orders were: NA HS9/355. Cornioley personal file.

p.129   On her second: Pearl Witherington Cornioley, *Code Name Pauline*, Kindle edition.

p.132   You have probably: NA HS9/1435. Szabo personal file.

p.132   At Gestapo headquarters: Basu, *Spy Princess*. It is very likely that Renée was Emile Garry's sister. This has often been asserted but never conclusively proved. In 1947 Renée Garry was tried by a French military court and acquitted of betraying Noor.

p.134   Noor began to scream: Jean Overton Fuller, *Noor-un-nisa Inayat Khan: Madeleine*. Vogt's account of the arrest, p.207.

p.135   'Give me your hand': Fuller, *Noor-un-nisa Inayat Khan: Madeleine*, p.208.

p.136   Finally she said to: Fuller, *Noor-un-nisa Inayat Khan: Madeleine*, p.211.

p.137   At one point in: Fuller, *Noor-un-nisa Inayat Khan: Madeleine*, p.212.

p.138   Marks went to Buckmaster: Leo Marks, *Between Silk and Cyanide* (HarperCollins, 1998).

p.138   *Sonja* was Weil's fiancée: Helm, *A Life in Secrets*, p.296.

p.139   As a result: Ray Jenkins, *A Pacifist at War*, p.98.

p.139   He replied a month: HS9/647/5. Hall's personal file.

p.140   He was introduced: Clare Mulley, *The Spy Who Loved*, p.166.

p.140   Before he handed it over: Fuller, *Noor-un-nisa Inayat Khan: Madeleine*, p.214.

p.142   'Cheer up. You're not alone': Fuller, *Noor-un-nisa Inayat Khan: Madeleine*, p.229.

p.143   Night fell and Starr: Fuller, *Noor-un-nisa Inayat Khan: Madeleine*, p.235.

p.145   They realised that: Fuller, *Noor-un-nisa Inayat Khan: Madeleine*, p.236.

p.146   The next day: Fuller, *Noor-un-nisa Inayat Khan: Madeleine*, p.241.

p.147   Meanwhile at his new: Jenkins, *A Pacifist at War*, p.101.

p.147   The interrogation report was: Déricourt file HS9/421.

p.148   She had grown tired: Nancy Wake, *The Autobiography of the Woman the Gestapo Called the White Mouse*, p.102.

p.149   Churchill raged against: Richard Overy, *Why the Allies Won*, p.141.

p.150   Around Christmas, Baker Street: Helm, *A Life in Secrets*, p.48.

Chapter 10: 'The life that I have …'

p.154   Through his efforts: M. R. D. Foot, *SOE in France*, p.312.

p.155   On 24 January 1944: NA/HS9/1435.

p.156   He described him as: NA/HS9/423.

p.156   She had fallen: Susan Ottaway, *Violette Szabo: The Life That I Have* (Leo Cooper, 2002).

p.156   They talked about: Foot, *SOE in France*, p.269.

p.156   Then they trudged: NARA/RG226(CF).

p.156   After arriving at the: NARA/RG226(CF).

p.157   He became indignant: NARA/RG226(CF).

p.158   Not far away: NA HS9/836/5.

p.159   On 8 April: Carole Seymour-Jones, *She Landed by Moonlight* (Hodder & Stoughton, 2013).

p.159   He asked her: NARA/RG/226 (CF).

p.159   When Maurice Southgate: Pearl Witherington Cornioley, *Code Name Pauline*, Kindle edition.

p.159   Pearl went in: Witherington Cornioley, *Code Name Pauline*, Kindle edition.

p.160   Other arrests followed: NA/HS9/13395/3.

p.161   When he was around: Nancy Wake, *The Autobiography of the Woman the Gestapo Called the White Mouse*, p.105. Nancy was wild even when under extreme pressure in the field. In an interview given to the *Australian News* in 2011, just before she died, Nancy summed up how she saw herself as a Resistance fighter. The article is headed 'Fearless Matriarch of Resistance' and she is quoted as saying: 'I'd see a German officer on the train or somewhere, sometimes dressed in civvies, but you could pick 'em. So, instead of raising suspicions I'd flirt with them, ask for a light and say my lighter was out of fuel ... A little powder and a little drink on the way, and I'd pass their posts and wink and say, "Do you want to search me?" God, what a flirtatious little bastard I was.'

p.161   Nancy's final training: NA/HS9/1545.

p.162   While Nancy was finishing: Ottaway, *Violette Szabo*, Kindle edition.

p.162   Marks, mesmerised by her looks: Leo Marks, *Between Silk and Cyanide*.

p.166   The briefing officer: NA/HS9/1545.

p.167   Once airborne Nancy: NA/177/HS6/570. Farmer's action report.

p.168   Southgate arrived to find: NA/177/HS6/570.

p.169   Sometimes she took: Author conversation with Bob Maloubier. I was able to talk to M. Maloubier on the telephone. We spoke for about fifteen minutes and agreed that I would call him later to arrange a visit. He died a few days later.

p.169   Across the Mediterranean: NA/HS9/612. 'Appreciation on proposed operation to prepare reception committee in Hungary'; quoted in Clare Mulley, *The Spy Who Loved*, p.170.

p.170   By now Virginia: NARA/190/140/844.

p.170   From America Virginia's: NARA/RG/226 (CF).

p.172   'I do not think': William Stanley Moss, 'Christine the Brave', *Picture Post*, 27 September 1952, p.30.

p.173   Seconds later he: NARA/RG226/M1623 rolls 6/7/8 René Dussaq Field Report.

p.173   Dussaq spent the: NARA/RG226/M1623 rolls 6/7/8 René Dussaq Field Report.

p.176   The two agents: Wake, *The Autobiography*, p.121.

Chapter 11: D-Day

p.177   Hundreds of similar: Leo Marks, *Between Silk and Cyanide*, p.521.

p.179   'They're trying to shake': Marks, *Between Silk and Cyanide*, p.552.

p.179 He was told: Max Hastings, *Das Reich*, p.78. Hastings was quoting Milton Shulman's *Defeat in the West*.

p.179 'Impression growing that the': Hastings, *Das Reich*, p.78. Hastings quotes the Army Group G War Diary.

p.180 Once more she just disappeared: Vincent Nouzille, *L'espionne*, Kindle edition.

p.180 Noor Khan read: I cannot be absolutely certain that Noor read about the invasion on the bottom of her food bowl.

p.180 They erected a large: Ray Jenkins, *A Pacifist at War*, p.154.

p.181 A signal went: Hastings, *Das Reich*, p.76.

p.182 Vera Atkins, who was: Hastings, *Das Reich*, p.22.

p.185 The woman who: Hastings, *Das Reich*, p.158.

p.185 In the yard: There are several differing descriptions of how Szabo was captured. I have based this on the testimony of Albert Tisserand who was the little boy mentioned. I have also used photographs of the farm and its surroundings as a basis for the details of the trees, railway line etc.

p.187 For a while there: Nancy Wake, *The Autobiography of the Woman the Gestapo Called the White Mouse*, p.127.

p.187 When in the end: Wake, *The Autobiography*, p.123.

p.188 In the morning orders: Wake, *The Autobiography*, p.130.

p.188 For days afterwards: NARA/RG226/M1623 rolls 6/7/8 René Dussaq Field Report.

p.189 A Resistance fighter: Pearl Witherington Cornioley, *Code Name Pauline*, Kindle edition.

p.190 The door was opened: NARA RG 226 (CF).

p.191 Virginia asked him: NARA RG 226 (CF).

p.192 The battle of Les Souches: Witherington Cornioley, *Code Name Pauline*, Kindle edition.

p.192 In the Vercors: Jenkins, *A Pacifist at War*, p.151.

p.193 In spite of the: Many historians claim that the Das Reich division was seriously delayed by the Resistance. In fact, the leading elements of the division reached the battlefield on schedule. I am indebted to Alan Ogden, late Grenadier Guards, for talking me through the logistical problems of moving a heavy armoured division hundreds of miles.

p.194 The next day: Wake, *The Autobiography*, p.133.

p.197 Descending around him: Elliot, NA/HS9/1648.

p.197 On 6 July, Andrée Borrel: NA/HS9/183.

p.199 To the right: Brian Stonehouse, unpublished diary.

p.200 In the officers' mess: Sarah Helm, *A Life in Secrets*, p.251. In her book Sarah Helm conducts a forensic investigation of what happened that day at Natzweiler-Struthof. Her investigation is described through the eyes of Vera Atkins, who interrogated survivors of the camp and also some of the guards who took part in the execution, especially Franz Burg. Atkins went on a post-war mission to find out what had happened to the missing women of F Section. Initially it was thought that Noor Khan was one of the four women executed. Noor was confused with Sonya Olschanezky, to whom she bore a striking similarity.

p.203   In the room: Helm, *A Life in Secrets*, p.259.

p.205   A few days later: Brian Stonehouse, unpublished diary.

Chapter 12: 'She led us like a man.'

p.206   On the night: Christine Granville, personal file NA/HS9/612.

p.206   The green light: Madeleine Masson, *Christine: A Search for Christine Granville*, p.182.

p.207   They told her: Joseph La Picirella, *Témoignages sur le Vercors*, quoted in Masson, *Christine*, p.188.

p.207   The town was alive: La Picirella, quoted in Masson, *Christine*, p.188.

p.207   There was a rumour: Clare Mulley, *The Spy Who Loved*, p.193.

p.207   He loved her: Xan Fielding, *Hide and Seek*, p.175.

p.207   He signalled to Brooks Richards: Mulley, *The Spy Who Loved*, p.201.

p.208   In the days: Ray Jenkins, *A Pacificist at War*, p.156.

p.208   Another read: Jenkins, *A Pacificist at War*, p.156.

p.208   The pilots waggled: Jenkins, *A Pacificist at War*, p.171.

p.209   People threw themselves: Jenkins, *A Pacificist at War*, p.171.

p.209   Their ammunition spent: Jenkins, *A Pacificist at War*, p.171.

p.209   For the rest of the day: Jenkins, *A Pacificist at War*, p.172; quoting Pierre Tanant, *Vercors*, pp.148–81.

p.210   'They don't want': Jenkins, *A Pacificist at War*, p.173.

p.211   Violette was moved: NA/HS9/1435.

p.213   No one appreciates: John Wheeler-Bennett, *The Nemesis of Power*, p.645.

p.213   Christine encoded Suttill's: Jenkins, *A Pacificist at War*, p.174.

p.215   Henri, her second in command: Carole Seymour-Jones, *She Landed by Moonlight* (Hodder & Stoughton, 2013).

p.215   'I am not sure': Pearl Witherington Cornioley, *Code Name Pauline* (Hodder & Stoughton, 2013).

p.216   In the foothills: Jenkins, *A Pacificist at War*,, p.185.

p.216   As she crossed: Arthur Funk, *Hidden Ally*, p.69. Also NA/72/ AJ/66/44.

p.217   On another occasion: Mulley, *The Spy Who Loved*, p.225.

p.218   By 26 July: Jenkins, *A Pacificist at War*, p.187.

p.218   General Blaskowitz, leader: Funk, *Hidden Ally*, p.56.

p.219   If they were: Nancy Wake, *The Autobiography of the Woman the Gestapo Called the White Mouse*, p.138.

p.219   The Germans did not: Jenkins, *A Pacificist at War*, p.187.

p.220   Noise from the crowd: Schley situation Report NARA/RG226/M1623 Roll 7.

p.222   The following day: Schley NARA/RG226/M1623 Roll 7.

p.222   Schley reported: Schley NARA/RG226/M1623 Roll 7.

p.222   The first part: Susan Ottoway, *Violette Szabo: The Life That I Have* (Leo Cooper, 2002).

p.223   By 12 August: Andrew Williams, *D-Day to Berlin*, Kindle edition.

p.223   They saw each: Ottoway, *Violette Szabo*, Kindle edition.

p.224   Nancy heard that: Wake, *The Autobiography*, p.142.

p.226   He told her: Mulley, *The Spy Who Loved*, p.229.

p.226   The men came: This description is based on a photograph in Wake's book *The Autobiography of the Woman the Gestapo Called the White Mouse*. It shows the Maquisards assembling outside Restaurant Tailhardat shortly before the raid.

p.227   In retribution for: American Army situation report NARA RG 226 M1623 Roll 8.

p.229   The streets of Paris: Matthew Cobb, *Eleven Days in August*, p.95.

p.229   Robert Alesch wobbled: US Army Intelligence Appraisal NARA RD226 Mi623 Roll 10.

p.230   Other Maquis commanders: Liddell Hart Archive, O'Reagan Papers, quoted in Mulley, *The Spy Who Loved*, p.244.

p.230   One bomb had hit: Guy Raymond, *Histoire de la Libération de Digne 14–20 Août 1944*, Les Petites Affiches, online edition.

p.232   A young assistant: Author interview with Noreen Riols.

p.234   Waem got out: What happened in the car is based on Xan Fielding's account in *Hide and Seek* and Ray Jenkins's interview with Francis Cammaerts, quoted in Jenkins, *A Pacifist at War*, p.193.

p.234   It was a very: Cobb, *Eleven Days*, p.71.

p.234   In the police station: Cobb, *Eleven Days*, p.127.

p.235   During the night of August: Cobb, *Eleven Days*, p.127.

p.235   Jumpy German soldiers: Cobb, *Eleven Days*, p.131.

p.237   Later the corpse: Schley field report, NARA/RG226/M1623 Roll 7.

p.239   A Grenadier Guards: From the diary and private papers of Major John Davie.

p.239   Inside the building: From the diary and private papers of Major John Davie.

p.239   Picasso finished his: Roland Penrose article in the *New Statesman* and the *Nation*, 16 September 1944.

p.240   One battle went: Seymour-Jones, *She Landed by Moonlight*, Kindle edition.

Epilogue

p.243 'I just had to turn': Peter Fitzsimons, *Nancy Wake* (HarperCollins, 2012).

p.244 The US ambassador: Simon Berthon and Joanna Potts, *Warlords*, Kindle edition.

p.245 'That's the end.': Clare Mulley, *The Spy Who Loved*, p.275.

p.245 In September 1944: NARA RG 226 (CF).

p.246 Before Pearl and: Pearl Witherington Cornioley, *Code Name Pauline*, Kindle edition.

BIBLIOGRAPHY

Abrahams, Paul, *La Haute-Savoie contre elle-même: 1939–1945* (La Salévienne Académie Chablaisienne, 2006).

Bailey, Roderick, *Forgotten Voices of the Secret War: An Inside History of Special Operations During the Second World War* (Ebury Press, 2008).

Basu, Shrabani, *Spy Princess: The Life of Noor Inayat Khan,* [Kindle edition] (The History Press, 2011).

Berthon, Simon & Potts, Joanna, *Warlords: An Extraordinary Re-creation of World War II Through the Eyes and Minds of Hitler, Churchill, Roosevelt and Stalin* [Kindle edition] (Thistle Publishing, 2013).

Binney, Marcus, *The Women Who Lived for Danger: The Women Agents of SOE in the Second World War* (Hodder & Stoughton, 2005).

Bleicher, Hugo, Colvin, Ian (ed.), *Colonel Henri's Story: The War Memoirs of Hugo Bleicher, Former German Secret Agent* (William Kimber, 1954).

Boothe, Clare, *European Spring* (Hamish Hamilton, 1941).

Boyce, Frederic & Everett, Douglas, *SOE: The Scientific Secrets* (The History Press, 2011).

Buckmaster, Maurice, *They Fought Alone: The Story of British Agents in France* (Odhams Press, 1958).

Burney, Christopher, *Solitary Confinement* (Clerke and Cockeran, 1952).

Carré, Mathilde-Lily, *I Was the Cat* (Four Square, 1961).

Churchill, Peter, *Duel of Wits* (Hodder & Stoughton, 1953).

Cobb, Matthew, *Eleven Days in August: The Liberation of Paris in 1944* (Simon & Schuster, 2013).

Cookridge, E. H., *They Came from the Sky* (William Heinemann, 1966).

Courvoisier, André, *Le reseau Heckler, de Lyon à Londres* (Éditions France-Empire, 1984).

Cowburn, Benjamin, *No Cloak, No Dagger* (The Adventurers Club, 1960).

Cunningham, Cyril, *Beaulieu: Finishing School for Secret Agents, 1941–1945* (Pen & Sword, 1998).

d'Albert-Lake, Virginia, Litoff, Judy Barrett (ed.), *An American Heroine in the French Resistance* (Fordham University Press, 2006).

Deacon, Richard, *A History of the British Secret Service* (Frederick Muller, 1969).

Delarue, Jacques, trans. Mervyn Savill, *The History of the Gestapo* (Macdonald, 1964).

Desprairies, Cécile, *Ville Lumière, années noires: les lieux du Paris de la collaboration* (Denoël, 2008).

Diamond, Hanna, *Fleeing Hitler: France 1940* (Oxford University Press, 2007).

Domenach-Lallich, Denise, *Demain il fera beau, journal d'une adolescente* (Éditions BGA Permezel, 2002).

Downing, Rupert, *If I Laugh: The Chronicles of My Strange Adventures in the Great Paris Exodus, June 1940* (George G. Harrap, 1940).

Duras, Marguerite, *La douleur* (POL, Paris, 1985).

Elliott, Geoffrey, *The Shooting Star: Denis Rake, MC, a Clandestine Hero of the Second World War* (Methuen, 2009).

Fielding, Xan, *Hide and Seek* (Paul Dry Books Inc./Folio Society, 2014).

Foot, M. R. D, *SOE in France: An Account of the Work of the*

British Special Operations Executive in France 1940–1944
(HMSO, 1966).

——Six Faces of Courage (Eyre Methuen, 1978).

——SOE: An Outline History of the Special Operations
Executive 1940–1946 (Pimlico, 1999).

——Memories of an SOE Historian (Pen & Sword, 2008).

Fourcade, Marie-Madeleine, OBE., trans. Kenneth Morgan,
Noah's Ark (Allen & Unwin, 1973).

Fuller, Jean Overton, The German Penetration of SOE: France
1941–1944 (William Kimber, 1975).

——Double Agent? Light on the Secret Agents' War in France
(Pan, 1961).

——Déricourt: The Chequered Spy (Michael Russell Publishing,
1989).

——Noor-un-nisa Inayat Khan: Madeleine (East-West
Publications, 1971).

Funk, Arthur Layton, Hidden Ally: The French Resistance,
Special Operations, and the Landings in Southern France,
1944 (Greenwood Press, 1992).

Furse, Elisabeth & Barr, Ann, Dream Weaver (Chapmans
Publishers, 1993).

Garby-Czerniawski, Roman, The Big Network (George Ronald,
1961).

Gilbert, Martin, The Second World War: A Complete History
(Weidenfeld & Nicolson, 1989).

——D-Day (Turning Points in History) (John Wiley & Sons,
2004).

Gildea, Robert, Fighters in the Shadows: A New History of the
French Resistance (Faber & Faber, 2015).

Giskes, H. J., London Calling North Pole (William Kimber, 1953).

Groussin, Gilles, La vie sous l'Occupation dans le canton de
Valençay (Self-published).

Haffner, Sebastian, trans. Oliver Pretzel, Defying Hitler: A
Memoir (Weidenfeld & Nicolson, 2002).

Hastings, Max, Das Reich: The March of the 2nd SS Panzer

Division through France, June 1944 (Pan, 2012).

Helm, Sarah, *A Life in Secrets: Vera Atkins and the Lost Agents of SOE* (Little Brown, 2005).

Humbert, Agnès, trans. Barbara Mellor, *Résistance: Memoirs of Occupied France* (Bloomsbury, 2008).

Jenkins, Ray, *A Pacifist at War: The Life of Francis Cammaerts* (Hutchinson, 2009).

Jucker, Ninetta, *Curfew in Paris: A Record of the German Occupation* (Hogarth Press, 1960).

Keegan, John, *The Second World War* (Hutchinson, 1989).

Kitson, Simon, *Police and Politics in Marseille, 1936–1945* (Brill, 2014).

Kramer, Rita, *Flames in the Field: The Story of Four SOE Agents in Occupied France* (Michael Joseph, 1995).

Larson, Erik, *In the Garden of the Beasts: Love and Terror in Hitler's Berlin* [Kindle edition] (Transworld Digital, 2001).

Le Chêne, Evelyn, *Watch for Me by Moonlight: A British Agent with the French Resistance* (Eyre Methuen, 1973).

Long, Helen, *Safe Houses Are Dangerous* (William Kimber, 1985).

Ludewig, Joachim, *Rückzug: The German Retreat from France, 1944* (University Press of Kentucky, 2012).

McDonough, Frank, *The Gestapo: The Myth and Reality of Hitler's Secret Police* (Coronet, 2015).

McIntosh, Elizabeth, P., *Women of the OSS: Sisterhood of Spies* (Naval Institute Press, 1998).

Maloubier, Bob, *La vie secrète de Sir Dansey, maître-espion* (Albin Michel, 2015).

Marks, Leo, *Between Silk and Cyanide: The Story of SOE's Code War* (HarperCollins, 1998).

Marshall, Robert, *All the King's Men: The Truth Behind SOE's Greatest Wartime Disaster* (HarperCollins, 1988).

Masson, Madeleine, *Christine: A Search for Christine Granville, O.B.E. G.M. Croix de Guerre* (Hamish Hamilton, 1975).

Miannay, Patrice, *Dictionnaire des agents doubles dans la Résistance* (Le Cherche Midi, 2005).

Michael, Robert & Doerr, Karin, *Nazi-Deutsch/Nazi German: An English Lexicon of the Language of the Third Reich* (Greenwood Press, 2002).

Millar, George, *Maquis: The French Resistance at War* (Cassell, 2003).

Mulley, Clare, *The Spy Who Loved: The Secrets and Lives of Christine Granville, Britain's First Female Special Agent of World War II* (Macmillan, 2012).

Murphy, C. J., 'The Origins of "SOE in France"', *Historical Journal*, Vol. 46, Issue 4, 2003.

Nicholas, Elizabeth, *Death Be Not Proud* (Cresset Press, 1958).

Nici, John B., *Famous Works of Art and How They Got That Way* (Rowman & Littlefield, 2015).

Nouzille, Vincent, *L'espionne: Virginia Hall, une Américaine dans la guerre* (Fayard, 2007).

Ottaway, Susan, *Violette Szabo: The Life That I Have* (Leo Cooper, 2002).

Ousby, Ian, *Occupation: The Ordeal of France 1940–1944* (John Murray, 1997).

Overy, Richard, *Why the Allies Won* (Jonathan Cape, 1995).

Paine, Lauran, *Mathilde Carré: Double Agent* (Robert Hale, 1976).

Pearson, Judith L., *The Wolves at the Door: The True Story of America's Greatest Female Spy* (The Lyons Press, 2005).

Pearson, Michael, *Tears of Glory: The Betrayal of Vercors 1944* (Macmillan, 1978).

Perquin, Jean-Louis, *The Clandestine Radio Operators, SOE, BCRA, OSS* (Histoire et Collections, undated).

Pidgeon, Geoffrey, *The Secret Wireless War: The Story of MI6 Communications, 1939–1945* (UPSO Ltd, 2007).

Pryce-Jones, David, *Paris in the Third Reich: A History of the German Occupation, 1940–1944* (HarperCollins, 1981).

Read, Anthony & Fisher, David, *Colonel Z: The Life and Times of a Master of Spies* (Hodder & Stoughton, 1984).

Riffaud, Madeleine, *On l'appelait Rainer* (Julliard, 1994).

Ruby, Marcel, *F Section SOE: The Story of the Buckmaster Network* (Leo Cooper, 1988).

Seaman, Mark (ed.), *Special Operations Executive: A New Instrument of War* (Routledge, 2006).

Seymour-Jones, Carole, *She Landed by Moonlight: The Story of Secret Agent Pearl Witherington* (Hodder & Stoughton, 2013).

Shirer, William, L., *The Rise and Fall of the Third Reich: A History of Nazi Germany* (Simon & Schuster, 1990).

Simpson, William, *I Burned My Fingers* (Putnam, 1956).

Suttill, Francis J., *Shadows in the Fog: The True Story of Major Suttill and the Prosper French Resistance Network* (The History Press, 2014).

Sweet-Escott, Bickham, *Baker Street Irregular* (Methuen, 1965).

Vader, John, *The Prosper Double-Cross* (Sunrise Press, 1977).

Vance, Jonathan, *Unlikely Soldiers: How Two Canadians Fought the Secret War Against Nazi Occupation* (HarperCollins, 2008).

Verity, Hugh, *We Landed by Moonlight: Secret RAF Landings in France 1940–1944* (Ian Allan, 1979).

Vomécourt, Philippe de, *Who Lived to See the Day: France in Arms 1940–45* (Hutchinson, 1961).

Wake, Nancy, *The Autobiography of the Woman the Gestapo Called the White Mouse* (Macmillan, Australia, 1985).

Ward, Irene, DBE, MP, *F.A.N.Y. Invicta* (Hutchinson, 1955).

Werth, Alexander, *The Last Days of Paris: A Journalist's Diary* (Hamish Hamilton, 1940).

West, Nigel, *MI6, British Secret Intelligence Service Operations 1909–1945* (Weidenfeld & Nicolson, 1983).

——*British Security Coordination: The Secret History of British Intelligence in the Americas 1940–1945* (St Ermin's Press, 1998).

Wheeler-Bennett, John, *The Nemesis of Power: The German*

Army in Politics 1918–1945 (Macmillan, 1953).

Wick, Steve, *The Long Night: William L. Shirer and the Rise and Fall of the Third Reich* (Palgrave Macmillan, 2011).

Williams, Andrew, *D-Day to Berlin* [Kindle edition] (Hodder & Stoughton, 2004).

Witherington Cornioley, Pearl, *Code Name Pauline, Memoirs of a World War II Special Agent* [Kindle edition] (Chicago Review Press, 2015).

Young, Gordon, *The Cat with Two Faces* (White Lion Publishers, 1975).

Ken Macalister and Frank Pickersgill's story is told in *Unlikely Soldiers: How Two Canadians Fought the Secret War Against Nazi Occupation*, Jonathan Vance (HarperCollins, 2008). This book uses material from SOE files to tell the story of their endeavours.

PICTURE CREDITS

INDEX